Cuban Currency

CULTURAL STUDIES OF THE AMERICAS

George Yúdice, Jean Franco, and Juan Flores, Series Editors

For more books in this series, see page 220.

Cuban Currency

The Dollar and "Special Period" Fiction

Esther Whitfield

Cultural Studies of the Americas, Volume 21

University of Minnesota Press

Minneapolis / London

Portions of chapters 2 and 3 were previously published in "Billetes buenos y falsos: el dinero en la reciente narrativa cubana," *Temas* 32 (January–March 2003): 32–37. Portions of chapter 4 appeared in earlier form as "Dirty Autobiography: The Body Impolitic of *Trilogía sucia de la Habana*," *Revista de Estudios Hispánicos* 36, no. 2 (May 2002): 329–51.

Published by the University of Minnesota Press
111 Third Avenue South, Suite 290
Minneapolis, MN 55401-2520
http://www.upress.umn.edu

Library of Congress Cataloging-in-Publication Data

Whitfield, Esther Katheryn.
    Cuban currency : the dollar and "special period" fiction / Esther Whitfield.
        p.   cm. — (Cultural studies of the Americas ; 21)
    Includes bibliographical references and index.
    ISBN-13: 978-0-8166-5036-1 (hc : alk. paper)
    ISBN-10: 0-8166-5036-5 (hc : alk. paper)
    ISBN-13: 978-0-8166-5037-8 (pb : alk. paper)
    ISBN-10: 0-8166-5037-3 (pb : alk. paper)
    1. Cuban literature—20th century—History and criticism.
    2. Authorship—Economic aspects—Cuba—History—20th century.
    I. Title.
    PQ7378.W55 2008
    863'.64093553—dc22
                                                            2007044595

Printed in the United States of America on acid-free paper

The University of Minnesota is an equal-opportunity educator and employer.

15 14 13 12 11 10 09 08   10 9 8 7 6 5 4 3 2 1

Contents

CHAPTER 1

Selling Like Hot Bread:
New Money, New Markets

"We're what's happening," declares Manolín the Salsa Doctor, in the chorus to a song that hit Havana's airwaves and streets in 1996. He continues, showing off: "We're what sells like hot bread . . . we're the greatest."[1] Even from the mouth of Manolín, the refrain is ambivalent: it is a challenge to rivals in the music charts that nevertheless lends itself to displays of national pride.[2] But when this same refrain becomes the epigraph to Pedro Juan Gutiérrez's novel *El Rey de la Habana* (1999), its rallying cry wanes and its potential audience is radically displaced. For although Gutiérrez lives in Havana, his novel, like much of the narrative I explore in this book, was to be published and distributed only outside Cuba, beyond the reach of those who listened to Manolín. Removed from the internecine ratings wars of Havana's musical performers and without a local audience to answer back, *El Rey*'s declaration has no one to impress other than its initially European reader, and no enunciating subject other than the novel itself. And yet it is precisely this relationship between the Cuban book and its foreign audience that Gutiérrez's five "Ciclo Centro Habana" (Centro Habana Cycle) books and works by other contemporary Cuban fiction writers bring to the table in my readings of them, each teasing out of it a different paradox. For, if Gutiérrez's epigraph can flaunt with confidence that the novel will take the market by storm, then it does so in a moment—the "special period in times of peace," the state of emergency that directed post-Soviet Cuba's economic and ideological course—when Cuban culture, newly accessible to travelers and armchair tourists alike, was in high demand abroad. *El Rey de la Habana*'s epigraph has an immediate irony—it introduces a destitute young man named Reynaldo for whom Rey ("King") is a glaring misnomer and whose life is anything but "the greatest"—but its context suggests that "somos" also speaks for Cubans more broadly, and that its audience is the readers in the more than a dozen countries in which Gutiérrez's novels would eventually be published.[3] "Somos lo que hay" becomes a winked acknowledgment of the value that Cuba's spectators have accorded it in a global economy of consumption. It is a bold confrontation with the hard-currency market that signals a significant turning point in post-Soviet Cuban fiction.

El Rey de la Habana was published at the height of a boom in Cuban cultural exports that swept the *Buena Vista Social Club* film and sound recordings across the globe and brought an escalating number of Cuban-authored books to the lists of powerful publishing houses in Europe, the United States, and Latin America. From among these books there emerged a subset that I call "special period fiction," published within a time frame that spans two closely related, if not exactly simultaneous, events in Cuba: the official inauguration of the "special period in times of peace" in 1990 and its less official closure in 2005, and the decriminalization of the use of the U.S. dollar in 1993 and its withdrawal from circulation in 2004.[4] "Special period fiction" was not merely published during these years but is also thematically attuned to the turmoil they presented and structured as an implicit critique of the relationships they engendered.[5] Pioneered by the exiled writer Zoé Valdés and much revised from within Cuba, this subset of the country's literary production is the subject of my book. Through a sustained reflection on the structure of money and of economic relations, I suggest that certain Cuban writers have addressed Cuba's cultural currency by making the U.S. dollar and other market-driven images—an impoverished but sensual population and architectural ruins that invoke a ruined social project—insistent figures in their work. The following chapters explore these writers' broader engagement with the troublesome commodifications of Cuban identity, with the tourist and publishing industries' roles in the paradoxical transformation of the Cuban Revolution into commercial capital, and with literary stagings of the confrontation between capitalism and socialism that closed the twentieth century. Their work elucidates what Cuba—and socialism, and Fidel Castro, and a whole register of by now iconic images—means for today's post-Soviet world. It addresses the fascinations, nostalgias, and hopes that these images incite and how they translate into markets for literature. "Special period fiction" represents but a fraction of Cuban literary output between 1990 and 2004, but through its rehearsals of the theoretical principle that writing authorizes money, on the one hand, and of the market interests that underpin the special period, on the other, it stands as both a barometer and a criticism of Cuban culture's changing value in a newly internationalized economy.[6]

Lingering with Gutiérrez's refrain, we might ask why he, or the "somos" that his epigraph ventriloquizes, adopts such a confident pose. Why this affirmation of self-worth in the explicit context of a market in which buyers are distinguished from sellers? Why begin a book by touting the idea of salability? These questions propel Gutiérrez's novels, and the scope of my study, from the local to the global and from the unilateral to the international commercial dynamics in which Cuban culture quite suddenly became engaged from the mid-1990s on; for this period is defined by the new economic relationships it brought into being, and no writer—indeed, no Cuban—could remain outside their orbit. Following the disintegration of the Soviet-driven Council for Mutual Economic Assistance, which had accounted for 80 percent of Cuba's foreign trade, the special period in times of peace, introduced as such by Fidel Castro in January 1990, saw Cuba plunge into a severe economic crisis.[7] The rhetoric of the Cuban Revolution has always invoked combat, from its battles against illiteracy in the early 1960s to the threat of invasion that it sustained long after the Cuban Missile Crisis, but the special period brought war closer. In announcing it, the government took a series of stringent remedial measures usually reserved for wartime, including cutting energy supplies, rationing certain food products and consumer goods, and worker redeployments ("Información a la población," 1). Scarcity became a staple, to which the government responded with the calls for valor and endurance that had punctuated previous decades. *Resolver* ("to resolve") and *inventar* ("to invent") overreached themselves as the verbs of the moment, becoming practices for survival whose structural proximity to artistic creation, or to making something of nothing, haunts the period's literature. These initial economic measures, and the more drastic ones that followed, would radically alter the country's social and cultural infrastructure, staging a heady encounter with capitalist markets.

Not until 1993, however, did the spirit of cautious reform reach its peak, and it is here—when the seeds of lasting cultural change were first sown—that my reading of special period fiction begins. The farthest-reaching reform measure introduced in the special period was the depenalization of the U.S. dollar. It was announced on July 26, 1993, in recognition on Fidel Castro's part that "life today, our reality, the dramatic situation that this unipolar world is living, obliges us to do that which we would otherwise never have done, had we capital and the technology to produce it."[8] As Archibald Ritter and Nicholas Rowe put it, by 1993 "the Cuban government was confronting a multidimensional economic crisis to which the old remedies—intensifying controls and regulations or mounting state-led campaigns and programs—seemed irrelevant" (430). The use of the dollar was discontinued in November 2004 in favor of a Cuban "convertible peso" *(peso cubano convertible)* that was already in circulation alongside the dollar but finally usurped it amid nationalist rhetoric condemning the U.S. government's "economic war" against Cuba.[9] Nevertheless, the brief decade during which the U.S. dollar was legal tender dramatically changed the course of both Cuba's history and its literature, demarcating the period that is the subject of this book. The dollar's depenalization in 1993 anticipated and enabled sweeping policy implementations among which the most significant for literary production are a November 1993 law decree allowing writers to negotiate contracts with foreign publishers independently of state organizations; the consolidation in April 1994 of a ministry of tourism, under whose aegis Cuba's physical landscape and social hierarchies would be dramatically altered; and a 1995 law to promote foreign investment in Cuban enterprise that would in practice extend beyond the government's joint ventures with outside corporations and deep into the informal sector. Although the dollar had sustained Cuba's black market since the onset of the special period, the penal codes of 1979 and 1987 had prohibited its possession by Cubans and its sudden elevation to omnipotence was dazzling. Between 1993 and 2004 the dollar could legally extend its reach beyond state-level transactions and into the pockets and lives of private citizens. It could be used by individuals in the government-run outlets that operated alongside, and as an indispensable bolster to, the far more scantily stocked stores that continued to charge in Cuban pesos and dispense according to the ration book. As is implied by the official name for these dollar stores, *centros de recaudación de divisas* ("centers for the recovery of hard currency") all money spent there was recuperated by the state. This justified the dollar's legalization, allowing the government to harness hard currency that would otherwise circulate illegally.

Adopting the dollar as Cuba's new currency involved ideological cartwheels—which Fidel Castro was obliged to perform in announcing the measure, and which were a factor in his 2004 decision to replace it with a "convertible peso" of equal value. The dollar is the standard-bearer of the United States, what Jean-Joseph Goux has called "a potent political symbol" (116) and Castro's July 1993 speech focuses at length on his reluctance to adopt the currency of Cuba's historic enemy. A persistent question among his economic analysts, he admits, was "whether we should accept the dollar just as it is, with its own colors, the very same banknote."[10] Moreover, the dollar's superiority over the Cuban peso set a pattern for social inequalities that the revolutionary project had sought to eliminate. Salaries continued to be paid in pesos while material goods were sold in dollars, so that labor hierarchies were distorted and service work that could earn dollars (waiting tables, guiding tours, driving taxis, prostitution) was valued over specialist professions. Society's deeply ingrained work ethic became increasingly obsolete as the depenalization of the dollar propelled Cuba's primarily agricultural-industrial economy, once artificially sustained by the Eastern bloc, to a more service-oriented economy geared toward non-Cuban consumers. Cuban society had long been fueled by the drive to produce—the nationwide struggle to harvest ten million tons of sugar in 1971 being just the best-documented of many examples—and the new mandate to serve, primarily through tourism, but also in other economic areas, had profound implications. Precisely because of these deep-running paradoxes, the U.S. dollar comes to be the emblem par excellence of the special period, and as such it is the protagonist of my study. The fiction I read here insistently, if implicitly, interrogates the U.S. dollar both as text and as the motor of a new society and publishing economy in which books circulate as politically charged artifacts and their authors are assessed for their authority as survivor-witnesses. In Cuba the dollar is a foreign entity domesticated at a cost, and fictional works of the special period weave its physical, intrusively intimate dimension into their very structure, making it a figure for relationships between writing and money that are both textual and contextual.

THE TOURIST DOLLAR

The dollar's avenues into Cuba were determined by the decade's cautious transition from closure to exposure, and from a rigidly institutionalized socialism, in place since 1961, to a reluctant embrace of capitalist markets. Having disappeared from daily life since the eve of the revolution, the dollar returned to Cuba via two new and previously unthinkable sources: remittances and tourism. By the mid-1990s, tourism had overtaken sugar—the root of Cuba's economic dependence on the United States before the revolution, and on the USSR thereafter—in terms of annual revenue, just as remittances and other forms of foreign investment had taken the place of the Eastern bloc's subsidies. In the phase of economic growth that followed the worst of the special period, remittances were Cuba's new crutch and tourism its new hope: both, inevitably, came heavily laden with meaning for Cuba's legacy of egalitarianism. Legalized by the Cuban government at the same time as the depenalization of the dollar and subject to fluctuating regulation by U.S. authorities, remittances from Cuban residents abroad, primarily but not exclusively in south Florida, grew rapidly over the course of the 1990s, although the informal practice of sending money to relatives in Cuba predates the special period.[11] Between 1992 and 1996 alone, remittances increased by 242 percent. Unlike other, state-mediated sources of dollars, they flowed directly to individuals, making them the greatest net source of dollars, although both tourism and sugar yielded higher revenues (Monreal, "Las remesas," 50). Consequently, their potency as a link between the resident and the exiled population—between those who had remained within the revolution, and those long repudiated for having renounced it—was vast. Pedro Monreal writes of this as yet another of the many paradoxes that characterize the special period, arguing that in taking the place of Soviet-bloc subsidies remittances accelerated Cuba's insertion in a global economy (49).[12] Although in June 2004 President George W. Bush implemented severe restrictions on remittances from the United States to Cuba, that the dollar should for so long have flouted such seemingly inviolable political borders as those between Cuba and the United States, circulating as the lifeblood of geographically divided families, reaffirms it as the special period's most subversive agent of change.[13]

Remittances make their way cautiously into fiction of the special period. "La encomienda" (The charge), Anna Lidia Vega Serova's short story that I read in chapter 3, for example, figures as a violation the unannounced gift of five hundred dollars from emigrated parents to the daughter they abandoned. In contrast, the advent of large-scale tourism takes writing by storm. The most remunerative weapon in a potent arsenal meant to spur foreign investment, the complex relationships engendered by tourism provoked radical revisions in the practice of fiction writing. These relationships altered the surface of Cuban life, dramatizing on a daily basis the encounter between socialist and capitalist economics and giving fiction a new thematic repertoire. More deeply, they provided the structural model for a "boom" in literary production. Cuba's booms in both tourism and literary exports were facilitated by the dollar and, in the relations of international exchange that they both perpetuate, each is particularly faithful to it. Because of this common structure, we might think of the dollar circulating through special period fiction as, in a very specific sense, a "tourist dollar"—one that both marks and problematizes the special period's subtext of intercultural exchange.

Tourism to Cuba had its heyday in the 1950s, when the island was championed as a playground for visitors from the United States. The trade embargo imposed by President John F. Kennedy in 1963 meant that high-spending, hard-playing American vacationers were replaced thereafter, and for three decades to follow, by "a small number of more frugal and less demanding visitors from the former Eastern Bloc" (Martin de Holan and Phillips 783). The late 1970s saw a brief thaw in U.S.–Cuba relations and a surge of Cuban American visitors, returnees rather than tourists, whose presence and relative affluence prompted widespread unrest and led to both the Mariel exodus of 1980 and President Ronald Reagan's renewed ban on U.S. citizens' travel to the island. In the decades leading up to the special period, Cuba's foreign tourist industry was severely limited by restrictions on joint ventures (for corporations) and, less officially, on contact with Cubans (for individual visitors), as well as by the country's underdeveloped accommodation and transportation infrastructure. But, heavily promoted after 1994 by its new ministry, tourism—consisting principally of Europeans and Canadians and the occasional embargo-flouting American—increased rapidly, from 340,300 tourists in 1990 to 1.7 million in 1999 (CEPAL Fig. X:2). The Cuban government's sole aim in promoting tourism from these ideologically suspect countries was to generate dollar revenues. It did so with considerable success, principally for the national coffers, but also for individuals who worked in tourism both officially—as direct employees of state-run tourist ventures, or as self-employed but highly regulated restaurateurs and landlords—and in the prolific unofficial economy. The tourist boom gave rise to a spectrum of unofficial service providers, from self-styled tour guides to tobacco resellers to *jineteros* and *jineteras,* the hustlers whose conspicuous presence has redrawn racial hierarchies and captured the imagination of writers and filmmakers in Cuba and abroad. Indeed, as chapter 3 proposes, the recurring narrative of a young Cuban woman's relationship with a foreign lover, which begins with Marilyn Bobes's "Ask the Good Lord" and resurfaces in the work of Souleen Dell'Amico and others, can be considered a pared-down, and morally problematic, prototype for the trade in Cubanness that materialized during the special period. Antonio José Ponte has called such relationships an exchange of history (Cuba's story) for geography (the promise of a ticket to somewhere else), and similar exchanges occur, in different guises, in other interactions that take shape during this period ("La fiesta vigilada," 45).

The benefits of new tourist initiatives to the Cuban economy were undeniable, but it is their impact on the country's social fabric and physical landscape that binds them so inextricably to literary production of the special period. As with the depenalization of the dollar, the government justified its decision to encourage foreign tourism with considerable difficulty, urging Cubans to adopt a spirit of sacrifice and to serve the tourist as a stand-in for serving the revolution. In July 1993 Castro expressed his regret that foreigners, rather than Cubans themselves, would enjoy the country's resources: "if we had the oil that Kuwait and other countries have, we would have developed tourism almost exclusively for the enjoyment of this country's nationals, but the current circumstances oblige us to develop tourism fundamentally for the enjoyment of foreigners."[14] In his closing speech to a conference on tourism in May 1994, a month after unveiling new measures to promote tourism, he insisted that these did not amount to a renunciation of the ideal of constructing socialism and were merely a pragmatic adjustment to the reality of Cuba's economic circumstances.[15] But the paradoxes of Cuba's decision to cater to foreigners were reiterated on a daily basis, in the register of characters and landmarks that tourism invented. Although the industry originally steered tourists toward beaches isolated from the Cuban population, its success soon surpassed these limits and, on the most populous of city streets, foreigners began to practice a dollar-funded leisure that was wholly alien to the labor ethic on which Cuba's socialist project had been constructed. The country's coastline was dotted with incongruous resorts and the oldest streets of Havana—which a UNESCO-funded restoration project has set apart from the rest of the city—with museums in various stages of reconstruction. Tourism put air-conditioned coaches, luxury sedans, and the oddly playful coconut-shaped "Cocotaxis," as well as blatantly nostalgic forms of transportation like the horse-and-cart and much-photographed American cars from the 1950s, on once empty roads. Restaurants, taxis, hotels, and hustlers became telltale signs that, after decades in which production had been both an economic strategy and a credo, Cuba was once again a service economy.

The U.S. dollar drove these changes, but tourism both allowed it to permeate the country's infrastructure and rendered visible its unequal distribution. It is no coincidence, then, that the tourist boom was closely followed by a boom in cultural exports, foreign-financed literature among them. Indeed, Cuba's tourist boom spawned a much broader cultural boom whose attractions and mechanisms of exchange are closely aligned with its own. From the mid-1990s, magazine articles, travel brochures, and product advertisements, as well as cinemas, music stores, and dance venues, inundated European and American consumers with a repertoire of visual images that became recognizably Cuban and was addressed critically by special period authors, particularly Pedro Juan Gutiérrez and Antonio José Ponte, whose work I turn to in chapters 4 and 5. Whether of old cars, old musicians, or old buildings; of pristine beaches, gleaming hotels, freshly painted colonial mansions, or smiling schoolchildren; the images that circulate outside Cuba replicate those that tourists in the country both see and photograph. Just how closely these images are aligned with the official attractions of the state-sponsored tourist industry, and how their deviations from these bear upon Cuba's particular sociohistorical status as a last but ailing bastion of socialism, is a question to which I will return. But there is without doubt a continuum between tourism on the ground, the travel brochures and articles that motivate it, the dozens of photography and coffee-table books of Cuba that invoke it from an armchair, the films that animate the experience and momentarily bridge distances both political and geographic, and, finally, the fiction whose anxieties and markets are the subject of this book.

"Booming" Again

The relationships promoted by the tourist industry are fundamentally economic and "booms"—be they in tourism or literature—merely rehearse these economics on a magnified scale. As the publication and promotion of Cuban fiction outside the country increased over the course of the special period, the term *el nuevo boom cubano* ("the new Cuban boom") was coined and given widespread currency. In 1997, Amelia Castilla and Mauricio Vicent titled an article in Spain's *El país* "Havana's literary explosion,"[16] heralding the proliferation of this metaphor throughout the Spanish-speaking world.[17] Although Cuba's post-Soviet boom in tourism may prefigure its literary counterpart, the "new Cuban boom" has a longer-established predecessor. The term invokes the Boom with a capital B that in the 1960s brought the novels of Gabriel García Márquez, Mario Vargas Llosa, Julio Cortázar, and Carlos Fuentes—to name just the four heavyweights of José Donoso's *The Boom in Spanish American Literature*—to an international readership (119). Naming the 1990s Cuban phenomenon a "new boom" is thus an attempt on the part of publishers, booksellers, and industry journalists to re-create the commercial success of the earlier Boom. Despite this new boom's being greeted with some skepticism by critics, there is no doubt that, on the one hand, the late 1990s saw a surge in publications outside Cuba of both new and reprinted books, principally novels and short stories, by Cuban authors; and, on the other, that this phenomenon shares certain traits with the earlier Boom. While tourism boomed during Cuba's special period, Spain's elaborate system of literary prizes pushed many Cuban writers to prominence. In 1997 Spain's highest literary honor, the Premio Cervantes, was awarded to the long-established Cuban exile Guillermo Cabrera Infante, and in the preceding year the runner-up of the commercially visible Planeta prize went to the then lesser-known Zoé Valdés. Thereafter, Cuban authors, both exiled and resident on the island, reaped awards all over Europe.[18] Between 1994 and 2004, Cuban writers were conspicuous on the lists of major international publishing houses, not to mention those of smaller presses with special interests in Cuba—notably the Spanish houses Colibrí, Lengua de Trapo, Siruela, and Olalla, and the Puerto Rican Ediciones Plaza Mayor (Strausfeld). Some of these were books by new authors, the cult of the young having fused with that of the undiscovered; and some were glossy editions of newly celebrated classics, often those long silenced but cautiously resurfacing in Cuba.[19] The 1990s witnessed the effective resurrection, within Cuba and outside, of writers who had been condemned to censorship and obscurity in the 1960s and 1970s. Familiar names from successive crackdowns—Guillermo Cabrera Infante, Virgilio Piñera, José Lezama Lima—were reprinted in Spain in the 1990s in handsome tributary volumes. As Jacqueline Loss has explored, the most dramatic reclaiming is no doubt that of Reinaldo Arenas, brought to life on screen in Julian Schnabel's adaptation of *Before Night Falls* and subsequently reprinted, translated, and represented in previously unpublished works on both sides of the Atlantic. Whether the decision makers in these publishing resurrections took their cues from Cuba, where a perceived loosening of censorship and relaxation of intellectual property laws during the special period coincided with the coming-of-age of an avidly learned young intellectual class and of a fledgling homosexual movement, or whether these authors' republication in Spain spurred interest in Cuba, is difficult to determine. The correspondence between this phenomenon and the country's economic circumstances, however, is unquestionable.

Some books on foreign publishers' lists, including Zoé Valdés's *Yocandra in the Paradise of Nada* (1995) and *I Gave You All I Had* (1996) that coincide with the beginning of the "new boom" and can be credited with launching it, address the deprivations of the special period directly and the dynamics of the "new boom" implicitly. Others invoke these themes obliquely if at all, and their authors—particularly Abilio Estévez and the late Jesús Díaz—expressed public disdain for Cuba's fashionable status, and for the consequent rush to commercialize its fiction. And yet the perception that Cuba is fashionable and that there should be an entire commercial apparatus structured around it provides the "new Cuban boom" with its first bona fide parallel to the Boom of the 1960s. Subsequent listeners to the earlier Boom heard it as a commercial phenomenon, a marketing ploy masterminded by Barcelona publishers to promote the work of a small number of Latin American writers to the world. The terminology is itself problematic, writes Mario Santana in his retrospective on the Spanish American new novel in Spain in the 1960s and early 1970s: "the use of the word *boom* to describe a literary phenomenon has often been criticized because it seems to express an abdication to the language and values of the marketplace" (33).[20] Writers associated with the Boom have agreed that their work does not have enough in common to justify their grouping on a purely narrative level (Cabrera Infante, "Include Me Out," 14–15). Although the aesthetic integrity of the novels remains sacrosanct, as Donoso is at pains to point out, there is a persistent charge that the "Boom" was invented to advance the interests of a handful of Latin American writers and an even smaller coterie of Spanish publishers.

That Spain should be the defendant in this charge is key to a second link between the Boom and the "new Cuban boom," one that draws the latter into the larger pattern of global commercial relationships that characterizes Cuba's post-Soviet period. This link is the market-driven deterritorialization of literature that arises when books are written in one place—Latin America in the first boom, specifically Cuba in the second—and published and sold in another. Such severing of a book's creation from its material production and consumption marked both "booms," albeit in different contexts and to differing degrees. Its result is an effective expatriation not of writers but of books and thence, in the case of the "new boom" whose books are rarely on sale in Cuba, a complication of their accessibility to readers. Many of the Boom novels were written in—or least from what we might loosely call the cultural perspective of—Latin America but were first published in Europe.[21] Ángel Rama claims that when Barcelona overtook Mexico City and Buenos Aires as the center of Hispanic book production, the Boom was born (51–52) and Spain's pivotal role in the promotion of 1960s Latin American literature is the subject of several recent studies.[22]

This export pattern—creation in Latin America, publication and distribution in Europe—is not the same for all Boom novels, the most famous example being García Márquez's *One Hundred Years of Solitude*, which was rejected in Spain but then catapulted to best-sellerdom by the Buenos Aires publishing house Sudamericana. It is, however, a sufficiently common pattern to set a precedent for the novels of the "new Cuban boom." As chapter 2 explores, Spain—and to a lesser degree France—was at the epicenter of both booms, for historical and cultural reasons. A shared language and a highly developed publishing industry have made Spain the most important publishing center for Spanish-language fiction, and Michi Strausfeld calls it the "Mecca" for manuscripts that found their way out of Cuba in the 1990s (22). Indeed, the Cuban boom had its beginnings with some of the Boom's first Catalan publishers—Seix Barral and Tusquets, for example—as well as with other more popular houses such as Planeta, Anagrama, and the Madrid-based Alfaguara. And, like the Boom, whose global commercialization was in part accelerated by translations into other languages, "the new Cuban boom" reverberated beyond Spain and France. Local versions spun off in English-, German-, Italian-, and Portuguese-speaking countries, and elsewhere in Europe and the Americas. These sites had to wait a year or two for translations, with local interest mediated by particular sociopolitical concerns: in the United States, for example, contemporary Cuban fiction had to be a stand-in for, rather than an extension of, a tourist's experience, given the restraints on travel imposed by the embargo against Cuba. At the same time, however, a burgeoning market in U.S.–Latino, including Cuban American, fiction provided in some cases a ready-made niche for Cuban writers. As Gustavo Pérez Firmat remarks with regard to the cover illustration of Cristina García's *Dreaming in Cuban* (a box of cigars marked "Exported from Havana/De Cuba"), U.S. markets for Cuban and Cuban American fiction have dealt in shared stereotypes of exoticism and prohibition (Pérez Firmat 137–38).

The Boom novels published in Barcelona returned to, and were read in, their authors' countries of origin, although their distribution was not without its difficulties. Although Latin American publishing houses, particularly the Mexican Joaquín Ortiz and the Argentinian Sudamericana, would come to play key roles in the distribution of Boom novels and had important partnerships with Spanish publishers, Donoso complains that until the late 1960s writers were dependent on friends and chance to bring them books (*The Boom,* 82–83). The expatriation of "new Cuban boom" novels was, however, more definitive, having been precipitated by the material deficiencies of the early special period and sustained thereafter by Cuba's economic infrastructure and legacy of censorship. Although, as Pamela Smorkaloff has demonstrated, the Cuban Revolution built up a vibrant and educationally oriented publishing industry between the 1960s and its "golden age" of the 1980s, this industry was plunged into crisis by the collapse of the Soviet bloc. A paper shortage and the departure of skilled technicians, among other factors, severely limited Cuba's capacity to produce books and reduced annual publications from an average of 2,339 titles in 1983–89 to just 568 in 1993 (Más Zabala 49). Material considerations shaped writing during these years in quite specific ways: it being unthinkable to publish a full-length novel, for example, the short story became many writers' genre of choice. As there were few opportunities to publish in Cuba and fewer constraints against doing so outside the country in the wake of the 1993 law that allowed cultural producers to negotiate their own contracts, writers looked elsewhere. Coinciding with the increased spectatorship that dollarization and tourism foisted upon Cuba, foreign publishers soon came to the rescue, either financing joint publications with Cuban editors or—as was increasingly the case over the course of the decade—offering individual writers hard currency contracts that the economic climate rendered irresistible. Thus was born "the new Cuban boom."

Even as the domestic economy and publishing industry recuperated toward the end of the decade, however, and more Cuban writers were able to publish at home, those who still chose to publish abroad were faced with persistent bars to the entry into Cuba of their foreign-published books. Cuban bookstores being state-owned, an impenetrable mix of economic considerations and tacit censorship meant that many of the books they imported, with the exception of the large number bought for educational distribution, tended not to be sold in pesos but in dollars and on the so-called *mercado fronterizo* ("frontier market") that was aimed primarily at tourists. "Frontier market" stores rarely sold foreign-published books whose authors lived in Cuba at the time, and even if such books had been on sale, the price tag would have put them beyond the reach of many residents.[23] The 1990s saw a number of Spanish- or Mexican-published novels reprinted in Cuba and sold in cheaper peso editions, but this is a privilege that appears sensitive to both content and resources.[24] Of the texts to be read in the coming chapters, only Pedro Juan Gutiérrez's *Tropical Animal* has to date been published in both Spain and Cuba, and I will return in chapter 4 to the significance of this novel's being set partly in Sweden and thus at a safe distance from the special period. For most of this period, the novels of Zoé Valdés, written from exile and blatantly condemnatory of the Cuban political regime, did not circulate openly in Cuba. Antonio José Ponte chose to publish his fiction in the United States, Spain, and Mexico rather than in Cuba and, although he stated more clearly than others that he wished to avoid censorship, his predicament is otherwise typical for writers who live in Cuba but publish abroad. These writers were physically separated from the circles in which their books were read and, conversely, they were deprived of the domestic audience that Edel Morales and Homero Campa describe, somewhat problematically, as "their natural readers."[25] This demographic does not account for the prolific and semiclandestine circulation of foreign-published books among writers and intellectuals on the island, which increased with the growth in academic travel to and from Cuba and accounts for the growing body of criticism in Cuban journals on works technically unavailable in the country. It does, however—like the 1960s Boom but through more institutionalized mechanisms—reiterate a dynamic wherein local literary production enters global markets at the expense of its place at home.

GLOBALIZATION AND THE CUBAN BOOM

Such dislocation is a feature familiar in postcolonial contexts, and it is complicated by theories of cultural globalization. In an essay on Latin American subaltern studies, Mabel Moraña describes the paradigm in which the colonial metropolis takes raw materials from Latin America in order to reprocess and package them elsewhere. The "new Cuban boom" has followed the paradigm's first two steps, but stalls at the third to which Moraña refers: the resale of the packaged product to its origin. The fiction that was taken from Cuba as "raw material" to be published and distributed abroad rarely made its way back into Cuba during the special period. Its entry, as I have outlined, was barred not only by the economic factors that restrict the circulation of foreign-produced literature in other postcolonial societies but also by state-level cultural policy. Indeed, globalization, understood as the largely deregulated movement of products across national boundaries, is a phenomenon to which Cuba came reluctantly, partially, and only as a function of the economic necessities of the special period. Discussing Cuba's relationship to globalization in the political and economic sphere, Pedro Monreal insists that "for a country such as Cuba, globalization should be faced . . . from a perspective of exceptionality" ("Globalization," 95). Consumer-based models of global identity such as that explored in Néstor García Canclini's *Consumers and Citizens* do not hold in the Cuban case. Unlike other sites where participation in cross-border communities of consumers has increased with globalization, after 1989 Cubans became more, rather than less, isolated from foreign imports. For three decades Cuba's extended transnational community, the Eastern bloc, had produced and consumed its own goods, and Cuba was able to consider itself part of a self-sufficient entity. But this position was complicated during the special period, as that community disintegrated. In response, Cuba looked elsewhere for both import and export opportunities.

The transnational circulation of industrial goods is usually followed, albeit in diminishing degrees, by that of cultural products (García

Canclini, *La globalización,* 150), but Cuba's post-Soviet participation in cultural globalization followed a particularly idiosyncratic course. As Ariana Hernández-Reguant puts it: "the experience of globalization [in Cuba] had little to do with faceless transnational corporations or the pernicious and ubiquitous presence of mass culture" ("Radio Taino," 390). Although Víctor Fowler Calzada insisted that Cuba's transition from socialism would be less harsh than it was in the former Eastern bloc, because the scenes of capitalist excess greeted with awe after the fall of the Berlin Wall became familiar in Cuba during the 1990s, he admitted that most Cubans were observers of, rather than participants in, such scenes ("The Day After," 43–44). The homogenizing cultural artifacts charged with having left their mark elsewhere on the global landscape—MTV music, McDonald's, and so on—faced legislative barriers to entering Cuban homes throughout the special period. With the exception of national television, which broadcast a limited number of U.S. and Latin American serials, music and other imports from metropolitan centers of cultural dissemination reached Cuba principally through informal channels. Unlike the late-capitalist locales that both produce for export and consume imported products, Cuba consumed few cultural imports and even fewer literary ones. Indeed, Hernández-Reguant calls for restraint in heralding special period Cuba's place in the global economy as consumption-based. She claims that cultural producers—in her study, the radio-show hosts, music promoters, and agents of Cuba's fledgling advertising industry who in the 1990s constituted a crucial nexus between the Cuban state and foreign market interests—are workers schooled in the revolution's labor ethic, and as such are primarily producers for whom the demands of paying consumers are but one in a series of considerations.

García Canclini insists that literature is of necessity somewhat exceptional with regard to globalization, and Cuban literature is indeed removed from even the precarious circuits in which literary imports and exports move elsewhere. In García Canclini's formulation, while most cultural industries can expand globally with English as their lingua franca, literature's linguistic specificity has limited its expansion to regional rather than global spaces. Spanish-language fiction, for example, circulates principally in Latin America; and although the mainly European conglomerates that control the industry have subjected Latin American literature to "best sellerization," they nevertheless define their markets according to already-existing national borders and often distribute high-profile authors only in their native countries (*La globalización,* 150–54). During the special period, Cuban-authored books were doubly exceptional in their relationship to global markets. Not only was their circulation in such markets, like that of other Latin American literature, dependent on the feasibility of translations, but they were also written in a context in which few foreign-produced cultural products—including Cuban authors' own foreign-published books—were imported. Hence Josefina Ludmer's observation that once the fall of the Soviet Union had simultaneously initiated Cuba's special period and Latin American neoliberal globalization, "Cuba . . . began to depend on foreigners, dollars and the Spanish book industry as much as the rest of Latin America did" is accurate,[26] but with the crucial difference that residents of other Latin American countries are purchasers from, as well as suppliers for, the Spanish book industry.

Like the agents in Hernández-Reguant's study who produce music and advertising, Cuban writers are also producers. Indeed, the 1993 laws that allowed them, like artists and musicians, to negotiate their own contracts simultaneously recognized their status as autonomous workers.[27] Writers' far smaller domestic audience means, however, that they occupy a different place on the special period's cultural landscape. The channels for the diffusion of literature are narrower than those for music, so that Cuban musicians reached both wider audiences and greater commercial success than writers; and yet while books circulate in greater volume than individual works of visual art, the much lower price they command per unit meant that during this period even the most widely read of Cuban authors were the poor relations of well-known painters. This somewhat peripheral position has a history: Cuban mass media, particularly in the form of television and radio broadcasts, were brought into the service of the revolution from its very inception and have long been assured of large audiences on national territory. Literary production, in contrast, remained under suspicion for the first decade of the revolution, reaching its height with the Padilla case of 1967–71.[28] Although, as Pamela Smorkaloff has documented, the Cuban Revolution's publishing industry subsequently tailored its offerings for a mass readership, one of the consequences of the industry's post-Soviet collapse was a sharp decline in domestic readers that only began to rise again at the end of the 1990s. Faced with this decline, special period literature began to occupy a new critical space, one that accommodated reflection on the changing status of culture and consumption.

Inasmuch as globalization's constitutive tensions are those between production and consumption, Cuba cannot be wholly immune to its implications, and the shifting geographies of these two terms are a principal focus of special period fiction. Just as changing patterns in the consumption of mass culture, as García Canclini, Arjun Appadurai, and others argue, have prompted more critical reflection at its sites of production, so the special period authors I read in this book take foreign consumption of Cuban culture as an opportunity.[29] They rehearse in their work the paradoxes of Cuba's marketability to audiences residing beyond its borders and beyond its socialist context. For when the country's production economy declined as a result of the Soviet Union's collapse, Cuba became less a site *of* consumption—that is, a place where consumers were themselves located—than a site *for* consumption. This is the double-edged sword of Cuba's cultural boom; and it is also the underside of cultural globalization more broadly, whose critics' more "anxious narratives," as Steven Feld describes them in the case of world music, center on the phenomenon's inherent commodification of ethnicity (145–71). A further counterpoint to the much-contested theory that cultural products' transnational circulation renders their sites of origin less active than those of their distribution is that the place of origin can itself acquire intangible value, for its association with either the technologically advanced metropolis or the distant and alluring periphery. In the special period, not only were Cuba's opportunities to export cultural products vastly expanded by new contact with capitalist entities, but the perceived opening of the country after years of closure also generated a market in witness accounts and images of the country itself. Along with the export of cultural products—music, film, and literature—went that of Cuba as a place and as a set of historically situated experiences.

THE POST-SOVIET EXOTIC

Fiction that draws attention to the marketability of its place of origin in order to question the very premise of that marketability is the subject of Graham Huggan's *The Postcolonial Exotic: Marketing the Margins.* Huggan addresses "the cultural commodification of postcolonial writing" (ix) from Asia, Africa, Australia, and Canada by a de facto coalition of agents: multinational publishers; "self-consciously prestigious" literary prizes (like Britain's Booker); and, most important, readers and writers themselves. He calls this phenomenon "the postcolonial exotic," instances being "when creative writers like Salman Rushdie are seen, despite their cosmopolitan background, as representatives of Third World countries; when literary works such as Chinua Achebe's *Things Fall Apart* (1958) are gleaned, despite their fictional status, for the anthropological information they provide; when academic concepts like postcolonialism are turned, despite their historicist pretensions, into watchwords for the fashionable study of cultural otherness" (vi). The phenomenon is post-colonial in its context—Huggan addresses former British colonies—but also in the sense that postcolonialism marks an "index of resistance, a perceived imperative to rewrite the social text of continuing imperial dominance" (ix). It is exotic in the sense that "exoticism describes . . . a particular mode of aesthetic *perception*—one which renders people, objects and places strange even as it domesticates them, and which effectively manufactures otherness even as it claims to surrender to its immanent mystery" (13). Exoticism here is both aesthetic and political; more specifically, it is "an aestheticizing process through which the cultural other is translated, relayed back through the familiar" (ix) that is subjected to a process of repoliticization, "redeployed to unsettle metropolitan expectations of cultural difference and to effect a grounded critique of differential relations of power" (ix–x).

The demands channeled by the "postcolonial exotic" are varied, but prevalent among them is that for a stultified set of images that serves to define a postcolonial site for a public to whom it is foreign—including, in the case of Salman Rushdie's *Midnight's Children,* a conspicuously "gastro-nomic imagery" that Huggan terms "the deliberately exaggerated hawking of Oriental(ist) wares by a narcissistic narrator" (xi). Just as Huggan resists identifying a homogeneous community of reader-consumers of the "postcolonial exotic," however, he reads postcolonial writers' roles in perpetuating the "postcolonial exotic" as both varied and ambivalent. Many, he claims, subscribe to a "staged marginality" but do so as a form of "strategic exoticism" that allows them to both undermine market and academic interests in postcolonial fiction and, at the same time, take advantage of them. "Strategic exoticism" denotes "the means by which post-colonial writers/thinkers, working from within exotic codes of representation, either manage to subvert these codes or succeed in redeploying them for the purposes of uncovering differential relations of power" (32); but its inherent danger, or its constitutive slipperiness, lies in the fact that it "might be considered less as a response to the postcolonial exotic than as a further symptom of it" (33). Increasingly prevalent across the English-speaking world and accelerated by the mechanisms of globalization, this "postcolonial exotic" intersects with the international English-language publishing industry, the discipline of anthropology, and tourism, to the extent that each of these involves mutual but cross-cultural perceptions and unequal relations of exchange.

Both the marketing of Cuban fiction by principally European publishers and the strategic self-presentation of Cuban authors correspond to Huggan's framework in important ways. The currency, or the popularity and booming transnational circulation, of Cuban literature is sustained by a similar roster of agents—publishers, prizes, readers, and writers—albeit initially in a Hispanic rather than an Anglophone context. The prevalent trend in marketing this literature is to cast it as representative of a spatially and temporally defined "special period" Cuba, despite some authors' actual or attempted distance from this newly valued locale. (Zoé Valdés, for example, lived in Paris when *I Gave You All I Had,* the subject of chapter 2, was published; Antonio José Ponte, to whom I turn in chapter 5, titles a collection of his short stories *Cuentos de todas partes del imperio,* translated as *Tales from the Cuban Empire,* as a gesture toward expanding Cuba's limited borders.) Cuba has become associated with an "exotic" aesthetic that, like the one Huggan describes, is largely a construction of outsiders' perceptions, desires, and appropriations. And, most important, Cuban writers—certainly those practitioners of a "special period genre," who are the subject of this book—engage in a form of strategic exoticism that allows them to both appease and critically undermine demands for clichéd representations of Cuba. The local color these writers peddle is tinged with hypersexuality, revolutionary slogans, and moral-cum-architectural decrepitude rather than Rushdie's ironic "markers of Orientalism"; but it is peddled according to similar cross-cultural mechanisms and with similarly contestatory undertones.

Tempting though it may be, however, to read the popularity of Cuba as a manifestation of Huggan's "postcolonial exotic" in which one thematic repertoire is merely substituted for another, to do so would be to overlook the historical differences that not only distance Cuba from the contexts to which Huggan refers, but also generate the particularities of Cuban fiction's markets and aesthetic codes. For to transpose Huggan's term to Cuba is to deal with the anachronism of a twenty-first-century experiment in socialism; and it is precisely this anachronism, and its anomalous status vis-à-vis late-capitalist societies, that accounts for Cuba's appeal. In short, where Huggan invokes "the entanglement of [the postcolonial's] ostensibly anti-imperial ideologies within a global economy that often manipulates them to neo-imperial ends" (ix), we might substitute "the Cuban Revolution" for "the postcolonial"—and in so doing unearth a qualitatively different set of paradoxes, rooted in nostalgia not for the world as it once was (i.e., for the colonial past, Huggan xiii) but for the world as some hoped it might be (that is, for the ideal of socialism). It is the particular paradoxes of Cuba's exotic, what we might call its "post-Soviet exotic" or "special period exotic," that preoccupy Cuban writers.

The marketability of things Cuban—including the increased publication abroad of Cuban fiction—coincides with the collapse of Eastern European socialism and the concomitant perception that Cuba's tropical version is in the throes of a slow death. That this should be a perception most persistently vocalized outside Cuba, rather than an internally endorsed state of affairs, is important as it aligns outsiders' ways of reading Cuba with Huggan's formulation of exoticism as "a particular mode of aesthetic *perception*" (13) that can consume without needing to comprehend. Moreover, the perception that the days of Cuban socialism are numbered, like broadly held stereotypes about postcolonial sites and peoples, both generates and politicizes a distinct aesthetic; for Cuba's historical predicament, the interests it incites and authors' engagement of those interests shape an aesthetic code common across several cultural forms. By "aesthetic code" I mean not only a thematic repertoire that is recognizably that of special period Cuba, but, more specifically, a series of recurring images and linguistic figures that invoke consistent meanings decipherable only in the context of Cuba's status as a last bastion of socialism. The sociohistoric basis of this code—or its specific location in the economics of the special period—is evidenced by the contrast in both context and content between the Latin American literary Boom of the 1960s and the special period boom in Cuban literature; for while the earlier Boom followed upon the triumph of the Cuban Revolution, the later coincides with the revolution's apparent demise. The wave of revolutionary fervor that brought the Latin American Boom's now legendary novelists to international attention had been sharply reversed by the 1990s. In 1962—the year Mario Vargas Llosa won Spain's Biblioteca Breve Prize, and a founding moment of the Boom—Fidel Castro had just come to power, and the outside world, particularly the left-wing intellectual movements then gaining ground in Europe and the United States, watched in excitement.[30] Almost four decades later, in the mid- and late 1990s, it was the swan song, and not the birth, of the Cuban Revolution that made the stuff of salable fiction.

The thematic content of the 1960s Boom is notoriously difficult to unify—discerning tenuous but common threads, Gerald Martin mentions "a quest or quests" and "a metaphor or metaphors for the course of Latin American history" (60)—and that of Cuba's "new boom," particularly the subgenre of special period fiction that this book addresses, ranges from blackouts to food shortages, illegal migration to sexual frenzy, crowded barrios to deserted ruins.[31] This fiction's broader aesthetic code draws these motifs into a more complex gesture that pits representations of authenticity (what Cuba is now) against stimuli of nostalgia (for what Cuba once was or might have been), thereby exposing ideological fissures in both the Cuban Revolution itself and outsiders' interests in it. This is a code, moreover, that is not exclusive to literary representation: its most prolific manifestations, in fact, are spawned by the tourist industry. Huggan identifies a mutually defining relationship between tourism and constructions of the exotic that takes concrete form in the close correspondences between the tourist boom and the literary boom in special period Cuba. The effective export of a set of geographically situated experiences motors each of these booms as, for the first time, Cuban tourist promoters and writers produce in heightened awareness of the models of consumption according to which their work will circulate. Distancing themselves from the less ironic tourist industry, however, writers take their texts as opportunities to put foreign consumption itself in the spotlight, exploring their own cravings for it (it is in their financial interest, at least, to be "consumed") and at the same time subjecting it to scrutiny, mockery, and censure.

Tourism, Fiction, Authenticity, and Nostalgia

Authenticity and nostalgia are both central to the idealized tourist experience, as Dean MacCannell and John Frow have demonstrated. MacCannell's foundational study, *The Tourist: A New Theory of the Leisure Class,* reads the tourist as a figure whose quest to experience modernity in its entirety is constantly compromised as mere experiences of differentiation between localities and peoples. Steered unwittingly toward this lower expectation, the tourist comes to celebrate differentiation and, crucially, to engage in a dialectic of authenticity whereby the assurance that he or she is witnessing "the real thing" is enough to validate the experience.

When this dialectic plays out along national or cultural lines, as it has increasingly with the growth and globalization of the tourist industry, these differentiations, and their basis in an assumed authenticity, take on greater dimensions. Frow problematizes MacCannell's reading of authenticity as based in a distinction between the "front" and "back," or presented and concealed, regions of a culture or place, arguing that this distinction serves to reinforce "those categories that associate truth with concealment, secrecy, and intimacy, and untruth with surfaces and visibility" (128). These are categories, nevertheless, that are clearly operative in the premium placed on exposure in tourism to Cuba, particularly given Frow's insistence that they perpetuate an imagined "other of modernity" that "exists outside the circuit of commodity relations" (129). Following from the internal complications of this valorization of a non-"modern" other, Frow proposes that the problem of tourism is both hermeneutic ("how can I come to terms with that which is Other without reducing it to the terms of my own understanding?" 130) and semiotic, wherein the very marking of authenticity as such undermines its status as unmediated. He concludes by identifying as a constitutive structural paradox of the tourist experience one wherein the quest for authenticity, although always mediated and doomed to disappointment, facilitates the commodification not only of material services but of immaterial relationships: "the product sold to the tourist industry in its most general form is a commodified relation to the Other" (150). As my readings of the specific content of special period aesthetics explore, it is this very relation—and its grounding in a supposed authenticity—that both Cuban tourism and fiction bring into relief, the latter more critically than the former.

Although a tourist site can be viewed as "authentic" because of its present appearance, its valorization as such is dependent on the tourist's often unwitting foray into the past. In fact, as Frow and Jonathan Culler concur, rather than being opposed to ideals of authenticity, nostalgia is constitutive of them. The quest to behold an authentic other is motivated by longing not only for difference, but for a difference that stands for innocence, simplicity, and timelessness: in short, for MacCannell's "premodern." Frow reads *The Tourist*'s front–back (concealed/superficial) distinction as itself nostalgic as, through it, "MacCannell retains a commitment to the categories of the authentic and the real, . . . postulated historically (and nostalgically) as lost domains of experience or referentiality" (128). Culler states the point in similar terms: "one of the characteristics of modernity is the belief that authenticity has been lost and exists only in the past—whose signs we preserve (antiques, restored buildings, imitations of old interiors)—or else in other regions or countries" (160). The belief that "other regions or countries" are repositories of lost authenticity is a spur not only to individual travel abroad but also to mass international tourism. This is particularly the case when the destination is a site of historical interest or of marked cultural difference; but, although it is so-called Third World tourism that bears the brunt of Frow's criticism, a nostalgically motored delight in the purportedly authentic provides a structural model for many tourist encounters.

Nostalgia, as Svetlana Boym explores it, is a curiously restless stance: it looks toward the past without really wanting to be there and, through a gentle form of masochism, enjoys the pain of longing. Once considered a medical condition, it is "a sentiment of loss and displacement, but it is also a romance with one's own fantasy" and "a longing for a home that no longer exists or never existed" (xiii). As a "home," Cuba is the resting place of distinct nostalgias, the best documented being that of the exiles who have left the country continuously since 1959. Explored as fantasy in Roberto G. Fernández's *Raining Backwards* and from a more conciliatory stance in works like Cristina García's *Dreaming in Cuban* and Ana Menéndez's *In Cuba I Was a German Shepherd,* exiles' nostalgic claims to a Cuban home "that no longer exists"—often recrafted by imagination and the workings of memory into a home "that never existed"—have been a staple of post-1959 Cuban American fiction (Álvarez-Borland, *Cuban-American Literature of Exile,* 91–147). Special period society cultivates its own nostalgias, both those of the regime for its first moments of victory (Ponte, "What Am I Doing Here?"; de la Nuez 169–72) and those that, as Jacqueline Loss has addressed, contribute to current rememberings of the Soviet years ("Vintage Soviets," 79–84). Cuba has served also, however, as a metaphorical home for non-natives, from the "political pilgrims," to use Paul Hollander's term, who flocked there in the 1960s and 1970s, to subsequent, less activist visitors and would-be visitors seeking refuge from their own worlds; for, like Boym's invocation of "a home that no longer exists or never existed," it is upon an ideal of a place that borders on the impossible, or the invented, that Cuba is founded as a tourist destination. Representations of this destination that circulate outside the country, as well as official and unofficial installations in situ, stimulate desires for a certain form of authenticity that, in turn, is shaped by historically and geopolitically specific nostalgias. Indeed, it is with a focus on post-Communist Russia and Germany that Boym comments on nostalgia's resurgence "as a defense mechanism in a time of accelerated rhythms of life and historical upheavals" (xiv), and this historical dimension redefines nostalgia as temporal rather than spatial. "At first glance," writes Boym, "nostalgia is a longing for a place, but actually it is a yearning for a different time—the time of our childhood, the slower rhythms of our dreams" (xv). The nostalgia that underpins tourists' attraction to socialist Cuba has a foundation in similarly distant temporalities, although Cuba's singular political status marks these as the pasts of both Cuba itself and of visitors' own ideological allegiances.

Cuba's official tourism industry did not set out to promote nostalgic longing for the past, even though it capitalized on the country's revolutionary and prerevolutionary history. At the onset of the special period, visitors were steered toward sites whose conception and appearance upheld the revolution's rhetoric of progress, however inconsistent these sites might have been with broader tenets of socialism. Thus tourists were welcomed to gleaming new hotels, built in joint ventures with foreign developers on clean beaches almost devoid of Cubans, and toward state-run museums that, despite their depleted exhibits and bedraggled facilities, at least kept the revolutionary project's noble visions intact. Havana's oldest colonial quarter was offered alongside its hotels and museums as the city's foremost tourist attraction. The old city was renovated and repolished, and its preservation presented as an investment in the economic future as well as pride in a once-reviled colonial past. Old Havana's restoration began with its designation as a UNESCO World Heritage Site in 1982 and was greatly accelerated in the 1990s under the direction of the city historian, Eusebio Leal Spengler, who had said of the area's viability for tourism that "not only is [the old city's] historical, cultural, and social value to be taken into consideration, but also its economic dimension, as the aim is to achieve self-financed, integrated development that will make investments recoverable and productive" (Leal Spengler 11). In 1995, the old city was declared an "Area of High Significance for Tourism." With an ambitious master plan that would return many of the quarter's buildings to their original uses, peopling them with actors pretending to ply colonial trades and with tourists accommodated in colonial-themed hostels, Leal oversaw a rehabilitation of Old Havana that critics chastised for its theme-park pretensions—for creating an "Old Havanaland," as Paul Goldberger puts it (60)—and for evacuating those for whom the old city was a natural habitat. "Thanks to the patience and efforts of a group of specialists in different fields," write Antonio José Ponte, "from the most tumultuously inhabited locale has emerged the least livable place."[32]

In the absence of native life in Havana's designated historic center, independent-minded tourists turned elsewhere, defying both the de facto segregation policies of the country's hotels to seek out the company and the stories of Cuban people, and shunning beautified historic buildings to delight instead in Havana's architectural ruins. They strayed toward more marginal attractions: toward inhabited streets, stores where people stood in line to buy goods in pesos, and buildings faded and fallen rather than freshly painted. This is the alternative tourist circuit, the one that Mauricio Vicent, longtime Havana correspondent for the Spanish newspaper *El país,* invokes in his July 2000 assessment of "the dark charm" that Cuba holds for foreign tourists:

> For some, like the Italian designer Luciano Benetton, it's primarily an aesthetic question: it's the pastel light that filters across porticos at seven in the evening, coloring Cubans' faces and Havana's chipped facades, making them one and the same. For others, there is a morbid delight in the political contradiction, in the contrast between Fidel Castro's khaki uniform and the city filling up with Japanese cars. In rickety Cadillacs and the 1970s political slogans—"Fatherland or death, we will overcome!"—that seem to make time stand still. In mojito cocktails from the Bodeguita del Medio, that make you feel young. In the way people look at you. In easy sex, that merges with the aesthetic of Numantia. "You have to go to Cuba—now, because it won't be the same later," say some. And Cuba's magic lies, too, in its status as an ideological theme park, as a last bastion of socialism. And in the libido aroused in entrepreneurs by the business opportunities that will come later.[33]

This register of attractions assigns specific content to the authenticity and nostalgia that shape tourists' and readers' experience of Cuba. In accordance with MacCannell's formulation, both the allure and the illusion of authenticity depend on the revelation of "back" regions, on catching glimpses not only of a country's tourist structures but also of how people there live and work. "The way people look at you," the way their faces are colored by the evening light, and the rickety Cadillacs in which they drive all offer such glimpses. But the notion of access, and consequently of authenticity, assumes a distinct charge in a place closed to consumerist tourism for decades and only now, in the special period, opening its ports. In the 1990s, Cuba's "opening" inspired a narrative of exposure that pervaded both the experience and the advertising paraphernalia of tourism, spawning voyeuristic appetites for intimate contact with Cubans and their previously "concealed" way of life. It is no coincidence that this appetite should coincide with the advent of *jineterismo* and the reemergence of prostitution in Cuba; nor, then, that Vicent should list under the country's attractions "easy sex." The tourist experience of authenticity in Cuba intersects with the tropical, often racially defined stereotypes that sustain much tourism to the Caribbean, as Polly Pattullo has addressed.[34] The worldwide popularity of Cuban music during the 1990s, for example, is no doubt linked to ideals of spontaneity and innate rhythm long associated with the Caribbean and revived, after a considerable hiatus, for the Cuban context, and to tourists' appreciation of apparently impromptu performances encountered away from programmed venues. Similar valorizations of authentic cultural expression underpin what Katherine J. Hagedorn has analyzed as "religious tourism," born during the special period and including public performances of traditionally private rituals and initiations of foreign citizens into Afro-Cuban religious orders (Hagedorn 219–27). Manifestations of authenticity are rendered especially valuable in Cuba by the relative newness of their exposure to foreigners, on the one hand, and, on the other, by the sense that the lifestyle of which they are part is under threat of imminent extinction. As Vicent writes, paraphrasing a typical tourist: "You have to go to Cuba—now, because it won't be the same later."

It is in this notion of something newly exposed but nevertheless about to expire, and about to do so precisely because it is an unsustainable anachronism in a post-Soviet, almost postsocialist world, that the nostalgic dimension of tourism to Cuba lies. Vicent identifies among Cuba's roster of unofficial attractions emblems of the socialist state, including Fidel Castro's fatigues, his 1970s political slogans, and the endurance that sustained his regime for decades in the face of a far more powerful enemy. But their uneasy coexistence alongside attractions of a different order suggests that the appeal of Cuban socialism resides less in the political system itself than in its contrast with both the encroachment of capitalism (figured here as Japanese cars) and the ravages of time (seen in the city's chipped facades). Nostalgia for the heyday of Cuban socialism is tempered in Vicent's paradigm by what he calls "morbid curiosity" at the system's surely doomed struggle to survive. In this context, tourist nostalgia takes on new objects that compete with what would otherwise be more straightforwardly the recuperation or perpetuation of the Cuban Revolution. Among these objects are the tranquillity of a necessarily slower pace of life, slowed less by the late arrival of modernity than by the stubborn rejection of capitalist technology and exemplified by prerevolutionary cars, although a broader interest in lives of material lack is also part of this repertoire. These same now-rickety Cadillacs are signs of a further nostalgia: for the hedonistic abandon of tourism in Cuba in the 1950s, that for U.S. citizens might also represent longing for calmer, less problematic relations between the two countries.

It is thus socialism as a relic, as much as the hope it once was for some and still is for others, that animates this tourist experience; so that the longing for "the time of our childhood, the slower rhythms of our dreams" that Boym sees as a temporal component of nostalgia is implicitly dehistoricized. Tourist nostalgia is directed at a vague past that is neither recoverable nor desirable for the present: from this perspective, socialist Cuba appears neither as an achievement to be mourned nor as an ideal to be sustained. Contrary to the conceptions of history that are central to revolutionary rhetoric, beginning in 1953 with Fidel Castro's assertion that "history will absolve me" and ever present in public commemorations of heroic events, the political project of the revolution enters Cuba's tourist circuit in a much-diluted version, its once highly charged symbols reduced to knickknacks. As Iván de la Nuez puts it, the figure of Caliban—claimed as a revolutionary in Roberto Fernández Retamar's 1971 essay—has been tamed. He is now "the actor in a theme park named Cuba, the opportune inhabitant of that fountain of nostalgias—of Lefts and Rights, of primitive *son* music and of Che Guevara, of Cabaret and the Sierra Maestra mountains, of Lezama Lima's *Paradiso* and pork served in *paladares*—that the island has become."[35] José Quiroga, in his study of memory and the perception of time in and in relation to Cuba, points to a similar phenomenon as a hallmark of the special period. Although in the early decades of the revolution iconic images of its leaders "beckoned viewers to be mobilized toward a permanent resurrection" (96), these same images operated quite differently during the 1990s, entering a "mode of production and reproduction . . . that understood its iconicity as the point of departure for the production of a trinket" (97).

Consistent with narratives of postmodernism, which Catherine Davies reads generally as "disenchantment with narratives of progress in the ideological and cultural spheres" (117n1), and in post-Soviet Cuban arts specifically as "a crisis of confidence in the Cuban 'supreme fictions'—a loss of faith in the state and the Revolutionary ethic" (112), the nostalgia that underpins tourism to Cuba is not a politically actionable response.[36] It is not a spur to revolution but rather to the contemplation thereof. Thus, in the special period, Cuba can stand as an ideological theme park similar to those that the collapse of Eastern European socialism brought to Germany, with the crucial difference that its attractions do not offer artificial reconstructions of slogan-splashed billboards, half-empty food stores, and Soviet cars but rather the real thing, populated by its original inhabitants.[37] To German-style "Ostalgie," special period Cuba brings a much-valued ingredient: the persistent and visible presence of native life.

That Cuba's function as a tourist attraction is dependent on historically defined renderings of authenticity and nostalgia is particularly evident in its versions of what Frow, drawing on MacCannell's term, lists as tourism's "markers," or representations.[38] Arguing for the centrality of photography to industrialized tourism, Frow includes as markers "brochures, advertisements, guidebooks, coffee-table books" (144). Given the voyeuristic impulse that motored special period tourism to Cuba, and the strongly visual dimension of the attractions visitors sought there—Vicent's invocation of a light that fuses human faces with architectural ruins being merely the most stylized on his list of images—it is not surprising that visual media should be the principal disseminators of the aesthetic code through which Cuba came to be recognized outside the country at this time and that fiction writers choose to engage. Often produced in Europe and the United States and marketed to readers and spectators outside Cuba, glossy photography books and documentary films with Cuba as their subject also saw a boom in the 1990s. Ana María Dopico's study of such foreign-produced photography books proposes that this boom, simultaneous with that of Cuban cultural exports more broadly, "reconfigures photography's documentary burden, integrating it into the wider sensual markets of music and tourism" (454). From books of photography by Gianfranco Gorgoni, Claudio Edinger, David Harvey, and René Burri, Dopico explores the complex basis of post-Soviet Cuba's allure, reading on its visible and ostensibly neutral surface an "ideological geography" (452) that holds "banal and ominous significance for a city that lives in multiple temporalities, a capital that is negotiating survival and ideology, improvising its daily life amid the shifting and mixed economies of third-world tourism and Cold War symbolism" (451). The propagandistic shots of new sports facilities and clean cityscapes that the Cuban government circulated during the 1970s and 1980s were replaced in the special period by two main subjects that Dopico, like Vicent, identifies as "the crumbling beauty of buildings and the apparently candid beauty of Cuban faces" (465). This special period iconography imposes spatial limitations that at the same time cloud thoughtful vision, through both its focus on Havana and its veneer of aesthetic, and thus political, harmony. In thus occluding complexity, photographs portray the city as both recognizable and readable, as "a consumable geography that symbolically abolishes everything else around it" (453). Photographs are particularly troubling, argues Dopico, as they deliver "an unrivaled Cuban light that must substitute for enlightenment in the viewer" (452). They replace travel to Cuba for U.S. citizens, if not for those of the European countries in which these photography books are published and for whom they are, rather, an extension of the tourist experience.

Of the numerous documentary exposés filmed in Cuba during the 1990s, Wim Wenders's *The Buena Vista Social Club,* based on Ry Cooder's Grammy-winning recordings of traditional Cuban music with a hastily assembled group of elderly musicians, was by far the most successful, and thus a chief propagator abroad of a repertoire of special period images. Dopico sees *The Buena Vista Social Club* as sharing with the photographs in her analysis "both visual tropes and a persistent romance with socialist decay and Latin essence" (486) and, as chapter 5 explores further, debate on this documentary both within Cuba and elsewhere emphasized similar contradictions. In a roundtable discussion hosted and published by the journal *Temas,* Cuban intellectuals expressed concern about the documentary's partial perspective, both on traditional music at the expense of more contemporary genres and on Havana as a physical entity. Musicologist María Teresa Linares charged the film with lingering on "scenes of the dilapidated houses, the dilapidated cars, of all the poverty that the embargo has caused," and with contrasting this Havana to a gleaming New York in an act of aggression that ignores the cause of decay: the U.S. economic blockade against Cuba.[39] These criticisms and others that I discuss in chapter 5 see in *The Buena Vista Social Club* an implicit and biased contrast between the decline of Cuba's socialist utopia and the vitality of its octogenarian inhabitants, who survive against the odds and in the apparent absence of revolutionary zeal. Such foreign-produced visual arts perpetuate the mechanism of tourism to Cuba, wherein the special period is consumed as a set of ideologically contradictory but visually palatable images. Their aestheticization of systemic decay and human vitality, and the location of these two in the same physical and eminently recognizable space, is a formal valorization of Cuban authenticity and the nostalgias it inspires.

From a context of profound economic upheaval, then, in which the U.S. dollar redefines not only Cuban citizens' means of buying and selling, but also their relationship to both the long-standing socialist project and capitalist societies, there emerges a distinct visual aesthetic. Engendered in the relative immediacy of tourists' encounters with Havana, this aesthetic coalesces in visual arts whose subject is Cuba but whose consumers are elsewhere, and whose producers are themselves outsiders. From their very conception, these representations are exclusive to the tourist circuit, and effective extensions of its booming industry. Such visual productions found literary counterparts in the 1990s, in the shape of sensationalized novels with titles like *Los placeres de la Habana* (The pleasures of Havana) and *Cuba: La noche de la jinetera* (Cuba: The night of the hustler), by the Spaniards Vicente Romero and Jordi Sierra y Fabra, and *Cuba and the Night,* by the U.S.-based writer Pico Iyer, each of which invokes a Havana of struggling socialism and of moral and physical decay. Travelogues published in English during this period (those by Andrei Codrescu and David Graham, and by Christopher P. Baker, for example) also tended to foreground both the island's status as temporal anomaly—as a timeless landscape flecked with fading billboards, ramshackle vehicles, and an ingenious people finding ever more inventive ways to survive—and their authors' bemused but charmed detachment from the scenes before them. Dopico reads such travelogues as "somehow thin and self-reflexive—still suffering from an unfulfilled appetite for the most essential register of travel writing: analysis by the native, the transparent heart and translated national body for the tourist text" (462). What she finds most disquieting about this ventriloquism on the part of foreign writers, as of foreign photographers, is its one-sidedness, its imposition of "a gaze that can rarely be returned (453) precisely because "native written discourse about Havana has suffered from censorship, export, and dispossession" (462). She continues: "'Metropolitan' genres like urban chronicles, political reporting, or cultural critique written by Habaneros in Havana have not exactly been plentiful in a time of economic transition and fluctuating government surveillance" (ibid.).

FICTION AND THE SPECIAL PERIOD

Dopico's reading does not address the burgeoning number of Cuban voices that made themselves heard—as live and recorded music, as film, as photography, and as text—both in Cuba and internationally, owing to the special period's unprecedented distribution of cultural products and, in the United States, to the Clinton administration's facilitation of educational and artistic exchanges.[40] The scarcity of "native written discourse" about Havana, Dopico writes, "reminds us that a metropolis forges its identity in print, circulating as a lettered city, rewritten daily in a vernacular that contests tourist illusions by revealing an urban *vida cotidiana*" (462). The claim that native discourse is best channeled through the written word, through the constitution of a "lettered city," leaves open the status of textual production in Cuba at this time. Often credited, particularly in the early 1990s, with standing in for state-controlled journalism, fiction over the course of the special period addresses the question of Cuban "voicing" or "returning the gaze"—and the many other challenges that the period presented—in subtle ways, often problematizing the invitation to bear witness as yet another instance of tourists' and readers' thirst for authenticity. Indeed, fiction written by Cubans, with publication abroad as a consideration but not always as a reality, has as ambiguous a relationship to foreign-generated images of Cuba as to the dramatic economic changes that were to expose the country to capitalist markets.

Writers of special period fiction explore these relationships by embedding elements of them in their work: not as explicit critique, but rather through a series of textual figures that afford their authors both distance from and complicity with Cuba's new socioeconomic order and its new geographies of publishing. Contestation in fiction of the dollarized period moves on from the assumed ex-centricity and formal experimentation that José B. Álvarez has read in the *novísimos'* "contestatory fiction" of the late 1980s and early 1990s, to accommodate strategic alignments with the market. It also, however, challenges its markets and the political changes that have stimulated them. In acknowledgment of the discomfiting but undeniable supremacy of U.S. money, the dollar bill becomes a fetish; but it also becomes a text whose inscriptions, like those of books themselves, determine its currency. Tourists become both naive and exploitative bedfellows, both observers and participants in city life, while voyeurs, both Cuban and foreign, operate behind every wall, making a public spectacle of intimate encounters. Misery is exposed without mercy for either its sufferers or its readers; it is put on show and on sale, calling into question the price of bearing witness. Architectural ruins provide the scaffolding for fiction but also assume tragically human forms.

The following chapters tease out the structure of these figures and scenes, reading them in their context and tracing the formal innovations that define them as special period fiction. The chapters pursue insistent questions: How does the partial dollarization, if not the complete globalization, of Cuban society and literature shape fiction of the subsequent years? How do Cuban writers, implicated in the dynamics of international publishing whether they live in Cuba or abroad, acknowledge a readership whose expectations are vastly different from those of the domestic and noncommercial markets in which their work would previously have circulated? How do they respond to the demand for authentic Cuban experience that pervades outsiders' investment in tourism and the arts? Do their fictional renderings of life in Havana sustain the nostalgic readings that Cuba inspires in other media? How does fiction address the dramatic vendibility of things Cuban? Uniting these is the broader question of what happens to a literature—thematically, formally, and commercially—when its place of origin becomes attractive to consumers for the very feature, its socialist revolution, that once spurned capitalist consumption. Pedro Juan Gutiérrez offers the beginnings of an answer in the refrain that opens this chapter; and over the course of readings to come others echo him with varying degrees of enthusiasm, apprehension, resignation, and opposition, in acknowledging that "we're what sells like hot bread."

Both the U.S. dollar's all-pervasive entry into Cuban territory and experience and the much-marketed images of vitality and ruin are challenged and complicated from the field of literature. The second and third chapters of this book take on the first tenet of special period fiction, the dollar; the fourth and fifth turn to the repertoire of images that tourism and its concomitant cultural boom—direct effects of the dollarized economy—generated. Several of the texts explored, including Zoé Valdés's *I Gave You All I Had*, Ronaldo Menéndez's "Money," and Pedro Juan Gutiérrez's *Dirty Havana Trilogy*, are set at least partially in 1993 and 1994, the harshest years of the special period, when Cuba initiated its painful transition to a dual currency. The dollar makes its way into the fabric of these texts, its presence or absence becoming defining factors in their characters' physical, mental, and spiritual survival. Characters chase the dollar; they inform, conform, and perform for it; they love, hate, and copulate for it. The dollar is a figure for many things: for corruption, disruption, and power games, but, overridingly, for relations between Cubans and foreigners. And yet in these fictions and others set later in the decade, meditation on the invasive, intimate experience of contact with the U.S. dollar is counterbalanced by a shrewdly external perspective on the special period, inscribed as a recognition of the interest that the period and its tropes hold for outside viewers. As I explore in chapter 2, Valdés's pioneering novel incorporates this interest, as do the more anxious short stories of Ronaldo Menéndez, Anna Lidia Vega Serova, and others that I read in chapter 3. I suggest in chapter 4, however, that it is the brash and crude revelations of Pedro Juan Gutiérrez's novels—their exposure of Centro Habana intimacy at its most raw, and its most marketable—that take on readers' voyeuristic curiosity most explicitly. That the appeal of the supposedly vibrant and authentic goes hand in hand with that of a peculiarly ideological form of nostalgia is no more evident than in the elegies and conspiracy theories of Antonio José Ponte's fiction and essays, the subject of chapter 5, where ruins become the architecture of a fragile and strangely defamiliarized Cuba. Motored by dramatic social and economic change, special period fiction challenges the images that advertised Cuba to the world and the currency—both the money and the vogue—that allowed them to do so.

CHAPTER 2

Dollar Trouble:
The Roots of Special Period Fiction

"I gave you my whole life," cries the cover of Zoé Valdés's 1996 novel, and we can almost hear the love-torn tones of the Cuban boleros for which each of its chapters is named. There is something missing, though: the lament lacks a subject, a singer to give it voice and to give "all I had," as Nadia Benabid's English translation puts it. This line about giving gives away little, but the strains of its painful exchange should resonate as we move from the nostalgia-laden bolero to Cuba's dynamic cultural boom. Here exchange is explicitly monetary—determined, in fact, by the U.S. dollar that was legalized as Cuban currency in 1993 to alleviate a severe economic crisis. *I Gave You All I Had* is one of the earliest works of a boom in Cuban literature that began to take hold in Europe and the Americas in the late 1990s, and Zoé Valdés is a pioneer of a subgenre of contemporary Cuban fiction that took as its material the "special period in times of peace," Cuba's post-Soviet decade of economic hardship. Amid the images of suffering, sex, and socialist bureaucracy that animate the special period literary landscape, sketched in particularly lurid brushstrokes in Valdés's early novels, a single figure stands out and motivates much of that period's literary production. That figure is the dollar, and this chapter traces its inscriptions and implications

35

in Cuban fiction. *I Gave You All I Had* showcases a particularly potent dollar, one whose layers of inscription both multiply its potential for profit and, in a dramatic move that takes its cue from special period economics, charts a newly lucrative relationship between Cuban writing and foreign money.

Zoé Valdés's place in contemporary Cuban letters is, by any measure, a contentious one. Cuba's Minister of Culture Abel Prieto reportedly called her work "a literary subproduct" and another common charge, whose double meaning this chapter will unpack, is that it is "touristic."[1] Yet the specter of her commercial success haunted both writers and fiction in Cuba in the last years of the millennium. Hers was a discomfiting specter for writers living on the island, for she was a prominent exile, having lived in Paris since early 1995, and authored both fiction and nonfiction as a harsh and uncompromising critic of Fidel Castro and the Cuban Revolution. Although she published poetry in Cuba and was still resident there when her first novel, *Sangre azul* (Blue blood), was published, it is for her post-1995 novels that she is best known. *Yocandra in the Paradise of Nada* was written in Cuba during the early years of the special period and smuggled to France, where it was published simultaneously with its Spanish original in 1995 (Santí 9). *I Gave You All I Had* was published in Spanish in 1996, having been a finalist for the highly publicized Planeta Prize. Although two other novels, both revisions of texts written in Cuba, were published in Europe during that same period—*La hija del embajador* (The ambassador's daughter) in 1995 and *Sangre Azul* in 1996)—*Yocandra in the Paradise of Nada* and *I Gave You All I Had* stand as landmarks in the course that fiction written in Cuba was to follow for much of the 1990s, and in how this fiction would be read and marketed outside the island. On the one hand, both novels were commercially successful and were among the first new Cuban novels of the decade to be widely translated.[2] More important, however, it is with these two novels that Valdés inaugurates a thematic and linguistic repertoire closely bound to the social and economic conditions of 1990s Cuba.

Both *Yocandra in the Paradise of Nada* and *I Gave You All I Had* are set at least partly in Havana of the 1990s, and both are woven from a signature blend of physical squalor, political excess, and sexual proclivity. *Yocandra in the Paradise of Nada* is told by Yocandra, who was born on "an island that had wanted to build Paradise" (1) and named "Patria" (Fatherland) by her fervently revolutionary father.[3] Yocandra's birth and loves—with the Traitor, a sadistic officialist who sends her back from Paris upon their divorce, and the Nihilist, with whom she conducts a lust-ridden affair upon her return to Havana—are told against the backdrop of a malfunctioning, misguided social system that empties Yocandra's life of both meaning and nourishment. *I Gave You All I Had* is more fantastic and sweeping in its panorama of the revolution but, in dwelling on Cuba of the 1990s, it exposes the same hopeless decay as *Yocandra;* for beneath their anti-Castro tirades and extravagant sexual experiments both novels ground an aesthetic that has its basis in material lack. They push the practice of *inventar,* a neologism in its 1990s sense of making ends meet, to new linguistic possibilities. *Inventar* stood alongside its then synonym *resolver* as the core verb of the special period, a hopeful euphemism for finding material sustenance where there was none.[4] *Yocandra in the Paradise of Nada* and *I Gave You All I Had* dramatize this enforced creativity and cast it as a literary practice, wherein nothingness itself breeds new language and new material forms. It is only literature, for example, that allows Patria/Yocandra to taste once-familiar fruits: "Ah, papayas! How well I remember you. You who can no longer be savored anywhere but in a work of literature!" (57).[5] *Yocandra,* whose Spanish version *La nada cotidiana* is a play on *el pan cotidiano,* "daily bread," crafts its title from the substance of nothingness, and its tale of a young woman's quest for fulfillment that quickly declines into a quest for survival in post-Soviet Havana sets a precarious foundation for an aesthetic of absence both inside and outside Cuba. Pedro Juan Gutiérrez builds upon it for his Centro Habana Cycle, as my fourth chapter explores; as does Daína Chaviano in *El hombre, la hembra y el hambre* (Man, woman, and hunger), written in Miami and published in Spain in 1998. *I Gave You All I Had* epitomizes this practice of material invention, as its heroine conjures up a mouth-watering meal from thin air: "She tries to remember what she ate yesterday. Yesterday, she ate nothing. She fed on sliced air and fried wind" (110).[6]

Following *Yocandra*'s lead, *I Gave You All I Had* elaborates upon *inventar* as both material survival and creative liberation but, published a year after the former's commercial success, it takes its engagement with the special period a crucial step further; for *I Gave You All I Had* incorporates into its design the new economic relationships into which this period of crisis steered Cuban fiction, and its strategies for doing so are the subject of this chapter. The novel tells the tragicomic tale of Cuca Martínez, a young woman abandoned by her lover Juan (or el

'Uan—the One) as the revolution triumphs, and left in Havana with no reminder of him other than the 1935 U.S. dollar bill that he pressed into her hand as he said good-bye. After three decades, during which the ever-yearning Cuca has given birth to his daughter and witnessed the nationalizations and literacy campaign of the 1960s, the failed sugar harvest of the 1970s, and the bureaucracies of the 1980s, el 'Uan returns to a Havana ravaged by the special period to reclaim not only his lost love but also his lost dollar. The dollar's serial number is the key to a Swiss bank account where Juan's gang, displaced by the revolution from Havana to New York, has stored its most valuable deposits. He retrieves the dollar, but his love is ill-fated: he and Cuca are again separated, and both she and Cuba are left to perish in a time warp where 1959 is barely distinguishable from 1995. This novel, as its critics have commented, has more controversial protagonists than the undercover dollar, among them its humor, its obscenities, its take on discourses of gender and nationalism, and its antagonism toward the Cuban political system.[7] But I want to let the banknote play the leading role, as its implications for Cuban writing in the new publishing markets of the post-Soviet period, where deals are made in hard currency and demands are driven by cultural difference, are far-reaching. Juan's dollar bill keeps the plot in motion, linking Havana to New York and the 1950s to the 1990s, and its peculiar features—the fact that it is technically obsolete and yet rendered valuable by its inscriptions—make it a particularly laden symbol in the context of a post-1993 Cuba where the U.S. dollar circulates legally. In its hyperbolizing of the properties and possibilities of the U.S. dollar, *I Gave You All I Had* not only showcases the special period repertoire of the earlier *Yocandra* but anticipates, embeds, and even caricatures the interest this repertoire would generate among publishers and readers abroad. This novel full of secret codes is itself a code to the special period: to how, in this time of economic and political crisis, the dollar both changed hands and changed meaning.

Cuca's first encounter with a dollar bill is conspicuously anticlimactic. It is 1959 and, fearing persecution for his clandestine and antirevolutionary activities, Juan has left her for what he insists will be a short time but is in fact more than three decades. He has sealed his good-bye with the banknote, imploring her to take care of his cherished possession. But Cuca fails to appreciate its significance, either for Juan or in economic life more broadly:

In her opened hand, she saw a 1935 dollar bill resting against her smooth, young palm. It was her first American dollar; she didn't give it much thought. What's the big deal? It wasn't all that different from our money, just a piece of paper in another language. She'd find a safe place for it, and she stuck it deep inside the flower pot where her malanga flourished. He would come back, as he always did, money in his pockets and love in his heart. And she sat down in a chair to wait. (58)[8]

Cuca's dismissal of the U.S. dollar—that is, her inability to take it as anything other than a piece of paper, or to interpret what is written on it—marks a crucial turning point in the novel. This is her last moment of innocence, the last in which she will be allowed the luxury of not recognizing the dollar, before a thirty-six-year hiatus that ends in 1995 with a chapter named for Carlos Puebla's song "Se acabó la diversión" (The party's over). In the first years of the special period, when dollars are legal tender but she has none, Cuca will no longer contemplate a dollar bill with anything but elation. In fact, the next time one comes her way—in the early 1990s, when she is treasure seeking in her neighbors' garbage and the wind slaps a soaking banknote against her face—its implications are bountifully evident:

Squinching her eyes, Cuca Martínez sees that *it* filters the light and is made of some kind of paper. She makes out large and pleasing letters, but these are framed and adorned by other signs that stump her understanding of that word—ONE—and the language in which it's written. She might be an old lady, but she's not that old (even though she may feel as old as Methuselah sometimes) and sharp as a tack. She moves her eyes side to side and back and forth and traps the fluttering green bill as it grazes the bone that used to be her cleavage. A dollar bill! God Almighty! Sweet Miracle of Lazarus, what'll she buy herself? What'll she buy? (112)[9]

Here Cuca's proximity to the dollar—it is spread across her face—impedes her immediate understanding of its inscription, but she is soon illuminated, and able to read both the dollar's wording and its significance. "One" now belongs to a lexicon she knows rather than to another language, and not merely because her lover, el 'Uan, is its namesake. In stark contrast to her indifference toward a dollar bill in 1959, in 1993 this one presents itself to her as a symbol that is no less than miraculous, for it translates directly into purchasing potential, into the incantatory

"What'll she buy herself? What'll she buy?" She subsequently runs through the inventory of possible purchases—"How about a lollipop! No, no, no—a Coca-Cola? Oh, come on! What'll XXL say if he hears I'm gaga for the drink of the enemy" (112)[10]—and it is clear to her that, thirty-six years after her first encounter with a bill of this denomination and in this language, it is now much more than a piece of paper.

Between Cuca's first and second readings of the dollar bill there lies a deep epistemological difference: not merely that between Cuca's youthful innocence and her later decay but, more broadly, between the impotence of the U.S. dollar at the beginning of the Cuban Revolution and a time and place—special period Cuba—where its potency is immense. The transition from the dollar as an inconsequential piece of paper to a bill whose language and potential are understood only too clearly is at the crux of both the novel and its implications for Cuban society. These implications begin in the relationship between money and the writing upon it, which itself lies initially—as Cuca's two encounters show—in the ability to read, or in a prior knowledge of the codes that authorize money. More specifically, Cuca's reading of the dollar bill draws us into questions about the nature of money and its dependence on writing; about the meanings and purposes of money in a socialist society, the particular example being the slogan-laden revolution masterminded by Fidel Castro; and, ultimately, about how fictional writing in a dollarized Cuba was to create and engage its own hard-currency publishing markets. These three questions, framed by the three values of the dollar in *I Gave You All I Had*—first as worthless, then as the price of a Coca-Cola, and finally as the key to millions—shape the course of my reading. They underpin the three relationships that structure this chapter: the first between money and writing; the second between Cuca's dollar and Cuba's; and the third between Cuban fiction and its new international markets.

"JUST A PIECE OF PAPER IN ANOTHER LANGUAGE": WRITING AND THE AUTHORSHIP OF MONEY

Cuca's initial dismissal of the dollar as a worthless piece of paper disallows a relationship between writing and value that is fundamental to the history of money. It is with this initial denial that we should begin, as it stands in contrast to the extreme proximity between writing and money that the novel's later special period chapters imply. In reading the dollar as "a piece of paper in another language," Cuca fails to recognize its role in the capitalist circulation of commodities formulated in Marx's *Capital*. A commodity, initially defined as "a thing that by its properties satisfies human wants of some sort or another" (1) has both a use-value, that "become[s] a reality only by use or consumption" (2); and a relative exchange value. Capitalist economics privilege the latter, which is the value a commodity acquires when it enters into "a social relation . . . with the whole world of commodities" (37); that is, when its value is measured against others'. Money is a "special commodity" (72) and "the equivalent commodity *par excellence*" (ibid.), its function being "to supply commodities with the material for the expression of their values, or to represent their values of the same denomination, qualitatively equal, and quantitatively comparable" (ibid.). Although money's value is measured in relation to those of other commodities, its properties go beyond theirs precisely because of the effective negation of its pre-"social" use-value. Unlike any other commodity, which "never assumes this form [exchange value] when isolated, but only when placed in a value or exchange relation with another commodity of a different kind" (35), money operates only in terms of exchange. "Its functional existence absorbs, so to say, its material existence" (107).

The question of money's materiality versus its power to represent other materials—or its always-redundant use-value versus its always-predominant exchange value—is central to both Cuca's contemplation of the dollar and capital itself. Marx's analysis of exchange value is dependent on the fact that the material from which money is made—be it gold or paper—is superseded by what the inscription on that coin or bill says it is worth. It is only thus, when its value in terms of "social relations" has eclipsed what it might be worth outside of these, that money can function as "the equivalent commodity *par excellence*." In this regard, it is revealing that in 1959 Cuca should see the dollar bill as not only of little importance, but as "a mere piece of paper"—in terms of its material use, or lack thereof, rather than for its potential in social relations; for the transition from material that is valuable in itself to the mere symbolization of value was profoundly disruptive in the genealogy of money. Tracing this genealogy, Marc Shell identifies three distinct moments of upheaval, each taking money to a greater degree of symbolization than the last. Shell begins his narrative of the sweeping ideological shifts in the meanings of money, and of their inherent relationship to language, as follows:

Between the electrum money of ancient Lydia and the electric money of contemporary America there occurred a historically momentous change. The exchange value of the earliest coins derived wholly from the material substance (electrum) of the ingots of which the coins were made and not from the inscriptions stamped into these ingots. The eventual development of coins whose politically authorized inscriptions were inadequate to the weights and purities of the ingots into which the inscriptions were stamped precipitated awareness of quandaries about the relationship between face value (intellectual currency) and substantial value (material currency). This difference between inscription and thing grew greater with the introduction of paper moneys. Paper, the material substance on which the inscriptions were printed, was supposed to make no difference in exchange, and metal or electrum, the material substance to which the inscriptions referred, was connected with those inscriptions in increasingly abstract ways. With the advent of electronic fund-transfers the link between inscription and substance was broken. The matter of electronic money does not matter. (1)

In *I Gave You All I Had* the dollar does not reach its final degree of (electronic) abstraction; on the one occasion when Juan tries to pay with a credit card, no shop assistant believes that it is backed by money and Cuca, in her clear-sightedness, takes the card for an absence of wealth (183–85).[11] Instead, the dollar's properties are effectively those of paper until the economic crisis of the 1990s, and the enhanced opportunities for moneymaking that this crisis ushers in propel it to progressively more spectacular levels of representation. It is precisely the dollar's condition as a piece of paper that facilitates this trajectory and its inherent ambiguities. As Kevin McLaughlin notes in the context of nineteenth-century discourse on virtuality, paper money was troubling "because it challenged the traditional identification of value with substance" (964).[12] The United States being the context in which paper money first circulated comprehensively, the dollar is an apt and early poster child for the duplicities of money; debate over these "dominated American political discourse from 1825–1875" (Shell 5–6). Banknotes enact what Shell calls the dissociation of "sign from substance," wherein their value lies in what is written on them rather than in what they (intrinsically, materially) are.[13] It is in this deeply important sense that writing makes money, or makes money what it is. Money eclipses the material value of paper in favor of a written endorsement that ascribes value arbitrarily.

Money, then, is dependent both on writing and on purchasers' recognition of that writing's authority. That these same tenets—writing, and an institutionalized belief in it—should also be those of fiction did not escape writers in whose societies paper money circulated widely, as Shell discusses in the case of Edgar Allan Poe's "The Gold Bug."[14] Credit is the principle that renders the circulation of fiction analogous to that of money: "credit, or belief, involves the very ground of aesthetic experience, and the same medium that seems to confer belief in fiduciary money (bank notes) and in scriptural money (created by the processes of bookkeeping) also seems to confer it to literature" (Shell 7). This structural proximity of money to fiction, and the analogous circulation of these two, becomes central to *I Gave You All I Had*'s embedding of its own reading market, when its dollar leaves the early revolution for the special period.

Cuca's misreading of the dollar in 1959 appears as an act less of ignorance than of unknowing resistance to capitalism, for it defies the meaning of writing and hence also money's potential for exchange. To Cuca, the piece of paper Juan has bequeathed does not represent value within a system of commodities to be bought and sold; rather than creating a symbolic value, the "foreign language" in which this bill is inscribed bears no message for her, and thus denies the bill its status as money. It is no more than a piece of paper—and, with this refusal of recognition, Cuca undermines the economic system in which she ostensibly participates. Although she repudiates this face of capitalism at a particularly appropriate moment—in the first years of a revolution soon to be declared socialist—her refusal to allow writing to make money is anticipated by earlier scenes in Cuban fiction. We might rewind to these briefly to better understand the strategies and about-faces that steer *I Gave You All I Had*. Where scenes from Alejo Carpentier's *The Chase* (1956) and Lino Novás Calvo's "La noche de Ramón Yendía" (The night of Ramón Yendía) (1942) call into question the value that writing ascribes to money, Cuca's first encounter does the same, only then to see this separation overwritten, and the dollar overencoded, as the novel relocates to the 1990s. Valdés's novel, that is, inserts itself in a genealogy of fiction that questions writing's authorization of money but eventually reaffirms this authorization, linking it to the market potential of authorship. Both Carpentier's and Novás Calvo's stories are set in the same moment of political crisis—Gerardo Machado's dictatorship, and the 1933 revolution that put an end to it—and both, like Valdés's novel, are structured around a chase through the streets of Havana. *The Chase,* moreover, is played to the movements of Beethoven's Eroica symphony, just as *I Gave You All I Had* is choreographed to a series of boleros. As its financial about-face makes it a particularly interesting model for the meanings of money in *I Gave You All I Had,* we should follow its lead first.

Pursued by the fellow conspirators whom he has betrayed, *The Chase'*s fugitive leaves a telling trail, charted by a consistent clue: a paper banknote whose claims to value are as elusive as the fugitive himself; for whether the bill that he entrusts to the prostitute Estrella and to the theater ticket collector means what it says is open to question. The note is, as Stephen Boldy has observed, one of several texts in *The Chase* that are consistently misread, and whose legitimacy turns out to be suspect (614). It is graced by "the general with the sleepy eyes," an inscription whose meaning seems to be that it is worth nothing in the monetary system in which it surreptitiously circulates; "and besides," states the ticket collector in what is almost the final word on the recently assassinated student, "he was passing counterfeit money" (122).[15] If, like many a fictional banknote before it, this sleepy-eyed bill is counterfeit, then it implicitly abdicates from the relationship between writing and money, or between inscription and worth, that is at the basis of modern-day money. Counterfeit money strips away the constructed correspondence between writing and value: its inscriptions mark the depletion of denotation, and the Cinderella-like return of the embellished banknote to its impoverished condition as paper. Reading the title of Charles Baudelaire's prose poem "Counterfeit Money" as boding of illegitimacy, Jacques Derrida argues that counterfeit money "is a sign and an incorrectly titled sign, a sign without value, if not without meaning" (85). Its meaning, that is, is related precisely to its subversion of value and to its indecipherable status. If the sleepy-eyed general on *The Chase'*s banknote is not to be taken at face value, then, like Baudelaire's counterfeit, this banknote disallows the dependency of money on writing. And yet this disallowance is not definitive. Derrida insists that there is a necessary element of uncertainty surrounding a counterfeit bill, as only while it is *perhaps* genuine can it sustain the belief—"the *credit,* the act of faith" (95)—that allows it to circulate; and it is just this possibility of legitimacy that surfaces at the end of Carpentier's novella; for the question of counterfeiting is resolved in favor of the correspondence between writing and money. A policeman promises to submit the counterfeit banknote in court and let its falsehood be proof of that of the deceased;

but an underhanded observation on the part of the narrator—slipped in between the policeman's own last words—turns the tables completely: "'Give it to me,' said the officer, seeing that it was perfectly good. 'It will have to be included as evidence in the case'" (122).[16] The policeman's recognition that the note is not counterfeit reinstates the possibility of a relationship between inscription and value, in a resolution that anticipates the ultimate affirmation of this same relationship in the closing chapters of *I Gave You All I Had*.

The threat that paper money might be relegated to its mere material condition is realized more definitively in Novás Calvo's "La noche de Ramón Yendía." Set in a climate of revolutionary turmoil that prefigures the one in which Juan will abandon Cuca, its hero is the humble Ramón Yendía, a rebel once coerced into cooperation with the authorities and fearful for his life now that power has changed hands.[17] Soon to be assassinated himself, in a case of mistaken identity rather than retaliation, the hero watches as a lone fugitive, pursued by a gang of armed and bearded revolutionaries, tries desperately to buy their mercy with money: "he zigzagged along furiously, throwing fistfuls of banknotes at his pursuers as he ran."[18] But the pursuers ignore his gesture: "they trampled over the banknotes, without picking them up, shooting at him."[19] They incinerate both the fugitive and his banknotes, ignoring the value inscribed upon the money and reducing it to its material, and thereby combustible, condition as paper. Like Cuca's refusal to read the words on Juan's dollar, the gesture of these 1933 revolutionaries coincides with the attempt to radically rewrite money, and what it might mean in society, undertaken by Fidel Castro's revolutionary project. In the 1933 revolution, a national labor strike that provoked widespread violence and forced Machado out of power, Hugh Thomas sees a portent of the rebellion that ousted Fulgencio Batista a quarter of a century later: "the revolution of 1959 followed in the wake of that of 1933 as the Second World War followed the First, or the revolution in Russia in 1917 followed that in 1905" (605). In this same vein, Yendía's recollection that during his childhood the word *revolution* stood in for national currency prefigures the rescripting of money that Castro's 1959 revolution initiated.[20] For although Che Guevara's ideal of a moneyless society was never realized, the subsidies, the rationing systems, and even the hermetic trading relationship with the Soviet Union in which Cuba was locked for over three decades limited the free exchange of commodities that, in a capitalist economy, is promoted by money and its powers of simulation.[21] Cuca Martínez remarks that over the first decades of the revolution "[m]oney had lost all meaning, large bills were a rarity nowadays—value, supply, and demand had been consigned to oblivion" (75),[22] and it is no coincidence that the special period, during which capitalist economics once again infiltrated Cuban society, should crudely jolt her memory.

From the outset of the revolution, both the production of Cuban banknotes and the inscriptions upon them—that is, their specifically textual aspect—were brought into the service of a broader social project. In August 1961 the government recalled all banknotes then in circulation and reissued a new series, in order to remove Cuban money from foreign control. Between 1934 and 1960, Cuban pesos had been printed in the United States and England, and Law 863 made relocating their production (initially to Czechoslovakia, and subsequently to Cuba's own mint) a matter of urgency: "we must immediately eliminate the insecurity and risk posed by the fact that the Cuban banknotes currently in circulation are printed by foreign companies who are effectively beyond the control of the Revolutionary Government."[23] The banknotes were redesigned and their old images replaced by the revolution's slogans and heroes, in an appreciation for money's powers of representation that had flourished during Fidel Castro's years as an underground guerrilla. His July 26 Movement issued numbered bonds, inscribed "Libertad o Muerte"("Freedom or Death") and depicting an armed warrior, in recognition of its debts to supporters in Cuba and abroad (*Numismática Cubana,* 39). Although the faces on the banknotes issued in 1961 changed little—with the exception of Carpentier's sleepy-eyed General Francisco Vicente Aguilera, who was replaced on the one-hundred-peso note by rebel army commander Camilo Cienfuegos, the mysterious victim of a 1959 airplane crash—their reverse sides sketched vibrant scenes of revolutionary life and struggle. These include Fidel Castro's triumphant entrance into Havana on January 8, 1959; the advance of the rebel army from east to west in late 1958; the large public rally to hear Castro's "Havana Declaration" speech on September 2, 1960; the landing of the yacht *Granma* on December 2, 1956, that marked the beginning of the rebels' invasion; the nationalization of foreign companies on August 6, 1960; and the rebel attack on the Moncada Barracks on July 26, 1953. Later illustrations would include factories and smokestacks of Cuba's "fifteen years of economic development" on a one-peso note to mark the anniversary of the nationalization of Cuba's bank in 1975 and volunteer workers on the reverse of a new three-peso note fronted by the already-iconic Antonio Korda portrait of Che Guevara in 1983. The year 1991, with the withdrawal of Soviet economic support, saw a general reissue of peso bills, on whose reverse side were emblazoned scenes and updated slogans from the ongoing, but increasingly precarious, revolution. Among these are "Guerra de todo el pueblo" ("All the people at war") and, on a one-hundred-peso note issued in 2000, an illustration of the "José Martí Anti-Imperialist Grandstand, City of Havana," the structure built outside the U.S. Interests Section to protest the detention in Miami of the rafter child Elián González. As Jean-Joseph Goux explores, paper money is always an opportunity to ascribe ideological as well as monetary value and, alongside the simple statement of numerical denomination, the revolution and its values have been written into Cuban paper money. The banknote as text reiterates the revolution's message with every private transaction.

The new notes of 1991 were issued during a serious paper shortage, and their valiant rallying slogans were soon to be severely weakened by the legalization of the U.S. dollar. The symbols and slogans that had sustained Cuba's revolution and economy for thirty-five years were to be effectively overwritten by the dollar's English, the "foreign language" toward which Cuca Martínez showed such disregard in 1959. No longer would the U.S. dollar bill be "not all that different from the national peso": both the dollar's distinction from the national peso and the fact that it is printed in a language other than Spanish in a country long vilified as Cuba's ideological nemesis were radically disruptive to the values of both the revolution and its money. In August 1993, shortly before creating a ministry for tourism and announcing measures to promote large-scale investment from abroad, the Cuban government legalized the U.S. dollar, which had long sustained a thriving black market, for domestic use. The Cuban peso, devalued and now unusable in the best-stocked stores, was rendered effectively impotent. This was not the first time in Cuba's history that the dollar had circulated—it had been used since the Republic was declared in 1902 and was official tender until 1951—but to return to the practices of that earlier period, characterized by the rhetoric of the revolution as a period of domination by U.S. interests, was an undeniable compromise for Cuba's economic autonomy.[24] As Goux's reading of it demonstrates, the dollar bill—graced by the face of George Washington and a series of highly charged signs and mottos—speaks a particularly forceful language of power:

Let us consider for a moment the one-dollar "greenback." Clearly this bank note was conceived in such a way that an emblematic power emanates from it and transforms it into a potent political symbol. It is a civil monument that, though made of paper, is nonetheless ceremoniously laden with all the insignia of the state's officialdom. (115–16)

In post-1993 Cuba, the dollar's proudly American inscriptions muscled out those of the country's domestic banknotes, and the revolutionary slogans of the national peso entered into a deeply ambivalent relationship with "In God We Trust." Alongside the dollar there circulated a second innovation of 1990s monetary policy, the Cuban "convertible" peso, also introduced with the economic reforms of 1993 and for the following decade on a par with the dollar only within national territory (Ritter and Rowe 433). In November 2004, sweeping changes put an end to the use of the U.S. dollar—a triumph for both the domestic currency that had been its impoverished avatar and for Cuba's anti-imperialist cause; for the false grandiloquence of the *pesos convertibles,* whose fronts reproduced stone monuments to heroes rather than the heroes themselves and whose backs all bore the same national shield, had previously betrayed their deference to the U.S. dollar. The colorful and proudly revolutionary messages on the nonconvertible Cuban peso, or *moneda nacional,* moreover, had been relegated to the obscurity of a parallel economy—to the bodegas that supplied a limited number of basic foodstuffs, to the purchase of bus and cinema tickets, to the longest line at the ice-cream stand—while the insipid convertible peso and its mighty escort, the U.S. dollar, stole the show. It is the glare of this U.S dollar, legalized for use by all Cubans but effectively the domain of those with jobs in tourism or families abroad, that blinds Cuca, both figuratively and literally, when a bill blows into her face at the start of the special period.

"El dolor del dólar": The Price of Pain

Cuca's appreciation of the second dollar to come her way, three decades after the first, reflects the weight of Cuba's newly legalized currency. In subsequent chapters, upon Juan's arrival in Havana, *I Gave You All I Had* charts both his return and the reentry of the dollar into the Cuban ideological lexicon with a pun. To the question of what the U.S. dollar might mean for Cuba, against the background of increasing tourism and international investment, or what Cuca calls "that abnormal normality to which we've become accustomed" (116),[25] the novel tweaks the word *dólar* to produce instead *dolor*. Puns, in Freud's words, "pass as the lowest form of verbal joke" (45) and in reflection of Cuca's recourse to her neighbors' garbage for sustenance, this one is drawn from a repertoire of street jokes born with the special period and recycled in both this novel and others.[26] This pun is one of the many in *I Gave You All I Had* that contribute to its peculiarly irreverent linguistic composition and that approximate the novel to a third Cuban literary precedent. *I Gave You All I Had* pays conspicuous homage to Guillermo Cabrera Infante's *Three Trapped Tigers* (1967), from its verbal exuberance, to its pastiche on Hollywood cinema, to its elegies of the fragile beauty of Havana nights. *Three Trapped Tigers* (TTT) was also published from exile and, like *I Gave You All I Had,* it showcases the potency of the pun—with the distinction that while *TTT*'s Bustrofedon, its compulsive wordsmith, plays with puns in apparent isolation from his political context, Valdés's novel puns narrowly and antagonistically, with the revolution and its attendant deprivations as the invariable targets.[27] *I Gave You All I Had* makes of *comandante en jefe* (commander in chief) *comediante en jefe* (comedian in chief), for example;[28] and of *plan jaba* (an early-1970s program that gave working women priority in grocery stores) *plan jeba* (189) ("the woman plan," in reference to prostitution).[29]

Against this constant wordplay, the pun on *dólar* and *dolor* stands out as especially potent. Indeed, it is *I Gave You All I Had*'s prototypical pun, the one in which the relationships that define both the novel and its context are plotted. By dramatizing a linguistic situation in which the U.S. dollar is substituted for Cuban pain, the pun invokes the profound disruptions precipitated by the economic reforms of the 1990s, disruptions that the dollar's dependence on writing extend into the orbit of fiction. The pun first appears in a comment on Cuba's health tourism industry, which, from the early 1990s on, marketed the country's famed achievements in medical research to develop a system of clinics for private, dollar-paying patients from abroad. Lamenting that these clinics are not open to her, as a dollar-less Cuban, Cuca remarks: "Just goes to show how dough *[dólar]* can be a palliative for woe *[dolor]* and how the woe-dough syndrome got started in the first place" (110).[30] This syndrome, wherein those who have no dollars to alleviate their pain must instead suffer a pain caused by the very lack of dollars, has given the French translation of the novel its title, *La douleur du dollar* (The pain of the dollar); but a further instance of the pun renders the diagnosis more complex. The first embrace between Juan and Cuca, upon his return to Havana to reclaim his 1935 dollar bill, elicits this miscommunication:

> "And you, Cucita, what have you done with the dough?" And, because her ears were clasped in an embrace and because of the headstrong notions women get when it comes to putting their men on sky-high pedestals, she heard "woe" *[dolor]* instead of "dough" *[dólar]*. (149)[31]

Puns operate through substitution: one word takes the place of a similar-sounding one to produce a second word that is funny precisely because of its incongruity with, and therefore its vestiges of, the first. Distinguishing them from what he calls "play on words proper," wherein "two meanings should find their expression in identically the same word," Freud claims that "it is enough for a pun if the two words expressing the two meanings recall each other by some vague similarity of structure or a rhyming assonance, or whether they share the same first few letters, and so on" (*Jokes,* 45). *I Gave You All I Had*'s pun on *dólar* and *dolor* moves the one word into the place of the other, and its spelling out of the process of replacement, "she heard woe *[dolor]* in the place of dough *[dólar]*," makes for a particularly nuanced exchange. On the one hand, while the dollar is in the place of pain, there is a degree of coexistence between the two that precludes the neutralization of one (pain) by the other (the dollar). In other words, both dollars and pain can be in the same place—as they are, in fact, in Cuca's newly dollarized Havana. Furthermore—and it is in this regard that the pun prefigures the predicament of special period Cuban fiction most insidiously— Cuca and Juan's first encounter puts a price on pain's existence, rather than on its elimination. This is not a straightforward transaction, like the one that Cuca imagines to be the privilege of patients at the tourist clinic, where dollars are given in return for the neutralization of pain. Rather, both the 1935 dollar's whereabouts and Cuca's pain are her secret and privileged possessions. It befalls Juan to elicit from Cuca the hiding place she long ago chose for the dollar, but the novel itself, in its relentless revelations of poverty and decay, exposes the suffering that has shaped Cuca's life since Juan left her at the start of the revolution. Cuca's *dolor* is physical and material, but it also has a more abstract dimension. It is the experience of isolation, abandonment, and waiting in silence.

To read Cuca's *dolor* as her secret is to step into both private and collective suffering, for the novel's most subversive pun is not on *dólar* and *dolor* but on *Cuca* (a diminutive for Caridad, Cuba's patron saint) and *Cuba*. The slippage from one to the other is minimal, such that it is Cuba's pain, as well as Cuca's, that Juan's quest for his dollar unearths. That pain is the property of both Cuca and her country is clear in the novel's closing lines, written by Beatriz de Jústiz y Zayas in 1762 during the capture of Havana by the English:

> You, Havana, capitulated?
> You in lament? and ruination?
> You under foreign domination?
> The pain of it, beloved homeland, the pain! (234)[32]

If Cuca's *dolor* is an intimate experience, guarded for many years and barely known to the outsider (Juan), then we might see Cubans' experience and their country's recent history as following a similar pattern. Tourism to Cuba was restricted and the country was largely off limits to foreign visitors until the mid-1990s, as tourist brochures and travel magazines of the special period, anxious to create a mystique, were quick to remind their readers. Through the tourist industry, Cuba's *dolor* enters into a relationship with the U.S. dollar, the currency used by foreign visitors, that exploits the intrinsic interest of this hitherto closely guarded locale. Thus Juan and Cuca's miscommunication charts a model of exchange, of dollars for *dolor,* in which new tourism to Cuba is at least partially grounded. This is a tourist industry in which relics of the revolution, or its stores of secrets, are prized, where memorabilia like billboards and miniatures of Fidel Castro stand alongside a less tangible sense of ideological anachronism as the country's attractions. The pun on *dólar* and *dolor,* then, foregrounds an exchange in which pain is not eliminated by foreign money but instead is purchased by it. Dollars produce *dolor* by their absence, or rather by their presence in some lives and their absence in others, as Cuca muses to herself outside the tourist clinic, thus reiterating the ideological and economic disruption that the dollar caused upon its initial legalization in Cuba. At the same time and in the same context, however, dollars purchase pain just as Juan persuades Cuca to part with her secret, such that the tourist industry, this novel, and, indeed, a broader fiction industry are shown to depend on the material and ideological paradoxes of Cuba's special period; for, to the extent that fiction set recognizably in this period is itself a surrogate for travel—to the extent, that is, that reading is a form of armchair tourism—its circulation, too, is modeled on the interplay of *dólar* and *dolor.*

The inscription on Cuba's newly coveted dollar bill, then, signifies two things: first, a degree of suffering for those who are condemned to merely longing for money; more broadly, though, it denotes a dynamic wherein foreign money can put a price on a form of experience and knowledge that is peculiar to Cuba. It is in this second capacity that Cuba's new currency dramatically alters the relationship between money and writing, as a further imprint on *I Gave You All I Had*'s dollar bill goes on to show. For it emerges that Juan's banknote is no ordinary dollar bill. Rather, it is one endowed with powers of representation beyond those, even, of the bill Goux describes as "a civil monument." It is inscribed not only with the insignia of U.S. might and the imposing "one dollar," but with two further figures: the number of a secret bank account and the code to access it. It is thus the key not only to Juan's future but also to a relationship between writing and money that is unfathomably profitable. Its layers of coding open up for the money/writing relationship a surplus of potential value and contextual meaning, so that an inscription on a dollar bill becomes a figure for literature in a market and, more broadly, for Cuban culture in a transnational marketplace.

The command that spurs Juan's return from New York to Havana in the early 1990s comes from the boss of his former gang. Juan's gravest error was to leave Havana without the banknote, and for it he has spent the past three decades at the mercy of the organized crime ring. He has now been chosen for the rescue mission: he is to recuperate the banknote he left with Cuca. The boss insists on its importance:

> We need the serial number, it corresponds to our most important account in Switzerland. The account has been off-limits for thirty-six years, there are nine gold threads, each in a different karat, woven into that dollar bill. We need the code to get to the account. (98)[33]

Like all banknotes, this dollar's value lies not in its material but in what it represents. Unlike most paper money, however, it symbolizes at three levels rather than one. Taken at face value, a bill marked "one dollar" would be worth just that amount—a considerable one in special period Cuba, as we know from Cuca's elation at her second encounter with a dollar, but a value nevertheless consistent with its denomination and exchangeable for goods of the same price. But a dollar dated 1935 is no longer legal tender in either the United States or Cuba, so that this inscription is in fact the most specious of the three.[34] The second inscription— the serial number that corresponds to a bank account—multiplies the value of the bill by untold thousands, symbolizing not a dollar's worth of exchange but an as yet unquantifiable reproduction of the bill itself. The third code, the numerically calibrated gold alloys woven through the bill to spell out the key to the secret bank account, might seem to restore money to its presymbolic state; that is, to restore the correspondence between money's substance and its sign. And yet, despite the gang boss's order that Juan guard the bill as if it were gold—"Guard it like gold . . . Our future depends on it" [89])[35]—it is not as gold that the bill is valued. Rather, gold itself becomes a sign, and as a substance is worth less than the riches that it symbolizes. Together, these three codes rewrite the potency of the dollar bill in Juan and Cuca's Cuba; for although paper money always symbolizes something, or some amount, that it is not, Juan's banknote is a performance par excellence: it is worth much more than it advertises, for its superimposed codes are a supernumerary value, supplementary to those of its apparent denomination. These codes allow the note to denote far in excess of itself and afford its bearer access to thousands more of its own kind. Moreover, despite its links to Juan's criminal underworld, this note is not a counterfeit. It does not negate the endorsement of money by writing, nor does it undermine the value of writing itself. Rather, it has a surfeit of both value and meaning, and it points toward a particularly productive relationship between writing and money.

Juan's dollar dramatizes the possibilities of writing on money, or of codifying writing such that it leads to financial gain. The Swiss account code is present on this bill as its serial number, which is one of its standard markings—but its implications are far from standard. To find a correspondence between this printed number and a lucrative bank account is to read closely and to give writing an enhanced function. It is, in a sense, to read the fine print and read between the weave; to take the creative and regenerative potential of writing beyond that which is stated by the banknote's officially backed face value. The dollar bill that underpins *I Gave You All I Had* suggests an unexpectedly productive relationship between writing and money, one that has inevitable implications for the context in which this novel is written and published; for there is, as we know, a necessary dependency between money and writing. Not only is money constituted as such by the inscription upon it but, furthermore, both money and fiction count on credit—or belief in their capacity to represent—for their circulation. Moreover, there is a third layer of dependency, or reciprocity, that reaches striking proportions with *I Gave*

You All I Had: just as money is authorized by writing, so literature is sustained by its paying readership or, more broadly and to include the various components that bring a book to circulation, by its market.

This third reciprocity, between fiction and its market, is written into *I Gave You All I Had,* or written upon its heavily encoded dollar bill; and it is this foreshadowing of a decade of literary history that, as I see it, positions Valdés at the vanguard of special period fiction; for if writing makes money, then, by doubling the denotative capacity of Juan's dollar bill and coding the denotation as the key to untold millions, *I Gave You All I Had* foregrounds the making of money in a double sense. This book both circulates images of Cuba's special period in a hard-currency market for literature and, through the double move effected by the overinscribed dollar, it encodes its own practice. Although it might appear anachronistic to read in *I Gave You All I Had* an inscription of the readership its publication would generate, we should recall that this novel was preceded by Valdés's *Yocandra in the Paradise of Nada*—which is replete with special period imagery but has no such starring role for the U.S. dollar. *I Gave You All I Had* comes in the wake of its forerunner's commercial success in Europe, so that the staging of a transaction between a Cuban and a foreigner—that, thanks to a pun, is also an exchange of *dolor* for *dólar*—is not merely fortuitous. Through its dollar and its pun, *I Gave You All I Had* inscribes a link between external and internal economies, between textual and contextual moneymaking. This doubly inscribed dollar bill is a means of inscribing the foreign reading market in the text, or of embedding and prefiguring a relationship that might otherwise be shy to acknowledge its financial basis. Writing makes money what it is, and *I Gave You All I Had* reiterates this relationship by mapping textual moneymaking onto the production of literature in a particular period—the special period—and a particular market.

WRITING IN THE MARKET

This market for Cuban fiction is the one that began to take shape in the mid-1990s, coinciding with both the harsh conditions of the special period and the foreign-oriented measures taken to combat them: the legalization of the dollar, the promotion of foreign investment in Cuba, and the dramatic expansion of the tourist industry. The attendant changes for Cuban writers were generated from both inside and outside the country. From within, they included relaxed regulations around intellectual property, such that state institutions were no longer required to be intermediaries in the negotiation of contracts between writers and publishers. From outside the country, there came a marked increase in interest on the part of foreign agents and publishers that culminated in the publication of an unprecedented number of new Cuban-authored books and, by 1998, widespread talk of a "new Cuban boom." Despite the geographic and political distance between Zoé Valdés and many of the Havana-based writers whose work was published both inside and outside Cuba during this period, her fiction catalyzed the foreign interests that would create the "new boom." Valdés's brand of special period fiction—sordid, damning, and unforgiving—almost had to see the light of day abroad, rather than in Cuba; and the trajectory of *Yocandra in the Paradise of Nada* and *I Gave You All I Had* in European publishing markets, particularly those of Spain and France, signals Valdés's pivotal, and paradoxical, role in promoting Cuban fiction of the special period abroad. Both Spain and France were important bases for the 1960s Boom that, spurred by interest in the Cuban Revolution, put Latin American literature on the map for European readers; just as Cuban fiction, impelled by the decline of the same revolution, gained a foothold in these two countries in the 1990s. The key to Valdés's success was to capture each of these two bases at the beginning of the special period and thus to blaze a trail for a "new Cuban boom" that mimics the 1960s Boom in its commercial structure—as a phenomenon whose marketing was carefully orchestrated—if not in its geographic extent. And yet, while the aesthetic experiments of the Boom kept their distance from the economics of "booming"—the preferred term of this movement's writers, among them Carlos Fuentes, being *la nueva novela* ("the new novel")—*I Gave You All I Had* is a landmark in the special period precisely because it copies and critiques the mechanics of a boom."[36] It dramatizes the intercultural relationships that sustain the "new boom" and, in so doing, both anticipates and deflects the criticism—specifically, as we will see, the charge that it is literature "for tourists"—that such a raw portrayal of special period Cuba was bound to invite.

More than three decades after the heyday of the 1960s Boom, Spain—where, as both Mario Santana and Mayder Dravasa explore, many Latin American writers lived and most published—became the epicenter of "the new Cuban boom." But at the turn of the millennium, Spanish publishers' interest in Cuban fiction demonstrated less the commitment to art of a political underground, as was the case in the 1960s, than

Spain's increasing economic power in Latin America, and particularly in Cuba, where the U.S. trade embargo kept out the strongest potential competitor. What was termed a Spanish "reconquest" of Latin America was particularly pronounced in Cuba, where Spain ranked high among foreign investors, notably in the tourist sector (Roy 119). From the early 1990s, Spanish companies were among the first investors in hotel construction and administration and, despite a cooling off of political relations after 1996, as the then newly elected José María Aznar forged ties with Washington to the detriment of Havana, the flow of Spanish investment remained strong through the 1990s (Haines). The fact that Spain sent large numbers of tourists to Cuba and has an important history of emigration in the prerevolutionary period contributes to the current popularity of Cuban culture in Spain, as did the island's more generally marketable aura of Caribbean exoticism. As Joaquín Roy writes in his account of a century of Spanish–Cuban relations:

> Cuba persists as an important reference point for Spaniards. It continues to be an object of familiar nostalgia, real or somehow romantically invented . . . In a complex world, the island is a geographic area of accessible dimensions for the Spanish businessman. At the same time, it offers a dose of exoticism through its racial diversity and its Caribbean location.[37]

Anthropologist Mette Rundle argues, too, that Spain's "Cuba-mania"— a loosely termed phenomenon of which the "new Cuban boom" is a specifically literary avatar—"is closely linked to currents of colonialist and revolutionary nostalgia and sexualized images of racial others" (2); and that it created a confusing context for Cubans recently exiled to Spain, who were often implicitly denationalized for their refusal to identify Cubanness with socialism. On the shelves alongside a spate of Spanish-authored novels such as Vicente Romero's *Los placeres de la Habana* (The pleasures of Havana) and Jordi Sierra y Fabra's *Cuba: La noche de la jinetera* (Cuba: The night of the hustler), new and newly published Cuban titles indicated an entrenched fascination on the part of Spanish readers with the simultaneous familiarity and strangeness of Cuba.

Zoé Valdés's two postexile novels stimulate this fascination and were among the first novels set in special period Cuba to be published in Spain. *Yocandra in the Paradise of Nada*'s Spanish publishers are Emecé, and *I Gave You All I Had* appeared with Planeta Editores, a commercial publisher ranked consistently among the ten largest in the country in the late 1990s.[38] In 1996, *I Gave You All I Had* won Planeta's annual prize and thus benefited from a high-profile advertising and marketing campaign (Strausfeld 19). By 1998 its print run had reached 169,000 and its sixteenth Planeta edition; by 2003 there were three separate Spanish editions, including one in Planeta's "Prize Collection" and another in its "Golden Successes" series.[39] Valdés's subsequent novels, most of which have been published by Planeta, have also met with a receptive commercial audience, but it was *Yocandra in the Paradise of Nada* and *I Gave You All I Had* that made her a figurehead for Spain's "new Cuban boom."

And yet, whereas the shared language made Spain's publishing industry the obvious one from which to launch new Cuban fiction, another place in Europe served as a springboard to launch the "new boom," specifically through the residence there of Zoé Valdés. Like the Boom of the 1960s, the dissemination of Cuban fiction in the special period had a French connection. From the nineteenth century on, Paris was home to many a Latin American writer deterred by Spain's political instabilities and colonial legacy, and both Jason Weiss and Marcy Schwartz have explored the allure of the French capital to a Latin American literary canon formed at least partly in exile. In the 1960s, Paris was a de facto center for Latin American literature: as the ill-fated founding there of the CIA-funded journal *Mundo Nuevo* showed, the city was designated as an ideologically more moderate alternative to Havana and its *Revista Casa de las Américas* (Rostagno 100–102). During this period the French capital harbored Latin American exiles and expatriates of divergent political inclinations, from the pro-Castro Julio Cortázar to Cubans fleeing the revolution. Notably, the Cuban writer Severo Sarduy established himself in Paris from the early 1960s, becoming a prominent member of the Tel Quel intellectual group and Latin America editor for both Le Seuil and Gallimard publishers (Hasson). Dissident Cuban writers who have not lived in France have nevertheless seen their work pass through its publishing circuits, the most prominent example being Reinaldo Arenas, whose work—with the exception of *Singing from the Well,* the only book of his published in Cuba—was smuggled to France and published there before his eventual exile to the United States in 1980. Arenas's *Before Night Falls,* in fact, was published in French before any other language (Hasson).

Valdés followed Cuban examples in securing a relationship, for herself and for her books, with France. Like Arenas's early novels, her *Sangre azul* was published in France while she was still resident in Cuba and the manuscript for *Yocandra in the Paradise of Nada* was smuggled out to France and Miami, although she had followed it into exile by the time it was published. Many of Valdés's subsequent novels were published almost simultaneously in French and Spanish, and her first two were well received by French reviewers. Erik Orsenna, a novelist and member of the Académie Française who makes a cameo appearance searching for his Cuban grandparents in *I Gave You All I Had* (189),[40] has compared her writing in *Yocandra in the Paradise of Nada* to that of Milan Kundera (Orsenna 1995), and her Yocandra to Gabriel García Márquez's Ursula Buendía (Orsenna 1997). Like Sarduy, Valdés came to occupy a highly regarded place in French life but in television and print media rather than in the rarified milieu of the *Tel Quel* poststructuralists. She wrote frequently in national newspapers and became a familiar face on French television; in 1998, she was invited onto the jury for the Cannes Film Festival, alongside cinematic stars Martin Scorsese, Sigourney Weaver, and Chiara Mastroianni (Valdés, "Cannes"). Her public persona was one of contrasts: both familiar and foreign, speaking the French language but holding strange and intractable political opinions; both a Cuban writer and "la plus parisienne des cubaines" ("the most Parisian of Cubans") ("Le nombre des romans," 69). This dialectic of the foreign and the familiar, of the exotic and the deeply intimate, shaped Valdés's persona in France as it did in Spain; and it was at the basis of her market appeal in these countries and elsewhere.

Valdés's overt contempt for Fidel Castro set her against the French intellectual majority on more than one occasion, most notably when she insisted that the Cuban child Elián González, found alone on the Florida coast in November 1999, should remain with his Miami relatives rather than return to his father in Cuba (Valdés, "La infancia ultrajada"). She was also one of the more outspoken opponents of France's participation in Havana's 2002 Feria del Libro and, together with the novelist Régine Deforges and the journalists' action group Reporters Sans Frontières, she called for a boycott of the book fair on human rights grounds (Lanon, "Plumes françaises"). France's long-standing appreciation for Cuban literature goes hand in hand with that country's broader political and cultural engagement with Cuba. The French cultural and political Left has a history of support for the Cuban Revolution: Jean-Paul Sartre, Simone de Beauvoir, Régis Debray, and others stood firmly behind Castro in the early 1960s and Christoph Singler has argued that even today the notion of a flailing and anachronistic revolutionary ideal merely fuels nostalgia for a lost Left, or "the recomposition of a myth that includes the fact that it is worn out."[41]

With regard to the impact and the popular reception of Valdés's work in France, Lillian Hasson's brief article on French editorial politics vis-à-vis Cuban literature, "Y en Francia, ¿qué?" (And what's going on in France?), is illuminating. Hasson is the French translator of Reinaldo Arenas, Severo Sarduy, and Zoé Valdés, among others, and her article is drawn from a survey of French publishers of Cuban literature, whom she asked a series of questions about their criteria for selecting authors. Most editors surveyed denied that a Cuban author's ideological position or place of residence affected his or her chances of publication. Few, however, failed to recognize that during the 1990s French readers' interest in Cuban literature was shaped by a pervasive "Cubamania" with regard to cultural imports more broadly, although one insists that the 1990s boom is "nothing compared to the boom of thirty years ago."[42] Although "Cubamania" may be good for sales, the editors debate whether it is good for literature, an argument that is echoed by Havana-based journals, as we will see in chapter 3. Zoé Valdés's French publisher is paraphrased lamenting the cultural overload that established a repertoire of Cuban stereotypes for French readers, stereotypes that, once ingrained, made it difficult to introduce writers who varied from the formula: "'Certainly,' confirms Alzira Martins, 'this fashion or mania provoked an excess of Cuban cultural products that was detrimental to their quality . . . Caricatures have come to be expected, and this harms the more worthy writers who don't coincide with a certain folklorish aesthetic, as this is understood by some cultural media in France.'"[43] That Zoé Valdés's novels have a causal relationship to this "caricaturing"—one of the more serious charges levied against the Cuban literary boom—is affirmed by another publisher, who claims that "there is no doubt that there is interest in things Cuban, an interest to which Zoé Valdés's success in France has contributed greatly."[44] The implicit argument is that Valdés's work—precisely because of its visibility and popularity in France—has set too narrow a standard for Cuban fiction; but this is a profoundly ambivalent criticism that can to some extent be only a measure of Valdés's international success. That Valdés should not only launch a market for special period fiction (for the caricatures to which Alzira Martins refers are without doubt those of the special period) but also mimic that market's internal dynamics, as she does in *I Gave You All I Had,* is evidence of the complexity of her legacy to Cuban literature of the 1990s. In Europe and beyond, Valdés's position as both a pioneer of "special period fiction" and a catalyst for its market coincides with a peculiar set of historical and geographic circumstances. She was one of the first, and certainly the most prominent, of young Cuban writers to have fled 1990s Cuba and to have secured the two coordinates against which the 1960s Boom was mapped out: Spain, where *La nada cotidiana* needed no translation, and France, where Valdés made her home in exile and whose publishers, as Hasson argues, had long shown faith in new Cuban authors. Having secured publication in both Spain and France, Valdés's novels, like those of Cuban authors who both preceded and followed her, would soon generate translations for other markets: in Germany, Italy, Brazil, the United States, the United Kingdom, and beyond. Although the publication of Valdés's work follows a trajectory carved out by Cuban writers before her, the Cuba in which her novels are set—post-Soviet, poor, and newly opened to the dollar and tourism—distinguishes her work from that of her predecessors. Reinaldo Arenas's *Before Night Falls,* surely the most grueling account of Castro's Cuba to be widely translated by the 1990s, is set in the 1960s and 1970s, while Guillermo Cabrera Infante, who after the mid-1960s could speak only from the distance of miles and years, revives the prerevolutionary period in much of his work. Although some of Valdés's later novels bear the traces of distance—such as the aptly named *Café Nostalgia*—both *Yocandra in the Paradise of Nada* and *I Gave You All I Had* portray the Cuba of the early 1990s from close quarters. The process of writing *Yocandra in the Paradise of Nada* during 1993 and 1994 was like "vomiting" for Valdés, a spontaneous reaction of physical and psychological disgust (Santí 7, 9). The immediacy of her novels, and its manifestation as both frenetic language and impassioned political denunciation, is what has most captured critics' attention. In a review article of Valdés's work, Philippe Lanon observes: "She writes a lot, no doubt too much. Her tales take off in all directions. They suddenly change tempo, form, and tone, as though a genie or a dream were pulling them along . . . Don't expect good taste, perfection, or unity of tone here. Zoé Valdés takes anything that wells up in her, desires and frustrations, and throws it onto the page as though time were burning away."[45]

The novels are distinguished by the rawness with which they portray special period Cuba, a rawness that readers of these and later special period novels—particularly readers of Pedro Juan Gutiérrez, the subject of my fourth chapter—would be quick to hear as an authentic testimonial of life in Cuba at this time. Few other exiled writers in the mid-1990s wrote with a witness's authority about post-Soviet Cuba: Valdés was one of the first to have lived in Cuba during this time and then to publish novels based on the experience. Her two novels break new social ground, stooping lower into the physical mire of the special period and addressing it more directly than writers either in exile or in Cuba had done to date. The later 1990s saw more writers living both inside and outside Cuba depict the travails of the special period. Gutiérrez stands out among the former, although Amir Valle, Miguel Mejides, and many others introduce the theme; the Miami-based Daína Chaviano, whose *El hombre, la hembra, y el hambre* (Man, woman, and hunger) won Spain's Premio Azorín in 1998, is an example of the latter. Within Cuba, the *novísimo* writers, of whom we will hear more in the following chapter, were heralded as great rule breakers in Salvador Redonet's first anthologies of their work—but their iconoclasm was more cerebral. Other published works of the early 1990s and earlier broke specific taboos, one of the most notable being the revolution's moratorium on homosexuality, but did not tackle Castro's regime as unequivocally as Valdés does. Perhaps the most brutal published portrayal of the special period to predate *Yocandra in the Paradise of Nada* and *I Gave You All I Had* comes in the detective novels of Leonardo Padura Fuentes, whose investigator Mario Conde probes the underworld of black markets and poverty with the pretext of solving crimes and was credited with supplementing the reports of Cuba's state-controlled newspapers in the early 1990s. Nevertheless, Conde operates with a subtlety and a degree of euphemism with which *Yocanda* and *I Gave You All I Had* summarily dispense.

Zoé Valdés's role in the reception of Cuban literature in the 1990s is intimately connected to her thematic repertoire, a connection that is elucidated by the workings of Cuba's tourist industry. This is the arena in which relationships between Cubans and outsiders—the relationships that radically altered Cuba's social landscape during this period—are negotiated most visibly, and, to consider Valdés's responses to it, we might turn to one of the more damning and prominent critiques of her fiction. For although the commentary by Jesús Díaz—published first as an interview with François Maspéro in the French newspaper *Le Monde* and then in the Spanish journal *Encuentro de la cultura cubana* in 1998—purports to be dismissive, it in fact identifies the key strategy through which *I Gave You All I Had* undermines the accusation that

Valdés's work is merely the pawn of its market. Díaz, a prominent writer and cultural official for the first three decades of the revolution, was also an exile from special period Cuba, having failed to return from a fellowship that sent him to Germany in the early 1990s (Strausfeld 14). He established residence in Madrid and, until his untimely death in 2002, was founding director of one of the most important Cuban cultural journals to emerge during the 1990s. First published in 1996, *Encuentro de la cultura cubana* was initially conceived less as an exile forum on Spanish terrain than as a neutral space for the contemplation and criticism of contemporary Cuban culture, as "a democratic meeting place, where antagonisms will finally be overcome: not only those that oppose Havana to Miami, but also those that exist within the exile community and within the island."[46] *Encuentro* has been a powerful base for the dissemination of literature produced within Cuba, for honoring the lifetime work of writers shunned hitherto, and for stimulating critical debate of a kind rarely seen elsewhere. And yet, when asked about Zoé Valdés, Díaz's response is distinctly censorious:

> Zoé Valdés's commercial success comes from her having written what a certain sector of the European public wants to read: a dose of feminism, a dose of sex, a dose of uprootedness, a dash of Lezama Lima. It's a form of literary tourism, in a moment when Cuba is becoming a paradise for cheap sex. The Cuban tragedy has been commercialized. Literature, true literature, is the impossible place where both tragedy and comedy try to find expression, the abyss and the ambiguity between which this century moves; all the complexity of human fate. What is needed is lucidity and madness and not an escape into characters who are nothing but ideological puppets.[47]

Díaz's assessment implicitly acknowledges that *Encuentro*'s commitment to a lasting Cuban culture, or to one that expresses "all the complexity of human fate," sits somewhat uneasily in countries like France and Spain, gripped by undiscerning "Cubamania." It is also indicative of a frustration, widely expressed among Cuban writers and critics during the late 1990s, with the apparent lack of discrimination in the initially European market for Cuban literature, and, more broadly, with the confluence of expectations and stereotypes generated by the special period's overexposure in music, film, and photography. The criticism of Valdés is leveled from one exile to another, and it is striking that, in its insistence on the values of art over those of the market, it echoes critiques aired in the journals of Cuban institutions, the subject of my next chapter. Despite Díaz's later insistence that "Cuban culture is one," Cuban criticism has tended to divide along distinctly political—and distinctly inside versus outside—lines. The virulence with which Valdés's work is disdained in both Madrid and Havana is indicative, to my mind, of a protectionism toward national literature that unites the most unlikely of allies and, consequently, of a profound unease with the encroachment of Valdés's novels upon this legacy.

Díaz's dismissal is far from clear-cut, and it cannot deprive Valdés of significance in contemporary literary history, for the sequence of demand and supply remains ambiguous here. Although there should be a considerable distinction between writing in response to what "a certain sector of the European public wants to read" and shaping that demand a priori, as I believe Valdés does, Díaz sets out a simple formula: "a dose of feminism, a dose of sex, a dose of uprootedness, a dash of Lezama Lima." Even if Valdés's novels could be reduced to this (which they surely cannot), then the fact that they craft rather than merely follow the formula should be taken seriously. In other words, to draw a strict distinction, as Díaz and many others have, between Valdés's novels and a "true" Cuban literature—"la literatura verdadera" (true literature) being the phrase chosen elsewhere by Abilio Estévez ("Méditations," 221), Francisico López Sacha ("Literatura y fin de siglo," 160), and Edel Morales (18), as well as by Díaz here—only to exclude Valdés from the canon on this basis, risks ignoring a major influence on the reception and production of Cuban literature in the 1990s. This literature could not exist in the absence of its market, and the fact that the market was changing beyond recognition leaves its trace on fiction both "true" and "false," as my subsequent chapters explore. Valdés's novels, particularly *I Gave You All I Had,* foreground these economic changes, offering a harsh and irreverent commentary on them.

Tourism is at the heart of Cuba's economic shift and it is also closely aligned with the awakening of foreign readers' interest in Cuban fiction, so that Díaz's phrase "literary tourism" is both apt and ambivalent; for there is a substantial difference between fiction that is "touristic" in the derivative sense that Díaz appears to give it, on the one hand, and a writing that closely heeds the mechanics of the touristic encounter in order to expose its ironies, on the other. If Valdés's novels offer an experience similar to that sought by the tourist, then they do so not only by showcasing Cuba's attractions but also, and more cannily, by mimicking the structures and relationships on which attraction is based. The pun on *dólar* and *dolor* is the paradigmatic example; a narrower one is the episode in *I Gave You All I Had* in which a Cuban teenager tries to tempt an aging Argentine tourist to a night of inexpensive sex, which foregrounds not the teenager's allure but the financial imperatives and ideological contradictions of the relationship he would initiate. "Aren't you ashamed of yourself, you, the child of such a great Revolution defiling the memory of Che?" asks the tourist, to which the teenager replies, "I have to eat, damn you; die, you old red bitch!" (187–88).[48] Although sales of Valdés's novels might benefit from the interest in Cuba that tourism has generated—seemingly the sense in which Díaz brings his charge of "literary tourism"—*I Gave You All I Had* in fact, in its constant mimicry of the inequitable relationships that tourism has instigated, offers a powerful critique of the industry. That Zoé Valdés should write into her novel the financial underpinnings of both tourism and literary production is a skilled move on her part; for it is one of the sad paradoxes of Cuban tourism that the very contrast between the past triumph of a revolutionary political project and the signs of its current decline, between cultural vibrancy and material and architectural decay, and between the state's previous coldness toward foreign tourists and its present needy embrace of them are all constitutive of the country's appeal. Tourism, and particularly so-called third-world tourism, runs the gamut of these paradoxes, as John Frow suggests in his analysis of the industry's dependence on "the semiotics of nostalgia" and "the commodification of reciprocal bonds" (150). Graham Huggan's study of the publication of postcolonial fiction implies that "marketing the margins," or the selling of books across political and economic lines similar to those between Cuba and Europe, tends to exploit similar paradoxes. As Huggan argues for the work of Salman Rushdie, for example, reproducing stereotyped images is not necessarily an unknowing move.

In rejecting Valdés's work as "a form of literary tourism," Díaz exposes the economic links between Cuba's writers, their readers, and a greater intercultural phenomenon of which both are part: a phenomenon fueled by the legalization of the dollar and whose blueprint has been set by the tourist industry, wherein that which is perceived as authentically Cuban is exchanged for money. To censure Valdés for subscribing to this phenomenon is to overlook the implications of her having inscribed it, as the founding motif, in *I Gave You All I Had;* for what is Díaz's claim that "the Cuban tragedy has been commercialized" if not a reformulation of *el dolor del dólar?* And is this potential capitalization upon the downfall of Cuban socialism not precisely what the pivotal exchange between Cuca and Juan foregrounds—as a commentary and, moreover, as a caution? Even if *I Gave You All I Had* predates what would be known as "the new Cuban boom," it is set and produced as the economic relationships of this boom are forming; and to embed these so centrally in the text, inviting consideration and questioning of them, surely exonerates the author from the charges levied against her. At the very least, she should be regarded as a critic of, rather than a mere participant in, the marketing of Cuban culture. Despite—and perhaps even because of—criticisms like Díaz's, Valdés's "special period fiction" is to be taken seriously in a consideration of Cuban narrative in the 1990s. There is more to the "commercial" charge than meets the eye; and *I Gave You All I Had,* underpinned as it is by the U.S. dollar, offers ways to rethink both writing and reading in the context of a country broadening its economic relations with the outside world and of a culture that is booming.

Returning to where we began, with a boom but also a banknote, we might reassess the implications of "moneymaking" in Cuba's special period. Moneymaking is inseparable from writing, even in the abstract; but the material context of special period Cuba, where the interests of investors, tourists, and readers meet, suggests further relationships between writing and money, and between fiction writing and profit. The English inscription on Cuba's newly depenalized dollar bill heralds a strong correspondence between foreign purchasing power and the formerly closed domestic economy and opens the way for a fiction writing very much of its time. The value attributed to the lived experience of Cuban socialism would facilitate, with the onset and advance of the "new Cuban boom," a form of exchange between reader and writer that was secured by foreign money. The expanding sphere in which Cuban fiction was published and read abroad during the latter half of the 1990s and early 2000s—a sphere dramatically broader than the protected national circuit to which it had previously been restricted—influenced both the quantity and the content of its production, as my next chapter goes on to explore. Through its founding pun on *dolor* for *dólar,* rooted in a relationship between a Cuban woman and a man who returns from afar, *I Gave You All I Had* anticipates the "new Cuban boom," its aftershocks, and its implications for the practices of writing, publishing, and reading. In this deeply resonant sense, *I Gave You All I Had* is a measure of the textual and contextual preoccupations that would mark Cuban fiction for the decade to come.

CHAPTER 3

Covering for Banknotes:
Books, Money, and the Cuban Short Story

"Money," the title of a short story by Ronaldo Menéndez, could hardly be more explicit about the cause of the social turmoil amid which it was written. Published in 1997, after the collection in which it is included won that year's Casa de las Américas prize for short fiction, Menéndez's story is set in late July 1994. Cuba was by then a year into its dual monetary system, with pesos circulating alongside dollars. Riots in Havana would soon provoke a Castro-sanctioned exodus of thousands of rafters to the United States.[1] The story's title is an English word, borrowed from the language of Cuba's most powerful currency and disruptive social force: the U.S. dollar. In giving the dollar pride of place, Menéndez's story, like others written and published in Cuba at this time, asks questions of Cuba's new economic order similar to those of Zoé Valdés's *I Gave You All I Had*. It challenges the government's legalization of a foreign currency, its promotion of tourism from capitalist countries, and its implicit condoning of transnational relationships that trade money for testimony. And yet these challenges are posed not from Europe, where Valdés's novel was written and published, but from Cuba, which places them in far greater proximity to the woes of the special period. That there should be common concerns about new market demands for Cuba and its literature in the work of an exile and vocal critic of Fidel Castro, on the one hand, and in that of writers schooled in and published by Cuba's official literary institutions, on the other, is at the very least surprising. Nevertheless, *I Gave You All I Had*'s critique of the price tags on Cuban experience that the new economic order heralded, contained conceptually in its repeated pun on *dólar* and *dolor,* finds echoes in the offerings of Cuba-based writers and publishers.

The following readings of fiction written and set during the special period explore the permutations of Valdés's *dólar–dolor* paradigm as it was recast in Cuba over the course of a decade. They consider the close correspondence the pun establishes between text and money, between fiction and publishing markets, and between insiders' experience and outsiders' voyeuristic desire. How, they ask, are money (in the abstract) and Cuba's dual currency (in the all-too-specific) figured in this fiction? How do writers who for decades had negotiated the demands of the revolutionary system adapt to the emergence of an international market for their work? And how do they negotiate the temptations of hard-currency markets, however remote the possibility of a foreign contract might be for many of them? Where do fictional representations of special period economic relations intersect with broader intellectual debates, in Cuba and elsewhere, about literature's relationship to its markets? To what extent do the relationships spawned by the tourist industry provide scenarios for fiction, and how do such scenarios imply their own allegories? Beneath these questions is the foundational one of writers' implicit critique of the changing coordinates of literary production in Cuba; for although the writers addressed here publish primarily in Cuba, the possibility of doing so abroad haunts their fiction. The market becomes for them a site of both opportunity and ethical struggle; and, as a consequence, their engagement with the dollar and its societal manifestations is both less overt and more troubled than Valdés's. They not only echo *I Gave You All I Had*'s critique of a political system that would trade in both material and ideological assets, they also register an implicit disquiet about the popularity of Valdés's work. At the same time, they anticipate the commercial success of Pedro Juan Gutiérrez, whose work in the late 1990s consolidated an image of Cuba that, as I address in chapter 4, would for many outside readers become synonymous with the special period.

Although the fiction published in Cuba between 1993 and 2004 is far from homogeneous, a distinct pattern emerges wherein literature's changing economic context is embedded in its themes and linguistic structures. These years are mapped out against the overnight disintegration of domestic institutional support for literature and the potentially lucrative attention of nonnational publishers, and writers cautiously negotiate between the old and the new, the Cuban peso and the newly depenalized U.S. dollar, the domestic and the foreign. With the legalization of the U.S. dollar, writers—among them the *novísimos,* whose emergence as a generation opened the decade—begin to engage in a textual practice that, in its linking together of writing, money, and sex, inscribes apprehension about the foreign market's glamorization of both Cuba and its literature. Stories by Ronaldo Menéndez and Anna Lidia Vega Serova, for example, simultaneously sexualize and textualize money, instating the dollar bill, the book, and the sexual encounter as an omnipotent triad. Rehearsed in the stories of a larger number of writers is the dramatization of a relationship between a Cuban and a foreigner—superficially a tourist and a visitor, but allegorically a writer and a publisher—that pretends to be romantic but is also economic. In revealing itself as such, the relationship unleashes a partly nationalist critique that resonates with a broader intellectual debate emerging at this time. Less combative than Zoé Valdés and less ironic in their strategies than the Cuba-based Pedro Juan Gutiérrez, these writers confront the special period with both fear and fascination. Unlike more commercially successful writers, their complicity with new economic demands is hesitant. Rather, they monitor an ambivalence toward the market that underpins both their work and others', intersecting with—but also, eventually, defusing—aesthetic and ideological debates that were hosted in Cuban cultural journals over the course of a decade. It is in this uncertain climate that writers resident in Cuba, and subject to the vagaries of its changing economic order, produce their version of the "special period genre." Through it, they engage a scenario of institutional and legislative change both economically and artistically, making their fiction a venue for both exploring and complicating the changing market demands to which literature was suddenly subjected.

New Markets, New Margins

For both material and historical reasons, the short story was the principal venue for Cuba-based writers' engagement with the early years of the special period. The paper shortage that followed the demise of the Eastern bloc gravely reduced the number of books published annually in Cuba from an average of 2,339 titles in 1983–89 to just 568 in 1993, of which only 143 issued from the Instituto Cubano del Libro (Cuban Book Institute), the principal publisher of literary texts (Más Zabala 49–50).[2] As they had since the 1960s, educational books took priority in resource allocation; but the paper shortage now meant that when fiction was published at all, the short story, requiring less material, was preferred over longer works. Several literary journals that in the 1980s had featured new fiction fell victim to the shortages. Publishing outlets were few and often improvised, as is ruefully acknowledged by the presenters of *Anuario Narrativo 1994* (Narrative annual 1994), an anthology compiled by the writers' union (UNEAC) between 1992 and 1993. "Cuba's paper crisis has reduced to previously unsuspected lows what was, until recently, its important publishing industry," begins the *Anuario,* adding that its ninety-five stories are evidence of "an activity that continues despite the fact that, for the moment, it does not get the editorial response it deserves."[3] Aspiring writers turned to "plaquettes," the pamphlets handmade from recycled paper that became a hallmark of the early 1990s; and the first four years of the decade—after which the Cuban publishing industry began to internationalize and recuperate—saw the heyday of "literatura de gaveta" (drawer literature), unpublished works kept indefinitely in someone's desk drawer.[4]

The privilege of publishing a novel in Cuba during the first years of the special period was reserved for seasoned writers and, until the launch in 1993 of the Cuban–Argentine Pinos Nuevos prize whose specific mandate was to disseminate the work of previously unpublished authors, brevity was a necessity for those seeking their first entrée into print.[5] These were often younger writers trained in the municipally run workshops that, as Pamela Smorkaloff has explored, were an important legacy of the campaign to eradicate illiteracy that the Cuban government waged with considerable success in 1961 (*Literatura y edición de libros,* 287; Fagen 33–68). Formalized at a local level in the 1960s and 1970s, the workshops brought into the popular sphere a literary culture that before the revolution had been the domain of a few (Smorkaloff, *Literatura y edición de libros,* 277–83). The workshops were open to anyone other than professional writers associated with the UNEAC and were often overseen by established authors and teachers. In these settings, characterized as "study centers and literary laboratories . . . that prioritize the concept of literary creation as practice, as conscious and sustained labor,"[6] the technical precision of the short story made it a useful pedagogical tool. The genre also allowed aspiring writers to participate in an established national tradition whose recent critics, among them Francisco López Sacha and Begoña Huertas, have traced it from its beginnings in the 1930s, through vicissitudes that map the revolution's evolving cultural policies, to the workshops of the 1980s whence was launched a concerted assault on the aesthetic and thematic parameters of Cuban fiction (López Sacha, *La nueva cuentística cubana;* Huertas, *Ensayo de un cambio*). It is in such terms that Salvador Redonet, a critic and professor at the University of Havana, heralded the generation of *novísimos,* writers who were born after 1959 and began writing in the late 1980s. In a fraught sense that was important to Redonet and that anthologists later in the decade would reiterate, they were "children of the revolution," and their work was thus conceived in both aesthetic and political terms.[7]

Confronted with the special period just as they began to publish, *novísimo* writers were to produce some of the most complex explorations of its new currency. Nevertheless, because the U.S. dollar is incorporated into the work of some and not of others, its legalization marks a gradual dissolution of any common project. After the mid-1990s the idea of a *novísimo* writing is neither new nor coherent, emigration and more insidious economic forces having dispersed its writers and distinguished among them. In the early 1990s, however, the *novísimos* and subsequent subdivisions that Redonet would name *post-novísimos* and even *trans-novísimos* (*Para el siglo que viene,* 13) constituted what López Sacha has consistently called "the Iconoclastic Generation" (*La nueva cuentística cubana,* 78; "Tres revoluciones," 3), and they were credited with breaking new ground in two broad ways.[8] Synthesizing the work of López Sacha, Arturo Arango, and Redonet, Alfredo Alonso Estenoz outlines these. On the one hand, the *novísimos'* innovations were thematic: "they introduced themes that until then had remained unpublished or postponed: a traumatic relationship to reality and institutions; the world of the margins, with its rockers, freakies, and other forms of 'alienation'; homosexuality, the anguished aspect of war."[9] At the same time, and somewhat in line with postmodern trends elsewhere in the world, they challenged the formal practice of writing: "they revitalized writing, subverting the traditional structure of the story and including elements acknowledged as postmodern: intertextuality, diverse voices, fragmentation, irony, pastiche, the relativity of centers and peripheries."[10]

José B. Álvarez describes the *novísimos'* discourse as "a confluence of thematic and formal innovation" (43). This dual innovation is the basis of their claim to a "marginal" position vis-à-vis Cuban culture's status quo, a highly problematic claim whose shifting value nevertheless heralds the short story's cautious entrance into the dollarized period. As Iván Rubio Cuevas points out, the thematic preoccupations shared by some, although certainly not all, *novísimo* stories locate them in opposition to a "center" that they nevertheless need for self-definition, approximately identifiable as the state in its political and cultural functions (83–84). "Marginal" themes include, in the words of Luis Manuel García, "drug addiction, sexuality as hallucinogenic, maladjustment, heavy rock, and alienation,"[11] all of which correspond to specific prohibitions set by the revolutionary government, as well as to a less nationally bounded counter-cultural movement. In its formal complexity, too, much *novísimo* writing challenges both the state-level directives toward popularizing literature against which Cuban writers had battled since the late 1960s and, more specifically, the conventions of its practitioners' immediate literary predecessors. One of these predecessors is Arturo Arango, whose rhetorical question about the stories in Redonet's first *novísimo* anthology *Los últimos serán los primeros* (The last shall be the first)—"to what extent can the short story, without losing its distinctive nature, cease to narrate, shred its anecdote, disregard the construction of character?"[12]—seems to mourn a more familiar, and more ordered, way of writing.

The *novísimos*' claim to marginality (perhaps more accurately thought of as critics' claim on their behalf) has, however, been subject to scrutiny precisely because of the fraught conceptualization of the margins in a highly centralized society such as Cuba's. Redonet qualifies the notion of a Cuban marginality, admitting that the *novísimos* "have a marginal attitude within the limits of what marginal can mean in a country like this."[13] Less cautiously, Víctor Fowler Calzada scorns a marginality that is self-imposed, asking of young Cuban writers, "Is their substance marginality or maladjustment?"[14] and suggesting, as will others later in the decade, that socioeconomic marginality is a more justifiable position than counterculture. With greater hindsight, Rubio Cuevas lodges three objections to the label "marginal" as it was assumed by and applied to the *novísimos*. On the one hand, he argues, the label occluded more subtle and formally interesting aspects of writers' work, while, at the same time, its thematic wellspring was bound to be quickly exhausted (81). Furthermore, writers were tempted to conform to a label that was commercially serviceable both inside and outside Cuba (ibid.).

Rubio Cuevas's argument that the *novísimos*' marginality was unsustainable because it lent itself too easily to market appropriations—

by the international publishers whose hold on Cuban fiction became ever stronger during the 1990s, or by the much less lucrative system of Cuban literary prizes—partly anticipates my own. The export value of a marginality perceived as particularly Cuban was indeed among the more pressing issues confronting writers as the U.S. dollar confirmed its place in society. And yet for some writers, among them erstwhile *novísimos,* this issue becomes less a limitation than an opportunity to redirect their much-feted iconoclasm toward global rather than local political structures. Their most daring texts chart, but do not necessarily comply with, a crucial relocation of the Cuban "margins" that is precipitated by the post-1993 cultural boom. The weakening of the *novísimos'* claim to marginality, as I see it, is due to a qualitative shift in the term's content that certain short stories would monitor with unease; for the "marginal" themes initially adopted by the *novísimos*—rock music, drug habits, petulant introspection—would be complemented over the course of the decade by a marginality far more attuned to outsiders' conceptions of how Cuban lowlife should look. By 1994 Arturo Arango, in his capacity as juror for that year's Pinos Nuevos fiction prize, noted a decline in *friqui* (freaky) and *roquero* (rocker) themes at the expense of a literature "that takes on material precariousness but also extends to notable changes in our way of life, in the scope and material value of literature and the relationship of politics to the arts."[15] Although the *roquero* movement is strong to this day, marking out its defiantly nonnational territory in the first issue of the journal *Rockstalgia* (2005), it is significant that, from the mid-1990s on, its fictional output should compete with stories more attuned to the difficulties of the special period.[16]

    This shift from *friqui* and *roquero* themes to others that embrace the material difficulties of life in the special period heralds a new conception of marginality, one that gains ground with the very changes in the value of literature to which Arango alludes. Geared at least in part to foreign readers, this new image of marginality is notably different from what is regarded as "countercultural" within Cuba. Its referents are less specific to episodes in Cuban cultural history and are reflective, rather, of broader and more internationally recognizable images of Cuba. Western models of counterculture give way to themes that emphasize Cuban difference from the world of foreign readers. The most internationally visible representations of marginality to emerge in Cuba in the mid-1990s are drawn along racial and economic lines. Pedro Juan Gutiérrez's "Ciclo Centro Habana" (Centro Habana Cycle), the first book of which was published in 1998, is the high-water mark of this shift in the value of marginality.[17] As I explore in chapter 4, however, the success of Gutiérrez's novels owes less to his relocation of the margins within Cuba—that is, to his local redefinition of counterculture—than to foreign valorizations of the contrast between his destitute, sexually depraved, and often Afro-Cuban characters and the still-socialist society in which they live.[18] Throughout the 1990s, dollarization drew the margins of Cuban literature closer to the "marketed margins" of Graham Huggan's work on postcolonial literature. It is precisely their recognition of this shift, and their attendant preoccupation with what it might mean for Cuban literature, that welds the stories of Ronaldo Menéndez, Ana Lidia Vega Serova, and others to the special period.

MONEYMAKING BOOKS

Ronaldo Menéndez's "Money" traces the shift in content and value of Cuban marginality that the special period was to present, registering both anxiety and critique toward it. Together with Anna Lidia Vega Serova's "La encomienda," "Money" stands as a landmark in textualizing the parameters within which writers would operate in Cuba's dual economy. Born in 1970, Menéndez was one of the *novísimo* writers introduced in Salvador Redonet's first anthology, *Los últimos serán los primeros* (1993), and he was initially classified by López Sacha as one of the generation's *rockero* (rocker) writers (*La nueva cuentística cubana*, 74). Both before and after his departure for Peru in the late 1990s, Menéndez was a frequent critic of contemporary Cuban fiction and its changing literary and economic status. In "Money" he rehearses a particularly textured version of these critiques, bringing together the dollar, writing, and sexual taboos to articulate ambivalence toward Cuba's new publishing economy.

"Money" narrates the never-resolved loss of thirty dollar bills, the balance of the $1,100 a young couple needs to migrate to Mexico. Without these thirty dollars, the would-be escapees are merely "frustrated emigrants,"[19] confined to a domestic space that becomes acutely problematic. From despair the lost dollars breed disruption, of both the family and the familiar. The story explores duality as duplicity and insinuates a disturbing proximity between Cuba's *doble moneda* (the dual currency, in which the U.S. dollar circulated alongside the national peso) and *doble moral*, a phrase much used during the special period to refer to ethical double standards. Indeed, the legalized exchange of dollars for pesos itself appears incredible.

> The money, that has now turned from $1,100 into $1,070, is money they have saved—the devil only knows how—over the course of a year; and not to exchange it, through a magical multiplication of banknotes, into its formidable equivalent in local currency, but rather to metamorphose it into tickets to Mexico.[20]

Moreover, the protagonist's search for his lost thirty dollars leads him to a duplicity that seems to emulate that of the dual currency. It is with the thirty dollars in his pocket that he commits his first act of falsehood against his wife, initiating a physical affair with another woman. When he returns to his lover's house to search for the money, he deceives her too, stealing from her bedside thirty dollars that, despite his best efforts, he cannot convince himself are his. One consequence of his dollar-inspired deception is a profound and irrecoverable disruption of domestic relations, for he is wracked with guilt at his betrayal and forced to accept that there can be no "happy end" (76) to such double-dealing. Another is the unequivocal coupling of money and sexual transgression. As he recalls his first illicit sexual encounter in graphic detail, the scene assumes the dollar's color and texture: ("his lover astride him, his jeans down to his knees, the green rug and the green money, blue jeans, green girlfriend . . .").[21] It is only during this encounter that his dollars are physically present and that they should be confused in his memory with the act of copulation is deeply revealing of the dollar's special period status as an erotic taboo.

The couple's unhappy ending lends itself to broader allegories about the disruption the foreign dollar might bring to the domestic scene, one that is further complicated by the presence in the story of the printed word; for it is not merely the household, or the monogamous relationship, that splinters under the strain of the thirty lost dollars, nor is the money confused only with sex. In a potent figuration of the authorial anxieties of years to come, the dollar is imagined between the pages of a book, thus affirming its proximity to literary production. Before losing them, the husband had placed his dollars for security inside a volume whose title is relayed only in code, as though it were too scandalous to be identified otherwise. Its author is named as Reinaldo Arenas, but it is only by reading between the lines that we can assume it to be *Before Night Falls:* "after naming the book, they both collapse as though they had just been given the results to a positive AIDS test."[22] Later, "they resign themselves before night falls completely, so that they can sleep."[23] The allusion is clearly to Reinaldo Arenas's autobiographical account of his persecution in Cuba and affliction with AIDS in the United States. Emilo Bejel reads *Before Night Falls* as developing both a critique of "institutionalized machismo" and "an implicit theory of creativity and sexuality" (141), and although it differs in tenor and subject from much fiction written in Cuba in the early 1990s, certain aspects of it, particularly its denunciatory stance toward the Castro regime, its celebration of homoeroticism, and its explicit sexuality, were to make a cautious reemergence as the decade advanced.[24] When the couple recovers their copy of Arenas's book, the money is not there; but the expectation that it might be, or indeed that it should be, leads to a series of associations that speculatively chart a course for literature in a dollar-driven market.

First, the husband pretends to sell the book, in order to justify his possession of the thirty dollars that he has stolen from his lover. He assures his wife that, in a local market where Arenas's work has long been censored, "it's a best seller for which they'll give me thirty dollars."[25] The potential profits of this best seller soon multiply, however, as the book is provisionally launched outside the local market. He takes the book to the seafront and throws it into the water, thus launching it away from Cuba. It is as he is about to do so that *Before Night Falls* appears to him not as a thirty-dollar best seller but as a stack of banknotes. Having already lent their color to the memory of a sexual encounter, dollars now present themselves as the pages of a book. "He takes out the Reinaldo Arenas book and flicks through it as one might flick through a wad of banknotes."[26] The book appears as an untold amount of money in an image that displays both prescience and preoccupation regarding what Cuban writing—and, particularly, intimate, self-revelatory, and graphically sexual writing—would be worth beyond national territory.

From its very title, then, Menéndez's story anticipates layers of complexity and dependence in the opening of new markets for fiction. "Money" is located inside a book (Menéndez's) in a tale of concealing money inside a book, such that the book becomes doubly a cover for dollars. In visualizing its pages as a wad of bills in the moment the book moves from domestic circulation into a broader international space, "Money" anticipates the movement of Cuban fiction beyond national borders and into lucrative foreign contracts. That books and money should be interchangeable not only for each other but also for sexual encounters anticipates the thematic roster that would sell fiction like that of Pedro Juan Gutiérrez—a roster on which intimate sexual revelations rank highly. In consonance with its theme of doubleness, however, the story retains ambivalence with regard to fiction's prospects. On the one hand, the stated lack of a "happy end" (76) implies that it is futile and ultimately destructive to look for money in books that are to be launched abroad. In this sense, the story might serve as a warning against venturing away from home ground. And yet its closing lines are profoundly inconclusive. The husband rejects the convincing answers that might satisfy his wife, in favor of opacity and self-abandon:

> instead of racking his brains for some extreme yet convincing pretext, he abandons himself to the image of the book that sinks under the inertia of its fall and then, although it seems it will float, vanishes from sight under the murky gray of the sewage.[27]

Rather than take a final stand on his own ethical shortcomings, the husband prefers to lose himself in the rise and fall of the book. In abandoning himself to this image, he willfully relinquishes self-control. He identifies with the book and, most important, allows himself to be carried along on the tide that takes it away from Cuba. Mesmerized by the book's movement, he abstains, in the last instance, from passing judgment. His critique of fiction's flow toward foreign markets, on the grounds that it ruptures domestic harmony, is tempered by both fascination and aspiration. It is with this constitutive doubling that "Money" sets a model for the special period short story.

The same trio that motivates "Money," namely, that of the book, the U.S. dollar, and the intimate encounter, is replicated in another short story published in 1998. Anna Lidia Vega Serova was living in her native Russia while *novísimo* writing evolved, but she returned to Havana in the early 1990s as the economic context of Cuban fiction was beginning to change. Víctor Fowler Calzada singles out Vega Serova's narrative for its concern with "the preeminence that foreign money has in our lives today,"[28] and her story "La encomienda" (The charge) articulates the anxieties of "Money" from the perspective of a young woman. The space in which "La encomienda" unfolds is domestic, cocooning, and sealed from the outside world, a confinement that, as Nara Araújo has commented, characterized the spatial parameters of *novísimo* writing.[29] But Graciela's domestic harmony is violently ruptured by a knock on the door, as she eats alone in her kitchen. She is unprepared for this rupture of her private space—"she was terribly ashamed that someone might see what she was eating"[30]—and even less ready for what it heralds, namely, a gift of five hundred dollars from her exiled parents. The bearer of the money "was a stranger and, what's more, a foreigner"[31] so that, from the beginning, these dollars appear as outsiders disrupting the familiarity of home.

As soon as she has received the dollars, Graciela hides them in a place that reiterates the proximity between writing and money introduced in Menéndez's story. The hiding place is another unnamed book, although its author is the perhaps less incendiary Dumas. Instinctively, she makes the book the repository for foreign money, relegating it to the highest shelf in the room to keep it out of temptation's way. Thereafter, like the lost dollars in "Money," Graciela's become an obsession. She counts them interminably and handles them to test their physical presence: "she sat on the floor and placed the money in front of her, in rows . . . She arranged the bills in piles of a hundred, put them one on top of the other to make a fan."[32] They distract her from her work and, as *doble moneda,* again inspire duplicity. She is reluctant to inform her boyfriend of the gift and so provokes an argument with him. In her obsession with not losing the money, she seeks ever more elaborate hiding places for it. These include the kitchen and the bedroom, where the money moves progressively closer to intimate areas. From the drawer she places it behind the mirror but determines that the most secure location is her underwear: "She made a little bag and hid the envelope inside it. She placed it in her underwear and fastened it with a needle."[33] From here it is temporarily misplaced but, after several minutes of panic, relocated in a place that "Money" has insinuated is evitable: under the bed. Quickly, then, the dollars confirm their association with the genitalia (her underwear) and the site of sexual encounters (the bed).

Graciela's hiding places inscribe a tightly structured paradigm for special period literary production. Money is identified with, or inserted in, books and, at the same time, with an intimacy that is inherently domestic. The implication echoes that of "Money": the exchange of books for money is facilitated by the offer of sexual revelations. Together, these two stories anticipate a material economy motored by interest in Cuban intimacy, and their figuration of the dollar-book-sex trio both challenges this economy and addresses its opportunities; for, like "Money," "La encomienda" allows ambivalence to persist beyond the end of the story. It closes with a reconciliation between Graciela and Jorge and a promise that she will share with him not only the fact of the dollars' existence but also the comforts that they will purchase. In the context of a broader analysis of women's writing as a site of resistance to socioeconomic change, Fowler reads in this closing scene a triumph of love over money: "the force that stands in opposition to the power of money is love."³⁴ In privileging "the utopia implicit in the ending,"³⁵ however, Fowler leaves open the very question that resounds in Cuban literary production from Menéndez's story on: what is the place of the foreign money in domestic utopias, or of the U.S. dollar in Cuban society? Amorous though Graciela's reconciliation with Jorge may be, it cannot exist in the absence of the five hundred dollars that she continues to possess, and she is obliged to integrate them into the life that they will otherwise rupture. Despite the torment to which they have subjected her, she must take them as an opportunity; and it is in this spirit that she invites Jorge to eat in a restaurant whose prices are in dollars. The story presents a moral conflict that, rather than reaching a utopian resolution, subsists uneasily alongside Graciela's pragmatic decision to participate in the dual economy.

LITERATURE TRUE AND FALSE

"Money" and "La encomienda" stand as barometers of a changing climate in Cuban letters. They echo and nuance debates about Cuban culture's encounter with foreign markets that gathered force from the mid-1990s on, following legislative changes in writers' and artists' rights to their intellectual property. One of many measures introduced to attract hard currency to Cuba, Law Decree No. 145 of November 17, 1993, allowed writers to negotiate their own contracts rather than involve a government intermediary, and at the same time established a ministry of culture registry for such works. A simultaneous decree established these rights for musicians, and they followed upon similar provisions enacted for visual artists in 1988. As Ariana Hernández-Reguant has explored, these law decrees, and the context of economic transformation in which they were implemented, radically redefined the role of the cultural producer, introducing "a new way to value artistic labor, no longer according to state standards but to market considerations" ("Radio Taino," 346). It is the problem of value, precisely, that incites debate and makes its way into fiction from the mid-1990s, as new forms of economic value threaten to undermine existing moral ones. The most sought-after contracts were inevitably those from foreign entities, among them music producers, galleries, and publishers, whose potential control of both the circulation and the content of Cuban cultural products caused considerable concern.

Musicians and visual artists were among the first to benefit visibly from the legislative and economic changes of the early 1990s, and they were the most heavily criticized for doing so.[36] Their ascendance to the top of a value system quite distinct from that of previous decades provoked heated questioning about the role of culture in special period society, and although literature was less lucrative, it was subjected to the same scrutiny. A principal forum for debate about the changing rewards for Cuban cultural production was the journal *El caimán barbudo,* the cultural supplement to the Union of Young Communists' newspaper *Juventud rebelde.* Once its publication had resumed in the postdollarized period, after a brief hiatus caused by the national paper shortage, *El caimán* hosted a roundtable debate on "the excess of frivolity displayed today in certain areas of our culture."[37] The debate's central question was "frivolity, mediocrity or marketing?"[38] This focus allowed a group of critics to reflect upon the opening of Cuban culture to foreign markets, addressing both the assumed lowering of standards and the opportunities that the opening entailed. Those assembled generally expressed concern about the market's effect on quality. The film critic Rufo Caballero, for example, stated that "following this opening, or the inevitability of this opening, many people are taking advantage in order to simplify serious knowledge, to trivialize culture."[39] The debate was not, however, without optimism for the future of Cuban culture, with Caballero himself admitting that "openings don't necessarily have to imply trivialization"[40] and the radio show host Camilo Egaña insisting that "we must start from the assumption that the market is not necessarily the enemy of culture."[41] In a sequel to this debate, titled "El rojo y el verde" (The red and the green, in reference to socialism's confrontation with the U.S. dollar), Fernando Rojas set the opening questions as "the market or the protection of art? The market or the development of a policy aimed at the youngest of us?"[42] and art critic Helmo Hernández answered in favor of engagement with international markets, claiming that for Cuban culture to remain outside "was like trying to cover the sun with one finger."[43]

The tenor of these two debates is telling: the hope that the future might hold artistic as well as economic opportunities is tempered by deep suspicion of the market and its neocolonial aspirations, as well as by the defense of values deemed to be both aesthetic and socialist. It is striking, however, that those debate participants who are less hostile to the market work in media more readily associated with mass diffusion (music, radio) and high rewards (the visual arts) than is literature. When similar questions about mediocrity and the market were raised in discussions restricted to literature, Cuban writers' responses were more pessimistic about the market's potential. Fiction writer Alberto Garrandés's comment that "everyone tries to do two things: not distance himself from the demands of the market and remain faithful to a personal poetics"[44] is exceptional for both its frankness and its pragmatism in a discussion dominated by alarmist laments. Rafael de Águila's "¿Pathos o marketing?" (Pathos or marketing?), published in *El caimán barbudo* two years after the frivolity debate, is one such cry of alarm. De Águila's argument is that young Cuban writers in the late 1990s were all too ready to be seduced by the prospect of a foreign publication, the result being a reduction of fiction to its themes alone and to a roster of salable stereotypes. An amalgam of these is his hypothetical story about "a freaky drug-addicted hustler whose parents left on a raft and whose brother is an anal sadist."[45] The reaction to his formulation was heated. And yet, although a response in the following edition of *El caimán barbudo* took issue with both de Águila's methods and his partial representation of certain authors and topics, it did little to dispel his concern about the survival of aesthetic principles faced with threats from an allegedly lowbrow publishing industry.[46]

De Águila pitted literature against the market in especially vivid terms but his concerns were reiterated by less dramatic contemporaries, in different venues and from markedly different geographic and political positions. Ena Lucía Portela, for example, describes the choice facing Cuban writers in 1998 as one between "literature," on the one hand, and "lettuces"—code for "dollar bills"—on the other.[47] The common line of argument establishes a consistent and strangely fearful rubric for the categorization of special period literature, for by 1998, when the international boom in Cuban literature was at its height, Cuban authors writing not only from Cuba but also from France and Spain had cast the market as literature's enemy. They classed fiction published during the special period in purist terms: it was either "true" or "false." Their recourse to this dichotomy raises pressing questions about writers' relationship to the values of revolutionary cultural policy, on the one hand, and to capitalist publishing, on the other. Why uphold an

ideal of "true" literature, opposed to a "false" one, in a field long clut-
tered with works of varying ambition? Why should such categories as
"true" and "false" surface or resurface at this moment, and what might
they mean in the political and cultural context of Cuba's 1990s? These
categories reveal the ideological tensions underlying Cuban literature's
shift from dependence on state institutions to dependence on foreign
publishers, and they elucidate the strategies with which fiction writers
engage the perils and promises of the international market.

Jesús Díaz, a Cuban novelist and critic whose involvement in the
first decades of the revolution was considerable but who took up residence in Madrid in the early 1990s, formulates an ideal of "true" Cuban
literature in explicit terms. In an interview with François Maspéro—
published first in the Parisian *Le Monde* in May 1998 and subsequently
reprinted in *Encuentro de la cultura cubana,* the journal of which he
was founding editor—Díaz's response to a question about "a boom in
Cuban literature" includes the following statement:

> Literature, true literature, is the impossible place where both tragedy
> and comedy try to find expression, the abyss and the ambiguity between
> which this century moves; all the complexity of human fate. What is
> needed is lucidity and madness and not an escape into characters who
> are nothing but ideological puppets.[48]

Díaz's appeal to "literature, true literature" is a clear attempt to distance
literature from the economics of its circulation and from a practice epitomized, as the preamble to his statement makes clear, by Zoé Valdés.[49]
Díaz opposes "true" literature not to "false" but to "touristic" literature,
thus locating falsehood directly in the relationships between Cubans
and foreigners that marked the special period. In imagining for "true
literature" a hallowed space, freed from the restraints of the possible
and abandoned to the joys of both lucidity and madness, he expresses
an ideal that was echoed by other writers at this time. Abilio Estévez,
whose *Thine Is the Kingdom* was to win France's prize for best foreign
novel in 2000, similarly invokes a "true" Cuban literature in a lecture
given in Mons, France, in December 1998. He claims that "the dividing
lines between true and false literature, between the novel, novelty, and
simple testimony, in a chaotic present like all presents, are not always
drawn with precision."[50] Sadly, he continues, adopting the terms of *El
caimán barbudo*'s debate on frivolity, it is those writers "who cultivate
banality and vulgarity"[51] who have the greatest audience, for which they

can thank "the strange caprices of fashion and the market."[52] Although
he acknowledges the ambiguity of the category of realist fiction, exemplified in the special period by exposés of material hardship, Estévez
upholds the distinction between true and false literature as firmly as
does Díaz.

Francicso López Sacha, in a retrospective on Cuban literature at the
end of the twentieth century, defines truth by negation. True literature,
he affirms, stands in opposition to "products of *marketing*" ("Literatura
cubano y fin de siglo," 160) like the novels of Zoé Valdés. "It is that
which is always produced at the margins of fashion, business, or political opportunity."[53] Also referring to the struggle of "true writers"
against "the traps set by merchants and bad politicians,"[54] Edel Morales
offers an analysis of the challenges that "booms" and "best sellers" pose
to Cuban literature. He begins his 1998 article "Literatura y mercado"
(Literature and the market) by taking best-selling American novelist
Stephen King to task for choosing to produce merchandise (6) when
he could create literature. It is this binary opposition, between the creation of literature and the production of merchandise, that in Morales's
reading faces Cuban writers. Some, Zoé Valdés inevitably being among
them, choose the latter path; and Morales poses the unanswered question of why they should feel obliged to do so. He closes by placing his
trust in those stalwarts who will uphold the standards of true literature,
but not before recognizing that the "best-sellerization" of Cuban literature constitutes an attack on "that which we have until now considered
to be values of the literary."[55]

These commentaries on the state of Cuban literature in the late 1990s
converge at two salient points. On the one hand, they each mount a personal attack on Zoé Valdés and her commercially successful novels; for,
as I argue in chapter 2, Valdés is both the pioneer of the Cuban boom
and the specter whose success subsequently haunts Cuban writers and
critics. More broadly, the commentaries share a faith in the existence of
"true" literature, a category from which works can be excluded on the
grounds that they are false (Estévez), touristic (Díaz), or too close to the
market (López Sacha and Morales). This faith erects a dichotomy that
intersects with long-established questions about art and its markets that
revolve around the unstable notion of value. A distinction between economic value and what Martha Woodmansee and Mark Osteen call "a
specifically *literary* form of value" (9) crystallized in Europe during the
Romantic period, when writers' refusal to equate the value of their work

with either its price or its popularity resulted in a notion of creative production "to which literary and composition studies in large measure still adhere" and which made "a work's ineffectuality—contemporary readers' indifference to it—a measure of the work's value" (ibid.). As the technical capacity to produce large quantities of books increased during the nineteenth and twentieth centuries, so did writers' concern with the conflict between commercial and artistic success. Twentieth-century modernism, writes Terry Eagleton, "is among other things a strategy by which the work of art resists commodification, holds out by the skin of its teeth against those social forces that would degrade it to an exchangeable object" (392); and yet, despite their attempts at isolation from the market, modernist writers had no choice but to engage it to some degree (Delany 335). Their resistance is reflected in Pierre Bourdieu's subfield of restricted production, in which profit is symbolic, in contrast to the subfield of large-scale production in which rewards are more clearly economic (Bourdieu 37–40). Social actors who proclaim economic disinterest have an interest in maintaining an alternative ideal of literary value.

Arguments that essentially pit writers against the mass market, or elite against popular tastes and consumption habits, would, however, seem to transpose uneasily to post-1959 Cuba. It was the revolution's explicit cultural policy to make both literacy and literature the domain of the masses and to redefine the role of the writer accordingly. The elite writer, elsewhere the custodian of literary value, came under fire from the beginning of the revolution. Fidel Castro's landmark "Address to Intellectuals" in April 1961 aired this problem publicly, and the intellectual formed before the revolution was subsequently dismissed in Che Guevara's "Man and Socialism in Cuba" (1965) as irrecoverably bourgeois, then ridiculed later in state-sponsored cultural performances.[56] It was at the April 1971 First National Congress on Education and Culture, in the wake of the Padilla affair that had alienated many of Cuba's foreign supporters, that the intellectual was most linked to moral weakness. "The cultural media," declared Fidel Castro in one of the event's most resounding statements, "cannot serve as a framework for the proliferation of false intellectuals who would convert snobbism, extravagance, homosexuality, and other social aberrations into expressions of revolutionary art, distanced from the masses and from the spirit of our revolution."[57] This declaration had vast repercussions, particularly for homosexuals (Bejel 103–5); and it inaugurated what Ambrosio Fornet termed, in a 1987 review of Jesús Díaz's *Las iniciales de la tierra* (The initials of the earth), "five gray years" of fearful, line-toeing literature (153).[58]

When the Congress on Education and Culture thus enshrined moral standards in cultural policy, it crystallized a redefinition of value that had long been gathering momentum. This redefinition pushes toward a third term wherein value is neither literary nor economic but, rather, revolutionary. Although neither "Address to Intellectuals" nor the Congress's Declaration addresses the question of value directly, it lies in their subtext, particularly in the latter's insistence that, on the one hand, the revolution has freed art and literature from the market demands of bourgeois society and, on the other, that aesthetic experimentation should be ideologically rigorous.[59] The question comes to the fore, however, in the speeches and documents of the First Communist Party Congress, held in December 1975. Castro's speech to this congress invokes a set of values—"cultural values," "the consecrated value of art," and "national values"—and presents them as proper to the Cuban people.[60] Without distinguishing between these values, it locates them in a collective imaginary that seems to predate capitalism—for it is capitalism that inspired artists' violation of them: "It [capitalism] stimulated sensationalism, easy entertainment, and an art of evasion. Resources were used to impair the cultural values of our people and falsify history."[61] The thesis and resolution on artistic and literary culture produced by this same party congress are even more insistent in their defense, and somewhat more consistent in their definition, of the relationship between revolution, culture, and value. It is socialism, according to this thesis, that gives art and literature "their real values": values that are explicitly not economic, for writers access them only through the material stability guaranteed by the revolution.[62] That the revolution purports to rewrite the notion of artistic and literary value is clear from the insistence on its having revaluated works of art in accordance with "the new values of the revolution."[63] This process of revaluation involves stimulation on the part of the revolution and response by the artist, both of which have a specific content. In an allusion to the socialist realist imperative in place at the time of this congress, cultural policy "must stimulate the appearance of new works capable of expressing, in their rich and multifaceted variety and with a clear humanistic conception, the multiple aspects of Cuban life."[64] The measure of a work of art's "value" and "transcendence" depends in return not only on its author's maturity and talent but also on his or her "ideological formation" (100). Although the documents from the First

Party Congress do not present a coherent thesis on revolutionary value, there nevertheless emerges from them a concept of value that, in banishing market interests and replacing them with those of socialism, would enrich artistic and literary production.

Pervasive though such a notion of value was in the public sphere of the 1970s, however, the Cuban writers and critics who paint special period works in terms of "true" and "false" are not advocates of it. They in fact conceive of themselves as its victims and opponents and they are highly suspicious of both market valuations of Cuban fiction *and* "revolutionary" values. Desiderio Navarro recounts that, from the late 1960s on, and with brief periods of exception, the artistic intellgentsia was largely excluded from the public sphere of revolutionary Cuba, and its notion of a purely literary value was debunked in favor of the newer, revolutionary form. Intellectuals' successive attempts at critical intervention were confronted by administrative measures of varying harshness, legitimized by a discourse that associated art with a defunct bourgeoisie and presented dissonance as an anachronism at best, and a security threat at worst (Navarro 359–69). It is with this legacy that Francisco López Sacha, in his introduction to a 1994 anthology of new short stories, describes fiction from the 1970s on as being in a battle between devils and angels. The devils in the duel are "the isolation, localism, regulations, and errors of cultural policy,"[65] the latter being more fully described as "an aesthetic and ideological program that postulated as supreme truths direct reflection, positive characters, evident bias, optimistic endings."[66] Sacha claims a triumph for the "angels" that he dates to the 1980s, when the short story began its return to experimentation and stylistic complexity (6). That the somewhat clichéd figure of the angel should represent such qualities is revealing of the predominantly formal criteria by which Sacha and other contemporary critics judge the value of Cuban literature. Defined both technically, in Sacha's insistence on structural coherence and closure ("Literatura cubana y fin de siglo," 59), and philosophically, in the ideal of an absolute truth that he, Díaz, Estévez, and Morales all invoke, their criteria are far closer to those of traditional intellectual elites than to the Cuban Communist Party's statements on the revolutionary value of literature.

These critics' insistence on "true literature" emerges as an attempt to retain literary value as such, as a hermetic code of its own, rather than surrender it to the values of either the revolution or the market. As James Buckwalter-Arias has demonstrated, this attempt, particularly insofar as it is directed at the cultural policy of the first thirty years of the revolution, is reiterated in novels and autobiographical narratives during the special period, as well as in critical essays.[67] "The partial re-absorption of Cuban literature by a transatlantic publishing market and the regime's diminishing control over cultural production," he writes, "make it possible for Cuban writers to turn the tables on the official revolutionary narrative by casting the individualistic, arguably roman-tic artist as hero and the government official, formerly vaunted as the people's representative, as antagonist" (364). This leads to a "flourishing of a pre- or extrarevolutionary aesthetic discourse" whose success in up-holding an uncontaminated artistic space is, nevertheless, compromised by its historical moment.[68] Indeed, Buckwalter-Arias suggests that the homage certain novels written during the special period pay to earlier figures such as José Lezama Lima and Virgilio Piñera is an acknowledg-ment that artistic freedom is by now (and perhaps always was) a mere fantasy (372), and that their authors, recognizing the extent to which their literature is politicized by its context, instead turn their attention to exposing "the relation between artistic performance and political ideology" (369).

New Parameters: Sociology and the Nation

Even those writers and commentators who embrace aesthetic values, as the antithesis of either revolutionary cultural policy, or what Jesús Díaz pejoratively calls "touristic literature," cannot avoid the implications for literature of economic change. It is the terms in which a different set of writers addresses these implications that interest me, as, in their fiction that engages the special period especially directly, these terms form a consistent and often critical subtext. As the market threatened to usurp revolutionary dogma as the antagonist of aesthetic integrity, a multilayered fear, most easily understood as both apprehension and ex-citement at a change in the status quo, was woven into the themes and structures of the decade's fiction.

The concept of value is at the core of this fear, and its shifts shape both intellectuals' debates, as I have suggested, and the material condi-tions of literary production; for the revolution's sui generis definition of literature's value had had practical implementations that granted writers a secure, if restricted, place in society. A generous system of subsidies and incentives, put in place in the early days of the revolution, largely freed both publishers and writers from economic concerns.[69] During this time, as Claudia Lightfoot puts it, "publishing houses functioned simply as editors and book designers"; "most importantly, they had no financial role" ("Publishing in Cuba," 10). Their protective cocoon was to be shattered by the policy of self-financing introduced to Cuba's publishing industry in the early 1990s wherein books, while still circulating in the unprofitable peso market, would have to also be competitive in dollars. Profits were not expected of individual books, many of which were targeted at Cuba's education system rather than the export market, but of the industry as a whole. The result was that works categorized as "for tourists" (Más Zabala 50)—among them guidebooks, histories of the revolution, and biographies of Che Guevara, as well as contemporary fiction—had to subsidize works for domestic consumption that were more aligned with the revolution's early ideals for literature.[70] That the domestic publishing industry should develop its own explicitly "touristic" interests and evaluations, aside from those that Jesús Díaz reviles as proper to the international market, exacerbated the need for writers and book producers alike to seek out foreign buyers for their work. The mid-1990s saw Cuba's national book fair adopt an annual rather than biannual schedule, and each year it was dedicated to a guest country, thus opening a further space for international trade.[71] Thanks to these and other measures, by the turn of the millennium the domestic publishing industry had improved considerably. Book production was almost at precrisis levels, and new regional publishing houses ensured more balanced representation of authors, and diffusion to readers, who lived outside Havana (Más Zabala 50–52). Nevertheless, the imperative to "self-finance" persisted, and it contrasted markedly with the decades during which both writing and book production were insulated from market economics.

For Cuban writers and critics, this imperative, and the concomitant legislation that allowed writers to negotiate directly with foreign agents, did not portend only the unknown terrain of commercial publishing. It also brought with it discomfiting déja vus that account at least in part for the above-quoted critics' impassioned defense of "true literature." The thematic content of literature concerns these critics because what they perceive as its increasingly privileged place in fiction of the postdollarized period replicates, rather than merely replaces, the centrality of theme—or the primacy of content over form—in earlier mandates to Cuban literature. Although strengthened by formal simplicity, the Cuban version of socialist-realist fiction that found official favor from the late 1960s, and particularly after the First National Congress on Education and Culture, had theme as its primary vehicle.[72] It is precisely with regard to thematic content that one set of demands on Cuban fiction appeared, in the 1990s, to give way to another that, although diametrically opposed to it in terms of ideological provenance, nevertheless threatened to resemble it in effect. As foreign interests in Cuban fiction increased and writers new to self-financing attempted to secure publishing contracts, the perils of socialist realism found a curious echo in critical debates. "Sociology," understood primarily as an intense thematic focus on Cuba's social failings, became the new nemesis of literature.[73] The objects of "sociological fiction" are parodically embodied in Rafael de Águila's grotesque amalgam of such unrevolutionary yet contemporary figures as the *jinetera,* the *balsero* exile, and the drug addict; and the term became a catchphrase for aspiring young writers who in the mid- and late 1990s might describe their vocation as "I do social fiction."[74]

Arturo Arango addresses the "sociological" phenomenon in a 1997 essay, where he proposes that foreign readers became less interested in Cuban fiction's literary merits than in the lived experience of its writers under a socialist regime.[75] The interest of European publishers and readers in particular, he writes, arouses suspicion: "Is it really literary or does it have a political, or even sociological, basis? Do they want to know how we write in Cuba or how we live in Cuba? What young Cubans write or how they think?"[76] This "sociological" interest originates, as did directives for socialist-realist fiction, on the demand side; but the demands of foreign publishers are qualitatively different from those of Cuban cultural policy and their effect, Arango suggests, is to dull distinctions between good and bad literature. Between high-quality fiction and some works offered by the Spanish market, he continues, "there is an abyss that can only be understood from the perspective of literature, but never if viewed with sociological curiosity."[77] The market for "sociological" writing, defined as such, calls into question the place of experience in literature and forces a renewed distinction between literary "truth" and a more denunciatory realism. It is in literature's interests, Arango suggests, and defenders of "true" literature concur, to steer away from "the country's daily reality"[78] and from writing—like that of Pedro Juan Gutiérrez, the subject of my next chapter—that is, or is read as, primarily testimonial.[79] "Sociology," then, appearing as an approximate and recontextualized version of socialist-realist principles, awoke a sinister ghost of earlier times.

THE PRICE OF THE NATION: TRANSACTIONS WITH TOURISTS

Critics' apprehension at a shift in the idea of value, on the one hand, and a return to prescribed forms of realism, on the other, is symptomatic of a broader fear: that of ceding national territory to foreign powers. Deeply ingrained in Cuban political discourse since before the nineteenth-century wars of independence and a founding principle of the 1959 revolution, nationalism was reaffirmed, and redefined, in the post-Soviet period.[80] The complementary agendas of anti-U.S. imperialism and international socialism that Castro's government had sustained for over three decades morphed, given the post–Cold War redundancy of the latter agenda, into a narrowly strategic exaltation of the nation's autonomy. Ariana Hernández-Reguant argues that as future-oriented political nationalism lost its relevance, culture was construed instead as a unifying force.[81] Radio campaigns promoted a national identity based on culture and community in a move that subtly replaced, even if it did not erase, the ubiquitous billboards that championed militaristic defensiveness.[82] In 1992, the Cuban constitution was amended to erase references to international socialism and proclaim José Martí as the ideological forebear of the nation, and the cultural nationalist writings of Fernando Ortiz and Jorge Mañach were reprinted (Hernández-Reguant, "Radio Taino," 119–20).

Writers' participation in this official move toward cultural nationalism was at best tenuous: although the economic benefits of flaunting a distinct Cuban experience in an international context became increasingly evident, both such benefits and the state-directed revival of cultural commonality aroused considerable mistrust.[83] Nevertheless, just as Rafael Rojas reads the special period essay as a venue for rewriting Cuban nationalism, so the nation's engagement with and difference from the outside world is the constitutive tension of much of the period's fiction.[84] Ronaldo Menéndez and Anna Lidia Vega Serova dramatize this tension as a rupture of domestic relationships (foreign money destroys the protagonist's marriage in "Money") and spaces (the dollar enters Graciela's home unannounced and proceeds to rupture the security therein), but it also underpins a much more common narrative. The relationship between the Cuban *jinetero/a* and the foreign tourist recurs repeatedly as the subject of special period short stories. Although

Arango lists the *jinetera* as one of the stock characters that foreign readers came to expect of Cuban fiction, and thus implies that this figure's
presence in any given text is merely a response to demand, writers' deployment of the cross-cultural sexual and economic relationship in fact
serves a more complex purpose. Like Menéndez and Vega Serova's foregrounding of money, books, and sexuality to explore the marketability
of sensationalized fiction, the figure of the *jinetera* mounts a challenge
to the special period and the demands it brought to fiction. Both the
frequency with which this theme recurs and its specific articulations are
revealing of the deeply problematic ways in which special period fiction
encounters its markets.

Víctor Fowler Calzada has read a series of stories on the *jineterismo*
theme, particularly those by women, as expressions of resistance to both
national crisis and the new power of foreign money.[85] He finds in these
stories, including two by Anna Lidia Vega Serova—"La encomienda"
(The charge) and "Billetes falsos" (Counterfeit money), in which a
woman performs a sex show for free rather than accept that her favors
be purchased—a feminine supplement (327) by means of which the
body takes control of the forces that would subjugate the *jinetera* and all
that she symbolizes. Chief among the *jinetera*'s symbolic designations,
for Fowler, is women's place in Cuban literature; for, as he concludes
in his reading of "Billetes falsos," "however much money tries to turn
bodies into objects, the key to these exchanges is in the hands of the
one who controls representation and, consequently, turns identity into
a performative act of inner freedom."[86] But an expansion of Fowler's list
of stories on *jineterismo* suggests that there is greater ambiguity, and less
outright hope, in the ubiquitous sexual relationship between a Cuban
and a paying foreigner. Ultimately, I propose, these stories—like those
of Ronaldo Menéndez and Anna Lidia Vega Serova that explicitly im-
plicate books in the exchange of Cuban sexuality for foreign money—
advance a defense of national space that nevertheless accepts as necessary writers' embrace of international markets. A reading of some of
these stories, and their place on the landscape of special period fiction,
consolidates and textures the critical debates on literature and its markets that arose during the special period.

Most stories that incorporate the *jinetera* or *jinetero* character have a
strong national component, such that the relationships explored are not
just between two lovers but between two countries. With some excep-
tions, the protagonist of the story is a Cuban woman, and her lover—

who invariably turns out to be her adversary—is identified by national-ity. This identification sustains a set of character traits that cast foreigners and their homelands as both alien and unwelcoming. Underpinning a number of special period stories, such typecasting shapes what might be thought of as a consistent moral caution against choosing the mate-rial comforts of the unknown over the familiar poverty of home. Fore-grounding the deceptions to which starry-eyed émigrées expose them-selves, the heroine of Marilyn Bobes's "Pregúntaselo a Dios" ("Ask the Good Lord") is ironically named "Iluminada" (Illuminated/Enlightened). She has left for a France where she is treated with coolness and contempt, with a husband in whom she finds no more than *la tendresse* (257). When it is too late—when, on a brief trip to Havana, she realizes that she can never really return—she acknowledges that Cuba is superior to France, morally if not materially: "if Cuba had more goods and they could get rid of the power cuts, it would be a place a thousand times better a country than this Tulús [Toulouse], crammed with wicked and selfish people, who look at you for what you've got, not for what you're worth (343)."[87] Souleen dell'Amico's "Contradicciones" (Contradictions) re-iterates Iluminada's story and its message. In France, its Cuban pro-tagonist is treated cruelly by a husband who keeps her under lock and key, blatantly denying her the freedom she sought in leaving Cuba. Her Cubanness proves to be of only superficial interest to the French, mask-ing deeper prejudices against her bad manners and assumed promis-cuity. Her regret comes in no uncertain terms, as she realizes the folly of having confused economic stability with happiness: "How stupid I was to think that I had my life sorted out, that I had found stability and that money would put an end to my anguish!"[88] Her romantic obses-sion with a blind man seals her fate as someone who has taken pleasure in not seeing the truth. No hopeful young woman, it seems from these stories, can leave Cuba without regretting her departure, for her expec-tations for happiness elsewhere will always be disappointed. This narra-tive advances a loyalty to Cuba that is based more in apprehension than in pride. Difficult though life may be in Cuba, the stories suggest, it is worse elsewhere, and the implicit distinction between moral and mate-rial well-being leaves no doubt as to where the moral high ground lies. With national boundaries drawn as firmly as they are in these stories, it clearly lies in Cuba.

Alongside this narrative of enlightenment, however, there emerges a dif-ferent conception of national affiliation, one that approximates Hernández-

Reguant's term "cultural nationalism" but is ultimately more opportunist than patriotic. Many stories that address the *jineterismo* scenario cast foreigners as recognizable stereotypes who compare unfavorably, in every regard other than in material wealth, to their Cuban partners. The Frenchmen in "Pregúntaselo a Dios" and "Contradicciones" are mediocre lovers who make their wives long for the assured machismo of Cuban men. The Swiss lover in Miguel Barnet's "Miosvatis" is easily duped into believing that his relationship with the woman of the story's title is monogamous on her part, when her sister has difficulty distinguishing him from other foreign boyfriends and considers him primarily as a ticket out of the country (83–84). The German women in Jesús Vega's "Wunderbar" and Miguel Mejides's "The Tropics" are targets of similar disdain. Vega's starving protagonist, a young and well-built Cuban who would steal to eat, is nevertheless reluctant to consort with the "incredibly fat and ugly woman with dyed blonde hair" (334) who seeks his attention.[89] In Mejides's story, Mrs. NG escapes from Frankfurt to the tropics in search of warmth and pleasure with "natives" (98), but is greeted instead by a lover who robs her and a band of Cubans who confuse her at every step. It is the North American woman who is ridiculed in Anna Lidia Vega Serova's "Erre con erre" (R and R)[90] for having given love, money, and a ticket out of Cuba to a partner for whom their lesbian relationship was merely a means to an end: once in the United States, the new émigrée settles into a heterosexual marriage. Tourists are cast in these stories as gullible, compliant, and mistakenly convinced that they are in control. Although on the one hand this would seem to be all the more reason to remain among Cubans, who are not only superior but also more streetwise, on the other it suggests a way of benefiting from relationships with foreigners on home turf; for if tourists can be consistently outwitted, then there is no need to take one's always regrettable leave of Cuba. These stories imply that there are profits to be reaped from enacting one's relationship with the foreign inside domestic boundaries.

Negotiating the national as it comes face-to-face with the foreign, then, these *jineterismo* stories embrace in two ways the idea of belonging to Cuba. On the one hand, national affiliation is affirmed through negation: escape to capitalist societies occasions suffering, repentance, and a final realization that although life in Cuba is difficult, it is less so than life elsewhere. In a second sense, however, the Cuban *jinetero/a* characters are aware of their allure and learn how to wield it strategically. Their stories play to the homogenizing expectations of foreigners—that on the part of foreign editors and readers, Arturo Arango has outlined, are expectations of hypersexuality, political dissidence, and material need ("Escribir en Cuba hoy [1997]," 17)—and yet counter them with equally superficial stereotypes of tourists. This countering strategy is explicitly the subject of José Miguel Sánchez (Yoss)'s "La causa que refresca" (The refreshing cause) that turns stereotypes of Cuba on their head with a searing typology of visitors' interests and hypocrisies. Its narrator is a young man who knows how to play the part expected of him: "in my features there is danger, the delicate risk of theft or venereal disease, but there is also the sweetness of sugar cane, sincere friendship, Rousseau's noble savage."[91] He meets this expectation, however, with a preconception of his own: that his foreign lover gives money to Cubans to assuage the guilt of privilege and facilitate a hedonistic abandonment to a situation that causes political discomfort. This stereotype of a sexually adventurous but politically oblivious European woman features in other stories that cast a Cuban man as *jinetero,* among them José Mariano Torralbas Caurel's "Último tren a Londres" (Last train to London) and Francisco García González's "Lo mío primero" (Mine first). In contrast to the effective emasculation to which the *jineteros* of these two stories are subjected, however, Yoss's protagonist responds with opportunism rather than acquiescence. His parting words to the tourist, "I absolve you and I leave you with enough guilt to return quickly,"[92] acknowledge that the charade in which they have both participated—he in the role of Cuban lover and she as carefree European—has served each of them well. Tourists, like the economic situation that has brought them to Cuba, are to be met on their own terms and taken advantage of.

This double narrative—of fearful attachment to Cuba, on the one hand, and of willingness to make the most of tourism, on the other—resonates with that of Menéndez's "Money" and Vega Serova's "La encomienda," both of which imply that anxiety about the dollarized economy does not have to preclude participation in it. Indeed, the juxtaposition of painfully ruptured domestic ties with the lucrative opportunities of foreign relations again meets the practice of writing in special period stories on *jineterismo.* As Fowler argues, some stories use the *jinetera* figure to address textuality as both political and artistic representation; that is, as affording women a degree of power in an economic and literary world dominated by others. But it is Marilyn Bobes's "Ask the Good Lord," published in 1996, that raises the farthest-reaching questions about the marketability and materiality of writing, questions that would under-pin the Cuban short story, contextually if not always textually, for the decade to follow. The story is narrated partly in the third person and partly through letters from Iluminada, the homesick *jinetera* unhappily married to a Frenchman. In adopting this epistolary form and casting its *jinetera* as the writer—of letters, if not of books—"Ask the Good Lord" allows a conflation of the relationship between its two characters with that between Cuban authors and foreign consumers. In exchange for material comforts for herself and her family in Cuba, Iluminada has given a foreigner rights over her, and it is precisely this exchange that causes her moral anguish. Cast as both a wife and a writer, Iluminada stands as a caution to others who might sell their rights to personal or intellectual property too naively. Iluminada, however, ultimately decides to return to France and to remain in the relationship to which economic circumstances initially tempted her. In dramatizing her emotional con-flicts as she makes this decision, the story explores the tensions that Menéndez and Vega Serova formulate through the figure of the dollar. What, they each ask, will be the fate of the Cuban writer, and of Cuban literature more broadly, if they enter into the economic exchanges with foreign entities that the special period offers all too readily? The response to which each story points, tentatively and even reluctantly, is that such opportunities are to be taken, although they can only be taken at a cost.

It is just this question of cost that these special period short stories explore, and rather than allowing it to map fully onto debates over val-ues that pit truth against falsehood, they cast it as a cool flirtation with both danger and opportunity. They resist determining whether or not fears that Cuban fiction would "sell out" to the international market were founded. Rather, they portray the relationship between demand and supply as volatile and inconclusive: from Menéndez's "Money," which ends with the mesmerizing launch of a Cuban book into inter-national waters; to Vega Serova's "La encomienda," which reiterates this union of books, money, and sex and gives it a more intimate and domes-tic setting; to the much-replicated theme of *jineterismo*, where national allegiances come into focus as a means of playing foreign interest at its own game. In making this economic relationship the theme and the motor of their stories, writers take on the doubts and possibilities that rocked special period Cuba, in the social as well as the cultural sphere. They address the changing status of production and consumption and consider what a transition from revolutionary and essentially moral values to those of the market might mean for both society and writing. Anticipating the central question of Pedro Juan Gutiérrez's work, the subject of my next chapter, they ask how Cubanness itself, and differing versions thereof, might figure into new trade practices between Cuba and capitalist countries. Yet they refuse to take a position on these questions, and it is precisely in leaving them open to interpretation that they both monitor and manifest the uncertainty of the special period.

CHAPTER 4

Markets in the Margins:
The Allure of Centro Habana

The cover of *Brudna trylogia o Hawanie* runs little risk of being mis-
understood. Published in Warsaw in 2004, it speaks an international
vernacular of erotica: a close-up photograph of a naked female body,
dark-skinned and glistening in the studio light, manicured fingers poised
suggestively over the crotch. And yet the relationship of the photograph to
the Havana of the title, and of that Havana to readers in Poland and the
other fourteen countries in which the novel was published, and between
these readers and Pedro Juan Gutiérrez, Cuban author of the original
Trilogía sucia de la Habana (Dirty Havana Trilogy), is perhaps more
puzzling. How can such an image represent post-Soviet but still-socialist
Havana? Why might readers outside Cuba be drawn to the book and to
what extent might they see in it, in 1998 when it was first published in
Spanish, an already-familiar Cuba? And, more important, how might
the text itself, aside from its cover art, sustain their attraction?

Gutiérrez may have disapproved of the Polish gloss on his book, but
its sexualization of Havana is nevertheless indicative of the different reg-
isters of reception into which the special period boom in general, and
his work in particular, were to take Cuban culture.[1] If, as my previous
chapters have proposed, the exiled Zoé Valdés was the specter looming

over Cuban critics' concerns about foreign threats to national literature, then the work of Gutiérrez, who lived among those critics in Havana and published his *Trilogy* three years after Valdés's *Yocandra in the Paradise of Nada*, incarnated their worst fears. To those defenders of a "true" Cuban literature, battling first against the dictates of revolutionary values and then against the capitalist notion of market value, Gutiérrez offers a dissonant alternative. The five books of his "Ciclo Centro Habana" (Centro Habana Cycle) redefine truth not as an aesthetic ideal—as per Jesús Díaz, Abilio Estévez, Francisco López Sacha, and others—but as testimonial revelation. Gutiérrez's fiction exposes lives of sexual abandon, moral depravity, and economic despair, all located unmistakably in 1990s Havana. This habitat bears so strongly upon its characters' fates that the fiction is sociological in a deeply organic sense, undermining the disdain, advanced by such critics as Arturo Arango, for readers who prefer sociology to art ("Escribir en Cuba hoy [1997]," 17). Indeed, the Centro Habana Cycle reaffirms, and at the same time complicates, images of life in Cuba that proliferated abroad during the special period and came to represent its zeitgeist. These are images that both tourists and readers wanted to see and were willing to purchase, suggesting a correspondence between demand and supply that was anathema to the guardians of Cuban letters.

Gutiérrez's renderings of the special period were in demand outside Cuba, where they achieved considerable commercial success. First published in Spain in 1998, *Dirty Havana Trilogy*, the first book in the cycle, was published in eighteen countries, and the sequels *El Rey de la Habana* (The king of Havana), *Tropical Animal*, *The Insatiable Spider Man*, and *Carne de perro* (Dog meat) in slightly fewer.[2] While Gutiérrez continued to live in a decaying tenement building in one of Havana's most run-down barrios, he became a cause célèbre in journals from Brazilian *Playboy* to the *New York Times Book Review*. At first, his notoriety was exclusively extraterritorial: although he had published poetry and fiction in Cuba in the 1980s, his subsequent turn to journalism had distanced him from the literary circles that would facilitate publication there.[3] Not until 2002 was an edition of *Tropical Animal*, the one novel of the cycle set largely outside Cuba, published by Letras Cubanas, preceded in 2000 by *Melancolía de los leones* (Lions' melancholy), short stories that did not form part of the cycle.[4] Critical attention in Cuba was slow in coming, despite Gutiérrez's high profile abroad. After some years of silence, a certain measure of approval was accorded *El Rey de la Habana*, significantly the only book to depart from the others' fragmented first-person narrative and thereby to both renounce testimonial claims and invite evaluation according to the formal criteria of the novel. Such cautious praise is exemplified by Francisco López Sacha's assessment that, although *Dirty Havana Trilogy* is clumsy, insufficiently elaborated, and too heavily influenced by Henry Miller and Charles Bukowski, *El Rey de la Habana* is "truly a novel with a thesis."[5]

La Gaceta de Cuba (The Cuban Gazette), one of the country's principal literary journals, included a critical article on the failure of utopianism in Gutiérrez's and others' work in late 2002 (Casamayor, "Cubanidades de un fin de siglo") and an interview with him in 2004 ("Animal literario"). This belated attention does not, however, dispel the fact that in the late 1990s, as Cuban literature reached the height of its international popularity, *Dirty Havana Trilogy* epitomized much that Cuban critics had considered bad about the "new Cuban boom." *Trilogy*, like the other books in the Centro Habana Cycle, offers sordid revelations of a society in despair and of individuals whose sexual appetites, in the absence of material and spiritual sustenance, are all they can hope to satisfy. That these themes, like those of Zoé Valdés's earlier novels, were well rewarded abroad might have compounded the fear—the subtext to much critical debate at this time—that, faced with the peculiar tastes that drove the special period marketplace, Cuban writers would simply sell out. And yet, despite his novels' supply of images that conform to the aesthetic and political expectations of post-Soviet Cuba watchers, Gutiérrez does not merely capitulate to international market demands. Rather, like Valdés and like the short-story writers of chapter 3, he takes advantage of the booming foreign market for Cuban culture in order to implicitly critique it. Embedding foreign readers in his texts as uncomfortable voyeur figures, he unmasks the sordid impulse behind much Cuba watching. "Somos lo máximo" ("We are the greatest"), the line that Gutiérrez takes from Manolín el Médico de la Salsa for the epigraph to *El Rey de la Habana,* becomes both a statement of attitude and a rallying cry, for his own work and for an entire era of literary production, as he simultaneously flaunts the interest that Cuba commands and exposes the base desires on which that interest is constructed.

Gutiérrez's strategies for mounting his critique are stealthy, and this chapter will attempt to chart them from their beginnings in the decrepit tenement buildings of *Dirty Havana Trilogy;* for *Trilogy* invents a Havana that is the center of gravity for both its protagonist and its sequels. To the extent that its appeal to readers is grounded in the morbid fascination with the decline of socialism that characterized foreign gazes on Cuba's special period, this is a Havana that reflects images of the city popularized outside Cuba by the visual paraphernalia of the tourist industry. And yet, unlike these much-circulated images, Gutiérrez's Havana is cast as largely inaccessible to tourists, and it is this quality of the texts' setting that ensures their allure. For in a Cuba that the special period and its large-scale promotion of tourism brought within closer reach, Gutiérrez's city still bears the seal of the unknown. Breaking this seal holds the promise of authenticity that, as Dean MacCannell has argued, motivates the tourist experience; and it is precisely this promise that Gutiérrez's narrative voice and authorial persona leverage to motivate readers. His books are marketed as "banned in Cuba," even though no such ban was ever announced, and their absence from Cuban bookstores, like that of many foreign-published books during the revolutionary period, was a function of both economic and political restrictions. The first-person narrative of the character Pedro Juan, protagonist of all the books in the cycle except *El Rey de la Habana,* gives them an unmediated quality that debunks Cuba's institutional claims to the Latin American *testimonio* genre in favor of a defiantly individualistic act of bearing witness. Positioning his fellow characters at the economic and racial margins of Cuban society and yet maintaining a distance from these himself, Gutiérrez's principal narrator recounts physically intimate experiences that further his marketable claims to authenticity. He offers his readers an entrée into a barely exposed underworld, only, however, to uncover simultaneously the paradoxes that accepting such an invitation entails.

Centro Habana and the Image Industry

Cuba's embrace of tourism in the early 1990s precipitated a boom not only in the country's cultural exports—generating new and vibrant foreign markets for its music, film, and literature—but, as Ana María Dopico has explored, in visual representations of Havana that were produced and consumed abroad. Among the most frequently reproduced subjects of glossy coffee-table books by European and North American photographers, writes Dopico, are "the crumbling beauty of buildings and the apparently candid beauty of Cuban faces" (465). These begin to constitute what we might think of as a consistent aesthetic code, or system of metaphors, wherein architectural ruins stand as readable figures for the decay of Cuba's socialist dream. Ruins, the subject of my next chapter, are indeed the most frequent figures in this code, and they have several symbolic functions. Ruins are joined in this visual panorama, however, not only by apparently candid faces, but also by a longer-established set of tropical clichés that hark back to the hedonism of the prerevolutionary era: carefree people devoted to the joys of music, dancing, rum, and sex. During the 1990s, these clichés once again became recognizably Cuban thanks to the efforts of foreign photographers and journalists, who showcased the return to the island not only of tourists' pleasure seeking but also of its attendant prostitution.

Gutiérrez's Havana is a city of both architectural ruins and loose morals, already familiar to those readers who know Cuba from its representations in tourist brochures, photo essays, and film, but promising a more textured city. His medium facilitates such texturing, and I will turn in the second part of this chapter to his strategic uses of autobiographical fiction. Supporting these strategies, however, is a contraction of the city's limits to an area that is both suffocatingly small and beckoningly deep, an area whose paradoxically marginal status, at the center of the city and yet home to its social outcasts, makes it particularly attractive in the context of special period fascinations with Cuba. This area is Centro Habana, the few square miles that lie between Havana's colonial core and the newer suburbs that developed during the twentieth century. *Dirty Havana Trilogy* maps out Centro Habana intricately and Pedro Juan, the narrator, rarely ventures away from its familiar yet oppressive haunts. For Rey, the protagonist of *El Rey de la Habana*, the return to Centro Habana—where his mother, brother, and grandmother died within minutes of each other—heralds the beginning of a new life (39). In the later books of the cycle, Pedro Juan attempts to distance himself from the barrio's suffocating hold, most extremely by escaping to Sweden and then to a dubiously idyllic ending on a rural farm in *Tropical Animal.* In *The Insatiable Spider Man* and *Carne de perro* he drifts toward Havana's beaches and outlying barrios in search of calm; but his primary home is still in a Centro Habana that persists as a magnet, or a perverse moral compass, from whose hold he can never entirely break free.

Centro Habana was consolidated as a municipality in the postrevolutionary period (Scarpacci, Segre, and Coyula 168–76), and the three barrios that form it—Cayo Hueso, Colón, and Barrio Chino— have a checkered history. Their houses were constructed principally in the late nineteenth century, as the city grew beyond the walls that until 1863 had enclosed the historical section (Lightfoot, *Havana,* 117). They were soon vacated by their middle-class residents who sought more space in newer suburbs, and by the 1950s successive waves of internal migration had made Centro Habana the city's most densely populated area (Scarpacci, Segre, and Coyula 79). This period brought American-style department stores and new apartment buildings to some of the area's streets, an elegant contrast to the gaming establishments, brothels, and poor rooming houses that hid behind closed doors (ibid., 99). New housing policies after the 1959 revolution did little to alleviate the congestion and decay: development initiatives privileged rural areas for the best part of the 1960s and the Urban Reform Law of 1960 diminished incentives for architectural maintenance. The revolutionary government focused less on reallocating housing than on eliminating the use of housing for profit (Hamberg 4), and Centro Habana's status as the most glamorous shopping district of the 1950s dwindled as stores were deprived of stock or became housing units. By the 1970s, it was too great a project to rescue many of Centro Habana's neoclassical homes, most of which by now housed dozens of families and were structurally neglected.

The advent of the special period found many of Centro Habana's buildings on the verge of collapse and its inhabitants living in poverty. Moreover, in the century since its homes were built, the area's racial demographic had altered dramatically. Following abolition in 1882, numerous freed slaves established residence in low-rent rooming houses, and the flight of many tenants after 1959 vacated living quarters for the poorer and darker-skinned Cubans whom the revolution championed (Hamberg 4). By the onset of the special period, Centro Habana's inhabitants, unlike those of historically wealthier suburbs to the west, were predominantly Afro-Cuban ("¿Entendemos la marginalidad?" 80). Cuba's state-directed tourism industry, crucial to the country's economic recovery efforts in the post-Soviet years, steered visitors away from Centro Habana. The colonial city, whose renovation began in 1982 with funding from UNESCO, was subsequently identified as a major economic driver of special period tourism (Leal Spengler 11), and hotels, restaurants, and other tourist establishments were concentrated in this district, to the detriment of Centro Habana's physical and economic survival. At a conceptual level at least, Centro Habana was once again walled out, to segregate not the intramural city's residents, this time, but its tourism.

And yet Centro Habana is not distant enough from the attractions of Old Havana and Vedado, nor from the much-photographed Malecón seafront, to be really off the beaten track. It is precisely this positioning, visible from the edges but considered somewhat dangerous, that makes of this area an attraction in its own right, for adventurous tourists and readers alike. It is its quality as partially charted territory that allows Centro Habana to stand as more authentically Cuban, and thereby more interesting, than the city's better-frequented tourist sites. Indeed, the one Centro Habana attraction that had established itself by the late 1990s speaks directly to the area's cachet as a stronghold of cultural experience. The "rumba del domingo," the Sunday-afternoon improvisation of Afro-Cuban music and dance held in Cayo Hueso's Callejón Hammel, was not originally targeted at tourists but was nevertheless embraced by them as less staged than performances elsewhere in the city (Lightfoot 12). José Quiroga describes Centro Habana as a "no-man's-land" (9), and for Claudia Lightfoot it is both an area that visitors should enter with caution (120) and "truly *habanero;* the forces of tourism have barely touched it" (ibid.). The extent to which this area or any other can be authentic or untouched in a sustainable sense is a topic for later exploration, but Centro Habana, as it is presented to tourists and other Cuba watchers, thrives on the perception that it harbors these qualities.

Gutiérrez's writing acknowledges and takes advantage of Centro Habana's dangerous allure to foreigners, an allure derived from just those characteristics that provoke Cuban characters' distaste. A woman from the Vedado neighborhood whom Pedro Juan, the narrator of all the books except *El Rey de la Habana,* invites to live in Centro Habana is scandalized by the prospect: "In Central Havana?! No, no, no, no! Not even if I were crazy! . . . [it has] a million horny black guys, and police, and crazy old ladies and disgusting old men, and cockroaches and rats and the sewers overflowing with shit" (*Tropical Animal,* 41).[6] And yet this same mélange of density and dirt entices non-Cubans. Pedro Juan comments on tourists' aroused trepidation as they peep from the seafront into the barrio's dark recesses, hoping to take a photograph without risking their lives: "the tourists don't enter the depths of hell. They prefer to take photos from the Malecón. It's a big adventure to watch the earthquake from the outer rim and avoid the epicenter" (*The Insatiable Spider Man,* 77).[7] It is just this Centro Habana—as the depths of a hell that is nevertheless so fascinating that it must be photographed—that Pedro Juan opens up for his readers, taking them where ordinary tourists fear to tread. It is a territory mapped out as streets and tenement buildings, populated by starving souls, scheming *jineteras*, and petty delinquents. Rafael Rojas notes the discrepancy between the official tourist circuit and the alternative one mapped in novels by Gutiérrez and Ena Lucía Portela. To an official discourse that emphasizes a comfortable synthesis of summertime pleasure and mestizo sensuality, he writes, "Cuban literature produces another touristic discourse: one that entwines the exotic charge of the city with danger, poverty, and violence."[8]

The urban street became associated with moral degeneracy in the early culture of the revolution, as Ernesto Capello has explored. The land reforms that were the hallmark of social policy in the early 1960s diverted attention and resources to the countryside. Rural areas, where the revolutionary struggle had begun, became the showpieces of its advance toward equality, at the expense of both Havana's architectural maintenance and its importance in propaganda campaigns. In response, Cuban cinema of the 1960s and 1970s, such as Tomás Gutiérrez Alea's *Memories of Underdevelopment* (1968) and Sara Gómez's *In a Certain Way* (1974), cast the city and its street life as dangerous and corrupt (Capello 4–7). Rather than shake off such casting, however, Gutiérrez's special period texts showcase it to the full. Physically, his streets are dirty and poorly maintained, constantly under threat from buildings that might collapse at any moment. They are filled with the stench of unprocessed garbage and the noise of the life that spills out into them around the clock. By day, people stand in the streets in interminable lines for their weekly food rations, fight and rob each other, gather to contemplate the latest suicide victim, and drink away their lives. By night, the streets are a popular venue for sexual trysts: vacant lots and alleyways are alive with "gays, guys on the prowl, men jerking off or young girls doing it for them" and the Malecón seawall that runs along Centro Habana's outer edge is a notorious haunt for couples who seek the relative privacy of its seaward side.[9] Opportunities for people watching abound in Centro Habana's streets, and they are seized upon by Pedro Juan as he both mimics and invites a similar, although inevitably less knowledgeable, stance on the part of camera-wielding tourists and curious readers; for the name of the bar that he frequents throughout the cycle, drawn as much to its philosophical resonances as to its cheap rum (*Tropical Animal*, 264), encapsulates the barrio's appeal. Centro Habana is "El Mundo" (The World): on the one hand, a world unto itself, seething with a life that is heterogeneous in its social composition but uniform in its misery; and, on the other, a microcosm less for what Cuba actually is than for how it can be most temptingly imagined.

Lining these streets, and lending them both physical and social structure, are the *solares,* overcrowded tenement buildings that are mired in Havana's urban history and stand today among the city's sorriest landmarks. Known variously since their emergence in the nineteenth century as *solares, casas de vecindad,* and *ciudadelas,* they are involuntary experiments in collective living often staged in the abandoned homes of the rich.[10] They have long been synonymous with squalor, as a 1945 doctoral thesis, subtitled "The Horrors of the Havana *Solar,*" makes clear in addressing "the painful tragedy of the bleak building where men and women trapped by poverty, damp, and pestilence argue in the darkness of their cramped homes."[11] The *solar* that grounds Gutiérrez's Centro Habana Cycle, the one on whose top floor Pedro Juan lives, was built in the early 1900s in the style of Boston and Philadelphia apartment buildings, but the fashionable ladies who once lived there have long fled, ceding their homes to migrant families from the countryside. It now draws photographers less for its grandeur than for the contrast between its former glory and its present decay. This *solar,* like all others in the cycle, is in ruins: "it's been forty years or more since they've repaired it, or even painted it. It's a complete shambles. There are sheets of cardboard and planks where there used to be window glass" (279).[12] As a physical structure it is constantly threatening to crumble, shedding bricks and plaster in ominous quantities as its aged building materials prove ever more inadequate: "When there were heavy rainstorms, everyone trembled in fear; because the building was so old, it was built of bricks, sand, and lime, no cement" (45).[13] Occasionally the building erodes, and one of *Trilogy's* more wrenching anecdotes describes the elderly lady, Dalia, who dies of fright in her bed as the wall of her bedroom tumbles into a hurricane-lashed sea (67–68).

The *solar's* crumbling infrastructure is clearly a figure for Pedro Juan's physical and spiritual ruin. In *Dirty Havana Trilogy* he is a broken man trying to reconstruct himself both psychologically and physically in the desperate times that are the early 1990s in Havana. At the same time as it provides a frame for his own ruination, however, the *solar* gives him both shelter and sustenance. It is only from its rooftop that he can look down upon Centro Habana and rise above its and his own devastation. "From up here, the whole city was dark . . . It looked bombed out and deserted, and it was tumbling down, but it was beautiful this city where

I'd done so much loving and hating" (224).[14] The *solar*'s function as scaffolding for both despair and hope supports what Odette Casamayor reads as Pedro Juan's existential conflict. The devastated landscape that he chooses to inhabit, she proposes, is key to his evolution from chaos to resignation: "More than a mere backdrop, this devastated landscape is an expression of a way of life and an existential choice."[15] At first, in the early special period that he survives in *Trilogía*, this conflict leads Pedro Juan to abandon all ethics, or at least to choose "an ethic of the absurd."[16] As he progresses through the years and through the texts of the cycle, however, "the protagonist seeks something else: peace and reflection."[17] Casamayor traces this progression from the turbulent ruins of Centro Habana to the shabby beaches of Guanabo, and Anke Birkenmaier reads a similar shift in *Carne de perro*, where Pedro Juan, wearied by monotony, finally evokes a stoical ideal ("El realismo sucio," 2). This is a stoicism prefigured in the very first book of the cycle, by the contrasting spaces and functions of the *solar*.

Given the historical context in which Pedro Juan attempts his spiritual reconstruction, his dilapidated *solares* must also represent the Cuban Revolution's systemic decay. As I explore in chapter 5, this metaphoric deployment of architectural decay intersects with a broader aesthetic of ruins rehearsed in special period fiction and visual arts. But the *solares* in Gutiérrez's books are not merely ruins, and their decay as a figure for Pedro Juan's spiritual and Cuba's ideological crises coexists with their portrayal as crawling with life. As Jorge Fornet puts it, the story of decline told by Centro Habana's poverty and architecture, if read as the decay of a national body, can accommodate the oppositional persistence of a beating heart, or life inside the *solares* (106–9). The *solar* is a sociological structure cast as zoological habitat, and this second casting, I propose, is at least as important as the first in shaping the books' appeal to their readers. As Antonio José Ponte has suggested, Havana's distinct visual appeal derives from its status as living, rather than inanimate, ruin ("What Am I Doing Here?" 15). Thus the Centro Habana Cycle animates the ruin, its *solares* being made not only of bricks, mortar, and other makeshift materials but also of human beings and substances. It may be "a labyrinth of rotten boards and pieces of brick" (322), but it is also where "people stifle in the heat, hungry and wallowing in shit" (ibid.).[18] It is itself a living thing, a monster with entrails inhabited by parasites that have buried their human dignity beneath the struggle for survival. "It's like a huge, clumsy monster that wallows around, breathes fire, and triggers earthquakes for six days and on the seventh day rests, gathering its energies" (171).[19]

The *solar* as a living organism allows Pedro Juan to delve more deeply into the animal life he observes on Centro Habana's streets and to cameo the predicaments of its individual members. The streets are populated by life-forms upon which he turns a distinctly zoological lens. His reference to the "fauna" of Centro Habana recurs in the first three books of the Cycle (*Trilogy*, 106, *El Rey*, 40, *Tropical Animal*, 268), and *Carne de perro* describes the dog-eat-dog defensiveness that the environment instills: in Centro Habana "you get used to living with your fangs and your claws sharpened, ready to destroy the first to give you a bad look."[20] In the streets, this "fauna" roams as a herd, staking out the urban jungle as its watering hole and its breeding ground. The pitifully overcrowded *solar,* on the other hand, corrals the fauna, at the same time allowing Pedro Juan to distinguish individual specimens from the herd and focus on their living and mating habits. These individuals include not only the "tropical animal," Pedro Juan himself, who gives the third book its name, but also "the morons" who perform all their bodily functions in the *solar*'s public spaces: "They shit in hidden places on the stairs. They pee everywhere" (140).[21] They also include elderly people who meet their death because of sexual exploitation (*Trilogy*, 323–32), vengeful women who castrate their wayward boyfriends (*Trilogy*, 170–73), and the butcher arrested for trading in human livers (*Trilogy*, 354–62).[22] The *solar*'s inhabitants spend their time mating, hunting, defecating, and dying, in an animal existence that effectively precludes cerebral concerns.[23] Although, architecturally, the *solar* is a frame for both Pedro Juan's spiritual ruin and the revolution's demise, it is also a cage in which to exhibit the sociological-cum-zoological composition of special period Centro Habana, as the title of one of *Trilogy*'s stories, "Salíamos de las jaulas" (We were breaking out of our cages), implies.[24]

In the absence of other options, copulating and excreting are the principal activities of the *solar*'s inhabitants, sealing their interests as primarily bestial. Sex offers one of the few opportunities for recreation, and those who are capable of doing so indulge constantly, while those incapable watch or fantasize. "Addicted to pricks" (*Trilogy*, 72 and 203) is one of the more frequent afflictions that Pedro Juan diagnoses among women, young and old;[25] and men of all generations, from the thirteen-year-old Rey who masturbates at the sight of his *mulata* neighbor (*El Rey*, 13–14) to the septuagenarian who in *Trilogy*'s closing episode mesmerizes a much younger woman with his expert technique, pursue quick gratification. Pedro Juan's own encounters are the most graphically described as, particularly in the headier days of *Dirty Havana Trilogy,* he barricades himself in the ultimately unsatisfying space of a private orgy: "Living in Olga's squalid room was like living in an X-rated film" (55).[26] Sex and dirt are complementary and barely distinguishable experiences, as Pedro Juan insists from the very first episode of *Trilogy:* "Sex is an exchange of fluids, saliva, breath and smells, urine, semen, shit, sweat, microbes, bacteria. Or there is no sex" (5).[27] Just as he and his neighbors wallow in the dirt of their physical surroundings, living between shit-smeared walls and using excrement to communicate revenge, so too are they drawn by each others' bodily excretions—"we inhaled each other" (50) being essential to foreplay.[28] Rey and Magda, the forlorn lovers of *El Rey de la Habana,* are the most extreme examples of this attraction to dirt: "Neither minded the other's dirt. She had a slightly bitter cunt and her ass stank of shit. He had fetid, white cream between the end of his prick and the hair around it. Their underarms reeked and their feet smelled of dead rats, and they sweated. All this excited them."[29] Sex and dirt, moreover, are principles not only for living but also for writing. To the extent that Pedro Juan presents a philosophy of writing, it is articulated as forcing his readers to "wake up and smell the shit" (*Trilogy,* 85).[30] "That's my profession: shitraker" (107), he insists in *Dirty Havana Trilogy,* and he later reiterates this vision: "an artist converts his shit into raw material. Construction material" (137).[31] Both the lives in the cycle and the mode in which they are narrated, he seems to suggest, are animal, driven by sex and defecation.

ZOOLOGY AND THE MARGINS

In an article on *El Rey de la Habana,* Ena Lucía Portela objects to readings that would cast this novel's characters as "a fauna of strange beasts to be seen in a zoo, from the other side of the bars" rather than as "Cubans you would see on the streets, nothing at all out of the ordinary."[32] Such readings, Portela claims, are a function of social prejudice, wherein the "average man" is taken to be of the middle rather than the lower classes. And yet it is Gutiérrez's texts themselves that repeatedly denominate Centro Habana's residents as "fauna," such that any prejudice is directed from within. The questions must then be why the cycle insists on a zoological portrayal of Centro Habana, what interest this portrayal holds for its readers, and how Gutiérrez's narrator negotiates between the inside and the outside of the cage. Josefina Ludmer's analysis of the character Rey provides some tentative answers: he is "a fundamental biological and territorial configuration that becomes a historically determined way of being (the special period)."[33] As a biological entity in a distinct national, as well as natural, environment, Rey comes to represent life in the special period. Rey and the Centro Habana that he inhabits, however, represent the special period in a particularly nuanced way, wherein representation anticipates reception, for the special period is crucial to Gutiérrez's fiction not only as backdrop but also as a series of images and expectations generated by its foreign readers. The texts' focus on Centro Habana as habitat engages readers' urge to experience Cuba intimately, an urge intensified during the post-Soviet period and motivated by a complex and often contradictory blend of desire, distrust, and cynicism. In this period, Cuba aroused a desire in tourists and readers alike to see and know a Cuba that the Cold War had kept off limits and, at the same time, a distrust of the official rhetoric that would obscure the sensual and personal dimensions of this place under a shroud of propagandistic optimism. Sympathy with voices perceived as dissenting and morbid fascination with the decline of socialism's grand dream combined to invent a roster of interests, a roster on which sex and filth, as markers of intimate and paradoxically uncontaminated experience, figure highly. That sex tourism features prominently in Gutiérrez's texts, and that *Tropical Animal* recounts foreign fashion photographers' penchant for "garbage and debris" (27),[34] implies that his casting of Centro Habana as habitat is attuned to the interests newly aroused in readers.

A locally and historically specific idea of marginality is crucial to the reception of Gutiérrez's books, both among their more enthusiastic Cuban critics and in the foreign markets in which they circulate most widely. The margins of these books' Centro Habana are peripheral not only to the European metropolis—home to many of their readers—but also, and more important, to the Cuban revolutionary project. The revolution counted among its early aspirations the eradication of economic disparity, racial discrimination, and prostitution, aspirations of which the special period landscape made a mockery. The margins were historically the territory of the Cuban Revolution, as it sought to bring into its equalizing center those who had been excluded from capitalist prosperity. It is with regard to this more local "center" that Gutiérrez's work pioneered a dramatic shift in how the Cuban margins were mapped in relation to both the revolution and Cuban fiction. As chapter 3 explained, in the early

1990s, Cuban literature's margins were claimed for young and icono-clastic writers whose largely delocalized concerns—rock music, drug use, teenage disaffection—allied them with countercultural figures outside the country. It was precisely in embracing a nonnational counterculture that they registered distance from the Cuban Revolution, although, as both Anke Birkenmaier and Iván Rubio Cuevas point out, they perhaps inadvertently perpetuated a domestically sanctioned practice of protest literature (Birkenmaier 41; Rubio Cuevas 87). And yet, over the course of the special period, as foreign markets for Cuban literature flourished, this iconoclasm ceded its marginal position to representations not only of dissonance with the revolution but also of difference from the met-ropolitan sites from which Cuba was being read. The characters of the Centro Habana Cycle, located both in the center of Havana and at the outer edges of Cuban society, came to occupy the margins that the times and their markets demanded.

Several critics have read Gutiérrez's relocation of the margins as evi-dence of the increasing irrelevance in Cuba of noneconomic forms of social exclusion, in the context of the overwhelmingly material con-straints of the special period. Although such critical readings are some-what more rooted in Cuban living conditions than in broader debates on marginality, in which gender, sexual orientation, nationality, and age as well as racial and economic status are all positions of exclusion, they nevertheless identify and coincide with one of the Centro Habana Cycle's strongest selling points abroad.[35] This is its constructed image of authenticity, of a life as peripheral to revolutionary ideals as it is to official tourist circuits. It is for its representations of a neglected lowlife that Víctor Fowler Calzada, in two articles published in Cuba that ad-dress the theme of marginality in literature of the 1990s, extols *El Rey de la Habana* and attacks contemporary young writers—implicitly the *novísimo* writers—for their self-imposed and self-indulgent retreat from society. As their own lack of experience leads them to depict neither criminality, incarceration, nor violence, and to rely on characters who are mostly university students and "alien to any antisocial practice other than the tendency to self-destroy,"[36] young writers' claims to marginal status are, in Fowler's opinion, baseless. He subsequently elaborates on the faux-marginal social status of these writers, who are "groups almost always of students, recipients, and practitioners of foreign cultural mod-els (rock culture), holders of clean criminal records and rebels primarily against their parents."[37] The incorporation of the word *marginality* into the lexicon of so-called countercultural writers constituted, in Fowler's words, "a semantic cleansing that was, at the same time, a social lie and an ethnic purge."[38] If the principal criterion for marginality is delinquency— as it must be for Fowler, given that the word comes from the language of police administration—then Gutiérrez's *El Rey de la Habana,* he insists, is one of the few works to give the margins a space in contemporary Cuban literature.

Ena Lucía Portela similarly addresses the distinct uses of marginality in Cuban literary production of the 1990s. Although Cuban writers had long been interested in the criminal underworld, she claims, the 1990s unleashed a torrent of such themes, to the extent that "incredible though it may seem, marginality becomes central or at least an obligatory reference."[39] She identifies three causes for this boom in literary explorations of Cuban lowlife: the material conditions in the country during the special period, the government and state-sponsored press's insistence on ignoring these conditions, and the foreign market's interest in unveiling them (64). These contextual motivations for writing do not preclude her from distinguishing between "falsified" and genuine marginalities and thus reiterating, but at the same time redefining, the terms with which other critics during the 1990s defended Cuban letters against fictional depictions of the special period.[40] "Falsifications," in Portela's reading, tend to be the domain either of exiled writers, who imagine but do not know firsthand the deprivations and delinquencies to which Cubans were driven during the 1990s, or of writers who live on the island but at a distance from its worst conditions and who, as a result, "aren't fluent in the subject, idealize or condemn, reproduce stereotypes, often have no clue what they're talking about."[41] Their distance and consequent falsehood with regard to Havana's lowlife stand in opposition to Gutiérrez's proximity and faithfulness and to his skill in remaining "rigorously faithful to the details."[42] Once again, accolades for a bona fide articulation of marginality are reserved for *El Rey de la Habana.*

Both Fowler's insistence that Pedro Juan Gutiérrez's rendering of marginal life is the only one to avoid "a social lie and an ethnic purge" and Portela's valorization of the lived experience of poverty intersect with Cuban social scientists' assessments of marginality as increasingly defined by economic and racial status. Some participants in a 2001 debate on marginality hosted by the journal *Temas* addressed the problem in resolutely abstract terms, implicitly locating its most severe manifestations elsewhere in Latin America and thus perpetuating the revolution's claim to have eradicated it on home ground, or proposing, as did the sociologist Mayra Espina, that in Cuba "marginality is a cultural and political phenomenon."[43] Other participants, however, were more candid. Particularly strident were those who locate the margins of the special period precisely where Gutiérrez does: in Centro Habana, in the *solar,* and in the severe poverty of Afro-Cubans. Echoing an argument long subdued in Cuba, and whose reemergence during the special period coincided with new critical forums for the discussion of race, Gisela Arandia drew attention to "a marginality that is closely linked to racism, to racial discrimination and prejudice."[44] This experience is especially acute, noted Arandia, in a barrio such as Centro Habana, whose living conditions are among the worst in the city and whose population is among the most Afro-Cuban (80). The *solar* in particular attracts prejudice toward its residents, claimed Arandia's colleague Bárbara Oliva (88). That the marginal position to which Arandia and Oliva refer should be charted by discrimination is an especially strong indictment of Cuban society, and that a roundtable on the question "¿Entendemos la marginalidad?" (Do we understand marginality?) should become a discussion of racism is indicative of the broad shift in values—social, cultural, and, indeed, commercial—that Cuba witnessed during the special period. The foregrounding by Cuban literary and social critics of subjects whose marginal position is defined by their socioeconomic and racial status intersects with foreign readers' privileging of subjects who are recognizably Cuban for this very same status, and it places Gutiérrez's books, mapped out against the margins of Centro Habana, at the vanguard of the period's literature.

Exporting Authenticity

The special period, then, saw in both literature and social analysis a restoration of the margins to the domains of class and race, a restoration whose most prominent literary manifestation is Pedro Juan Gutiérrez's Centro Habana. That this new valorization is in fact a revalidation of the disenfranchisement that motivated the Cuban Revolution is not lost on the literary critics who address it. Fowler, for example, chastises the *novísimo* writers for their neglect of the very sectors of society that Pedro Juan Gutiérrez would revisit, while Portela aligns Gutiérrez with what she calls the enlightened left."[45] Moreover, it is not only the revolution's broad struggle against inequality that this critical repositioning of social exclusion revalidates: it has a more direct target in the body of criticism that formed around Latin American *testimonio* writing in the 1980s and 1990s. *Testimonio* was initially heralded for publicly voicing the collective struggles of Latin America's socially oppressed and it was warmly embraced by the literary establishment of the Cuban Revolution. Miguel Barnet's *Autobiography of a Runaway Slave* (1966) was considered a pioneering example of *testimonio,* and the implementation of a biannual Casa de las Américas prize for the genre in 1970 sealed its paradoxical institutionalization within Cuba. Goffredo Diana has traced the genre's demise as a vehicle for protest in Cuba, owing precisely to its strong institutional presence, and both Margarita Mateo and Ronaldo Menéndez have addressed the *novísimo* writers' reluctance to assume its ideological legacy. As John Beverley implies in his essay "The Margin at the Center," the margins have a troubling place and value in *testimonio* criticism. As *testimonios* circulated in geographic and political contexts distanced from those in which they were produced, they were appreciated not only for their content, but also for their provenance. Such valorization of *testimonios* as unmediated in fact made little sense, given the necessary invention of a transcriber; but it nevertheless granted them a status as authentic, or as "auratic" in Alberto Moreiras's formulation, that became one of the thornier issues in *testimonio* criticism.

A similarly problematic equation of socioeconomic and racial margins with authenticity is implicit in Fowler's reading of *El Rey de la Habana.* It is more pronounced in Portela's insistence that, unlike others' renderings of Havana lowlife, *El Rey* is "a truthful, incisive, accurate novel,"[46] an assessment that becomes firmly rooted, thanks in part to the foundational role of authenticity in the tourist industry, in the reception of Gutiérrez's work outside Cuba. Portela acknowledges the privileged price that supposedly authentic representations of Cuba command in the international marketplace, commenting that "the literary value, very much a function of the commercial value, of all these books is determined . . . by the more or less evident link established between them and real life in Cuba right now, by the notion of 'authenticity.'"[47] And yet she persists in attributing this highly prized quality to *El Rey de la Habana,* insisting that its dialogues are to be recognized "for their truthfulness, their authentic rhythm and coloring, their faithfulness to the details of Havana slang."[48] Although she does not go so far as to brand the novel as "authentic" in its entirety—indeed, she observes that its recounting of real incidents in itself "would not bring any guarantee of authenticity"[49]—her reiteration of this term in the context of Gutiérrez's work does much to validate it.

In thus associating Gutiérrez's work with authenticity, Portela raises questions that are crucial to the special period, its literature, and the reception thereof both in Cuba and in the foreign contexts that are in some ways akin to the *testimonio*'s centers of dissemination. For, beyond the somewhat redundant question of whether or not Gutiérrez's work is or can hope to be "authentic" lies the issue of why it should be read as such, in this particular historical moment. Why, for example, should Gutiérrez's representations of his novels' milieu—namely, Centro Habana—be so attractive? And what are the particular strategies, both rhetorical and commercial, through which the Centro Habana Cycle assures authenticity? How, that is, do Gutiérrez's narrators and his marketers conspire to construct and present his work in this way? The cycle, I suggest, takes advantage of the presumption of authenticity that its characters' marginal status invites, in order to mount a challenge to the cross-cultural desires and dynamics that would position them as such.

Gutiérrez's Centro Habana might have become recognizably Cuban outside the country because of its coincidence with the aesthetic codes of the tourist industry, but it has a less established place in Cuba's literary traditions. Havana is both the setting and the protagonist of much Cuban fiction, as Ineke Phaf and Emma Alvárez-Tabío have explored. Álvarez-Tabío's analysis finds a city whose portrayals shift over time and that perhaps most resembles Gutiérrez's in the nineteenth- and early-twentieth-century novels of Cirilo Villaverde and Miguel de Carrión, whose streets are paved with danger and whose *solares* shelter women of uncertain repute. In Miguel Ángel González-Abellás's reading of this novel, for example, the *solar*-dwelling *mulata* who gives her name to Villaverde's *Cecilia Valdés* remains barely changed in *Dirty Havana Trilogy*; and, indeed, Pedro Juan's lover in *Tropical Animal* is compared to Cecilia Valdés (13). And yet, Villaverde's classic bears the standard of an antislavery novel and a difference-reconciling "national romance," to use Doris Sommer's term, thus raising it from the squalid urban context that the Centro Habana Cycle refuses to leave.[50] Indeed, the cycle's grounding in Centro Habana draws it closer to nonliterary traditions. Chief among these is the urban mythology and spiritual status of the *solar* that date from the mid-nineteenth century and witness a revival—predictably, one that is partly driven by tourism—in popular music of the special period. Carlos Venegas Fornias describes the prerevolution *solar* as a residence whose inevitably collective practices inspired distinct forms of cultural expression. "The Havana *solar*," he writes, "was the pillar of a culture centered on the *barrio* (neighborhood). Popular in the sense that everyone participated in a communal life, the *barrios* developed identities and created the stereotypes of Havana's urban culture, such as the *gallego* (a Spanish immigrant), the *mulata,* and the *negrito,* all of whom were used as characters in Havana's burlesque and comical theaters" (22). As Robin Moore argues, the emergence of these vernacular characters from the *solar* furthered the integration of Afro-Cubans into national culture in a double-edged way. While popular theater gave visibility to working-class Afro-Cuban music and dance, it also, "by disseminating frequently derogatory images of black street culture and artistic expression, conceived and performed almost entirely by white Cubans," perpetuated discrimination against Afro-Cubans (41). Aside from generating such stereotypes, however, as a home and refuge for large populations of Afro-Cubans, the *solar* was also a cradle for spiritual expression. The rumba, the spontaneous yet highly coded dance form that is central to "a collective festive event, a gala meal, a carousal, or a high time," flourished here, particularly in the late nineteenth and early twentieth centuries when slaves freed from the plantations, where it had originated, settled in urban areas (Daniel 17–19).

After the revolution, as the worst of the *solar*'s squalor was cosmetically cleaned up, its place in popular culture weakened, although it persists as a setting in Julio García Espinosa's film *Un día en el solar* (1967). It is in the late 1990s that the *solar* is reclaimed—specifically in *timba* music, the urban genre that developed over the 1990s as the sound of the special period. Largely developed among Afro-Cuban men, *timba* embraces the *solar* as a repository of noninstitutionalized spiritual culture, its ironic, hard-hitting lyrics recuperating this deeply symbolic space, along with a sense of blackness previously subdued by the revolution's egalitarianism (Hernández-Reguant, "Havana's *Timba*"). *Timba* recuperates the *solar* for its significance to Afro-Cuban culture and community, but not without acknowledging the value that these in particular, and that private life in Cuba more generally, have acquired during the special period. *Timba* music, in fact, was one of the more successful cultural exports of the special period, and consequently the one most vociferously criticized for its commercialization (García Meralla 56–58). The *timba* artist Isaac Delgado, for example, sets his song "Solar de la California" in the *solar* that in 1997 became a Center for Popular Yoruba Culture Studies, sponsored by the national artists' and writers' union (UNEAC) and a French research organization (Arandia Covarrubia 2).

Drawing his refrain from the Eagles' "Hotel California," Delgado sets up a direct opposition between the Vedado section of Havana, which he compares to Madrid, and the more authentic Centro Habana. Those visitors who want to know "el verdadero Habana" (true Havana), he claims, must brave the streets of Centro Habana and venture into the *solar*.[51]

Delgado thus claims the Centro Habana *solar* as the habitat of a distinctly local population and at the same time advertises its appeal as such to those visitors who are in search of true Cuban experience. It is in this double move that Gutiérrez's Centro Habana Cycle finds its strongest parallel, as the novels zoom in on the intimate details of private lives *and* capture tourists' and fashion photographers' attempts to do the same. Nevertheless, Gutiérrez's narrator maintains a crucial distance from the Centro Habana habitat that renders his books' claims to authenticity, and their critics claims on their behalf, clearly strategic; for, while *timba* music, in Ariana Hernández-Reguant's argument, can simultaneously tout and revere the *solar* as a site of Afro-Cuban community and religious tradition, Gutiérrez's work is spectacularly lacking in such reverence. There is little spirituality among his *solar*'s Afro-Cuban residents; they are distinguished, rather, as overwhelmingly physical, libidinal beings, who impress the Pedro Juan character with their abandon to the most depraved of sexual acts.[52] In an early review of *Dirty Havana Trilogy*, Achy Obejas discerned in the novel "an insistent sexism and racism . . . that can't be explained as either cultural difference or benign in content" (115), a racism that manifests itself not only in Pedro Juan's preconceptions about his neighbors but also in theirs about each other. His lover Gloria, for example, swears that she will never sleep with another black man "because they're bums, liars, useless pigs, and their pricks are so long they give you pelvic inflammation" (297).[53] These unquestioned racial hierarchies, voiced by Pedro Juan or ventriloquized for him by others, represent for Obejas "a cool overall detachment, a disdain almost, that Gutiérrez might be aiming as much at his readers as at his characters or even himself" (115).

It is detachment, precisely, that defines Pedro Juan's position vis-à-vis the other inhabitants of the *solar;* the building is filled with Afro-Cubans but he, crucially, is not one of them. Pedro Juan is identified as an outsider to the *solar,* both by race and by birth, recognized by others as new and untrustworthy.[54] While the character Rey, in *El Rey de la Habana,* is more closely bound to the Centro Habana *solar,* having been raised there by a mentally impaired mother, he too, however, keeps his distance from the barrio's Afro-Cuban inhabitants, subtly reiterating Pedro Juan's prejudices. The result of such detachment, particularly on the part of the Pedro Juan narrator, is, on the one hand, the effective silencing of these inhabitants. On the other hand, the same detachment enables the embedding of an observer figure within the texts themselves, a figure who both mediates representations of life in the *solar* and, crucially, offers a model for the voyeuristic but necessarily distanced reader.

AUTOBIOGRAPHY AND DISTANCE

In adopting this stance, wherein life in the *solar* is exposed by an inside observer, Gutiérrez's narrator radically reorients the testimonial voice. He appropriates this voice for an individual who is situated very close to, but not within, the collective experience that is both the foundation of his anecdotes and a primary attraction to those who read them from both inside and outside Cuba. Assuming an explicitly derogatory distance from the community around him, he commandeers the collective experience of life in special period Centro Habana and takes advantage of its appeal to outsiders in order to voice a far more individual intimacy. In so doing, he shifts the referent of first-person writing from plural to singular, a significant shift in itself given the legacy of collective, testimonial writing in Cuba. Although neither the institutionalization of *testimonio* nor the simultaneous promotion of revolutionary narratives of social betterment eliminated autobiographical writing, for decades they provoked its adoption of guises that muted its focus on the individual. Roberto González Echevarría's essay on post-1959 autobiographical writing in Cuba emphasizes the genre's inseparability from the revolution, its driving question being "If you are reborn, who is the new child . . . and how does he differ from the one who died and was left behind?" ("Autobiography and Representation," 569). Nevertheless, González Echevarría suggests that within Cuba writers resorted to coded forms of autobiographical writing, such as the roman à clef, or to personal histories of transformation consistent with the revolutionary project, while more explicit introspection, as well as expression of discord between the individual and society, were limited to exile writing.

With the exception of *El Rey de la Habana,* Gutiérrez's books present themselves as deeply autobiographical, despite *Animal tropical*'s prefatory disclaimer—absent from the other books in the Centro Habana Cycle and omitted even in *Animal*'s English translation—that "this novel is a work of fiction. Any resemblance to real circumstances or people is a coincidence."[55] Their narrator's trajectory through the special period and his physical appearance correspond closely to those of Gutiérrez himself, as described in interviews and advertised prominently on the jacket covers of his books; and, as if to satisfy the requirements for Philippe Lejeune's "autobiographical pact" in which "the author, the narrator and the protagonist must be identical" (5), narrator and author share the name Pedro Juan. Gutiérrez elaborates on his relationship to the Pedro Juan of *Dirty Havana Trilogy* in a 2004 interview with Marilyn Bobes, insisting that "that Pedro Juan is excessively autobiographical, so much so that I have never reread the book because it's too painful for me,"[56] and presenting the character as an act of masochistic revenge against the author himself whose life, like those of many in Cuba in the early special period, had reached its lowest point.[57] The Centro Habana Cycle is certainly presented as Gutiérrez's own story by its foreign publishers who, like those who tout *Carne de perro* as "defiantly autobiographical and raw," rarely distinguish between the author and the narrator.[58] Although the Cuban establishment has historically disdained autobiography, foreign publishers prize the genre as revelatory of unofficial dimensions of life in Cuba, a contrast that implies an explanation beyond that of literary quality for why *El Rey de la Habana,* the only book in the cycle to be written in the third person, was preferred by critics in Cuba but passed over by several foreign publishers.[59]

The autobiographical undertones of the Centro Habana Cycle's narrative voice are sealed by the uncompromisingly personal exposure that it foists upon his readers. Gutiérrez has called *Dirty Havana Trilogy* a "striptease" ("El Rey de Centro Habana"); and the narrator of *Tropical Animal* reiterates this as a figure for first-person writing: "To write in the first person is like taking your clothes off in public" (48).[60] The Centro Habana Cycle foregrounds physical intimacy between its characters and, in so doing, forces it between the narrator and his readers. The insistent wallowing in sex and dirt that are the hallmarks of Gutiérrez's Centro Habana are at their most vivid, and their most aggressive, when the lens turns on the narrator himself. This is a perspective that maximizes proximity, and one of its more succinct examples is the frequently quoted line "I like to smell my armpits when I masturbate" (140). "The smell of sweat turns me on," continues Pedro Juan, extending an invitation to his readers to be similarly excited.[61] It is an invitation consistent with Pedro Juan's philosophy of writing "to jar people a little and force others to wake up and smell the shit" (85),[62] but it welds this philosophy specifically to self-writing: readers are not only to experience excrement as a metaphor for reality, but they are to enjoy the functions and excretions of Pedro Juan's own body. Self-writing, as Gutiérrez implies with his reference to *Trilogy*'s striptease, is self-exposure, but in the Centro Habana Cycle's case it is a particularly engaging form of exposure. It both assumes and demands its viewers' interest in the narrator as a physical being, an assumption that acquires a visual dimension on the informational Web site, www.pedrojuangutierrez.com, that Gutiérrez began to administer from Havana following the success of his novels abroad. Lacking the sexual explicitness of the fiction, the site's many photographs nevertheless displayed Gutiérrez in various states of suggestive repose and included a section titled "En la intimidad" (In intimacy). Thus Pedro Juan the narrator, closely shadowed by Gutiérrez the author, forgoes the collectivity of *testimonio* for the exhibitionism of autobiography. He co-opts the communal experience of the Centro Habana *solar* in favor of a resolutely individual and inescapably physical persona, a stance that ultimately aims to both excite and admonish the reader.

Firsthand experience, then, is not offered in Gutiérrez's texts as collective. Indeed, although they peddle images of communal life in the *solar,* they keep from this life a duplicitous distance that renders highly problematic their relationship to special period valuations of authenticity; for the narrating Pedro Juan speaks from a periphery that does not map exactly to Centro Habana's margins. His is a seeing, knowing, and selectively participating position that is more aligned with what Graham Huggan calls "staged marginality" than with the experience of the books' other characters. Huggan's term "denotes the process by which marginalised individuals or minority groups dramatise their 'subordinate' status for the imagined benefit of a majority audience" (xii); importantly, the process "may function in certain contexts to uncover and challenge dominant structures of power" (ibid.). It is no coincidence that the term should be adapted from Dean MacCannell's work on tourism, where "staged authenticity" refers to tourist operations' attempts to eliminate their appearance as such and to create instead the impression of undisturbed, unobserved life and work (MacCannell 91–107). In post-Soviet Cuba, the staging of both authenticity and marginality, as defined by MacCannell and Huggan respectively, corresponds to the sudden interest turned upon the country as a tourist site and the subsequent market not only in pleasure travel there but in sharing native experience from afar, be this through cinema, photography, music, or fiction.

While MacCannell locates authenticity with the occupants of a visited site and its staging with those sites' managers, Huggan makes his alternative term, "staged marginality," the domain of the writer and privileges literature as the stage for a marginality that is both complicit and critical. Writers' "staged marginality" stands in opposition to what is frequently designated as the academy but is defined more broadly, in Huggan's reading, to include the global reading market. This idea of staged marginality as opposition is complicated in Gutiérrez's cycle not only by the books' initial although decreasing distance from "the academy," construed in Huggan's work and in the postcolonial theory from which he draws as an Anglo-American, university-based arbiter of political claims. It is also rendered questionable by the uneasy transference of terms like "subordinate" and "majority" to a context long governed by socialist principles. The global reading market, in contrast, is a force to be reckoned with by both Huggan's postcolonial authors and those of Cuba's boom. As discussed in chapter 3, revolutionary ideals as a controlling social force ceded ground over the course of the special period to the demands and possibilities of the dollarized economy. Although these two distinct sources of power permeated society as a whole, the Centro Habana Cycle, with its stridently autobiographical voice and insistence on Centro Habana as zoological habitat, allows little opposition to either power via any activity other than writing. Writing, as Pedro Juan's philosophy of the vocation reiterates, is the purest act of resistance, and it is in this regard that the peripheral position from which he speaks breaks away from the margins in which his books are set. It is in their capacity as writers that both Pedro Juan the narrator and Gutiérrez the author address the new power of the international reading market, foregrounding and challenging the relationship between local experience and its distant consumers.

Although Huggan names Salman Rushdie, V. S. Naipaul, and Hanif Kureishi as exemplary practitioners of "staged marginality," he does so in the context of a broader phenomenon, the "postcolonial exotic," that has multiple architects. "The cultural commodification of postcolonial writing [and] the exotic appeal attributed to putatively 'marginal' literatures and cultures" (ix) that drive this phenomenon are produced, he argues, in a tacit collaboration between corporate publishers, literary prize committees, academic critics, and, ultimately, writers themselves. Like the "postcolonial exotic," the Cuban literary boom of the 1990s was fueled by a similar collaboration. And yet, with the work of Pedro Juan Gutiérrez, as with that of Zoé Valdés, the pioneer of the Cuban boom, there is an important distinction to be made between the role in this collaboration of the book industry, broadly construed, and those of the author and narrator. However close these roles may seem, and they are certainly more so in these cases than they are in fiction less closely attuned to the material conditions of the special period, they are separated by a crucial space that becomes that of critique. If the book industry can be understood to include not only publishers but also distributors, sellers, and reviewers, then articulations of its interests are printed in a range of materials, from the illustrations, author biographies, copy, and excerpted reviews on the books' covers, to newspaper and magazine reviews.[63] Elements of what Gérard Genette calls the "paratext" give the book not only a self-contained presence but also a socioeconomic one in the world outside (1–15), and the published commentaries of parties not directly involved in the production of the book itself, such as reviewers and critics, can serve to reinforce the messages, or the marketing strategies, of the book's producers.[64]

In the case of fiction of the Cuban boom, extratextual layers of commentary are powerful and usually consistent with one another. They tend to reiterate what I have called an aesthetic code, common across several areas of cultural production, whose images invoke consistent meanings decipherable only in the context of Cuba's status as a last bastion of socialism. As is perhaps to be expected, the covers of the five books of Gutiérrez's Centro Habana Cycle tout the brutal realism of their portrayals of life in Cuba. The stories in *Dirty Havana Trilogy*, claims the jacket of this book's first Spanish edition, "reveal for us a thoroughbred writer, an implacable chronicler of a country and a time that are contradictory, terrible, fascinating."[65] The Spanish- and English-language editions of all five books introduce the author's biography with a reference to his selling ice cream on the streets at age eleven, in a transparent attempt to cast him as a social outcast. Such promises to reveal are reiterated by the sexually suggestive cover photography of almost all editions of the books: the Polish *Trilogy*'s is the most explicit, but it is by no means the only one to make the bare *mulata* body speak for the book as a whole. Newspaper reviews, too, took up the theme, to the extent that their comments are appropriated abundantly as supporting material for the publishers' claims. "A brazen, cruel, authentic voice" is the quote by the *Ajoblanco* reviewer Paco Marín included in the

Spanish edition of *Trilogy*.[66] "*Dirty Havana Trilogy* is probably the most honest depiction of life under Castro to have emerged in recent years," states the *National Review* report reprinted in the second U.S. edition of this book, and the U.S. edition of *Tropical Animal* quotes *Time Out London*'s assessment of it as "a book that shows the heart of Cuba with total honesty." Publishers' copy thus attempts to reap for reading the profits of tourism. It generates, and independent reviewers tend to perpetuate, vicarious excitement at seeing into a society perceived as both newly within reach and on the verge of collapse. Uncensored exposure, filtered through both social marginality and sexual intimacy, becomes a major selling point.

THE SIGHTSEER SEEN

The author's interest in exposure, however, is more than a mere sales pitch. Although Gutiérrez's insistence that he is oblivious to the demands of the market is surely to be regarded with skepticism ("Animal literario," 37), his response to those demands is carefully calibrated. It involves a strategy, for which the narrator Pedro Juan serves as a primary vehicle, wherein readers are invited as participants in the characters' physical activities only then to be ridiculed and chastised for the very desires that would make them accept the invitation. This is a somewhat sadistic rendering of what Doris Sommer has called a "rhetoric of particularism," in which minority writers engage their readers enough to advance a political agenda but ward off the empathy that would annihilate difference (*Proceed with Caution*, 1–31). The Centro Habana Cycle deploys similar tactics, but its political agenda is muted, at least as regards the regime that its foreign critics would have its author denounce more openly.[67] Rather, a target of its derision is outside interest itself. Gutiérrez stages marginality in order to enlist curiosity, depicting general misery as the backdrop to an intimate and sordid self-portrait. This staging, however, has a crucial second step that is a further act of exposure: that of Cubaphilia's own sordidness and squalor.

René Prieto has read the raw sexuality of *Dirty Havana Trilogy* as a ruse to expose its readers to Cuba's devastation: baited by desire, they are confronted with suffering (386). But with this ruse, the Centro Habana Cycle does more than alert its readers to the existence of suffering: it forces them to recognize their own implication in a relationship—to the writer, the book, and their context—whose basis is primarily economic. This relationship is drawn in terms that are as demeaning to the reader as they are accusatory. Nevertheless, in revealing it the cycle recuperates some ethical ground in the debate over market versus literary-cum-moral values that, as chapter 3 discussed, erupted in Cuba during the mid-1990s. For, close though Gutiérrez's books may be to the market, in terms of both their perpetuation of a distinctly salable aesthetic and their sales figures, they nevertheless incorporate a challenge to the interests by which that market is driven. They mount this challenge through the deployment of certain figures whose presence on the Centro Habana landscape is closely linked to tourism. Through a finely constructed analogy between sightseeing and reading as visual acts, the reader becomes an increasingly awkward onlooker.

Reflecting the growth in Cuba's tourist industry, tourism penetrates further into Centro Habana as the cycle progresses. And yet, despite their increasing presence until *Carne de perro,* where Pedro Juan's escape from his barrio erases them from the scene, visitors are always outsiders, their attempts to experience Centro Habana life thwarted not only by cultural distance but by the narrator's explicitly exclusionary naming of them. Foreign characters are usually *turistas* (tourists), marking their transient, outside status. If they are distinguished any further, it is by a national denominator: they are "the Mexican" (*Trilogy,* 69), "the German woman" (*Trilogy,* 164–69), or "German, Spanish, Italian and French architects" (*Tropical Animal,* 289), precisely because they cannot be Cuban.[68] They wander the streets but rarely enter the *solar;* if they do so, it is generally to complete a pre-agreed sexual transaction that serves to further mark them as foreign. It is only when, in *Animal tropical,* Pedro Juan spends several months in Sweden that a foreign woman is more than just that, although his insights into Agneta as a sentient and physical being only reaffirm his preference for Gloria, the Cuban siren. *Tropical Animal* is structured by the uncomplicated opposition of cold (Sweden, Swedish women) to hot (Cuba, Cuban women). As such, it is a sustained example of a dominant story line in 1990s Cuban fiction wherein, as chapter 3 indicated, the encounter between a tourist and Cuban underscores the superiority of the latter. Although, as the Centro Habana Cycle advances through the special period, tourists are occasionally taken to task on ethical grounds—in *Tropical Animal,* for example, Pedro Juan accuses of indecency "a tourist who displayed her gold in a country where people are starving" (214)[69]—the prevalent portrayal of tourists is not as irresponsible but as transparent and gullible. The jogger in *El Rey de Habana* who makes his way through Centro

Habana's ruins clad in designer sportswear "evidently didn't understand a damned thing,"[70] while the German woman who has married a now-ostentatious Cuban has no say in her husband's decision to spend the night at the beach with a pair of *jineteras* (*Trilogy*, 168–69).[71]

Tourists do not merely move around Havana, however. They look, recording what they see, and, as photography increasingly becomes the medium through which Havana is made recognizable abroad, they are often captured taking photographs—of a heavily policed robbery (*El Rey*, 197), of life among the ruins *(Tropical Animal)*,[72] of the earthquake that is Centro Habana (*The Insatiable Spider Man*, 77).[73] This focus on visual action as well as physical movement is important because it facilitates the identification of the books' readers not only with the tourist but also with the equally present figure of the voyeur. Voyeurs are everywhere in Gutiérrez's Havana, seeking self-sufficiency in a world where even sex, as Pedro Juan experiences it all too frequently, can cost money. Scenes of voyeurism punctuate the cycle at almost regular intervals, reminding readers that watching and being watched are crucial to their enjoyment of this text. Indeed, voyeurs have an increasing presence in Cuban fiction of the special period, where they are figures for state vigilance, clandestine eroticism, and, more insistently as the special period wears on, for curiosities and desires directed at Cuba from abroad.[74]

Gutiérrez's voyeurs are not necessarily tourists. In fact, they rarely are; but nor do they need to be for the cycle to relegate its foreign readers to watching in excited nonparticipation. The intimacy with Pedro Juan to which his autobiographical exposure obliges his readers affords them vicarious access to his own experience as a voyeur. Pedro Juan is often an onlooker to others' sexual activity: sometimes in public places, as one in a group of viewers of a tryst on the Malecón seawall (*Trilogy*, 191–92),[75] and sometimes alone in his apartment, either surprised by a spontaneous orgy on the adjacent rooftop (*Trilogy*, 122)[76] or with the help of the peephole he has cut in the wall of his bathroom for this very purpose (*Tropical Animal*, 62).[77] When he is in this position, his readers watch with him, observing every detail of others' sexual encounters; and they must thus recognize that even when Pedro Juan is a participant in such encounters, their own standing remains fundamentally unchanged. Thus the narcissistic scopophilia that Laura Mulvey reads as fundamental to viewing modern cinema, and in which pleasure "comes from identification with the image seen" (162), is thwarted by the reiteration of scenes from which Pedro Juan himself is excluded.

Reading is a visual and not a physical activity, and although its pleasures might be transporting, as Roland Barthes has claimed, they do not constitute active participation in the Centro Habana habitat that Gutiérrez depicts.[78] His books' foregrounding of both the tourist and the voyeur serves as a frequent reminder of the reader's fundamental exclusion from life as it is lived, and sex as it is purportedly indulged, in special period Cuba.

The Centro Habana Cycle, then, constructs the voyeur's position as one of impotence, not only in the sense signaled by René Prieto, whereby Pedro Juan's failed masculinity makes him watch rather than act (384–85), but also because it is a position that is repeatedly exposed. If, in accordance with Freud's analysis of scopophilia ("The Sexual Aberrations," 22–23; Mulvey 161), watching while remaining unseen might retain for the voyeur a degree of power, then it is precisely this power that Gutiérrez's characters deny their observers. Voyeurs are unveiled as such, for the objects of their attention know and exploit the fact that they are being watched. In *El Rey de la Habana,* Magda delights in the humiliation to which she can subject the group of fearful, embarrassed men who gather around to masturbate as she and Rey reunite in the Parque Maceo. She is "addicted to the men jerking off, to teasing them for their faces that are bold at times and at others frightened, evasive and distanced, while all the time they move it up and down."[79] His success as a writer established, the Pedro Juan of the later books revels in similar reactions to his work. Women call on him, sheepish but aroused by what they have read (*Tropical Animal,* 10, 63);[80] and he is unsurprised to hear that readers gather to masturbate over the Brazilian edition of *Dirty Havana Trilogy* (*Tropical Animal,* 301).[81] That he considers it an act of generosity to provide the voyeur with a spectacle to drool over does not preclude his satisfaction at being able to provoke such reactions.[82]

This undermining of the onlooker's urge to remain unseen cements the conceptual proximity between reader, tourist, and voyeur, a proximity that Gutiérrez exploits to unmask special period Cuba watching as fundamentally sordid. Both watching and the desire to do so unremarked are constitutive of the essentially liberal quest for authenticity that, in MacCannell's formulation, drives the tourist experience (MacCannell 96–98). Gutiérrez's narrator thwarts this quest by drawing attention to the fact that sexual activity in the texts, like his own marginality and the authenticity of his Centro Habana, is staged for its audience. This staging, moreover, has an economic component—for, in the particular context in which the Centro Habana Cycle is set, reading, tourism, and watching are all money-generating activities. Tourism and publishing each have buoyant markets focused on special period Cuba, markets whose interests and aesthetic codes coincide and that Gutiérrez reduces to a particularly sordid market in watching. His sexual performers' willingness to be watched, and their delight in their power to humiliate their observers, establishes this market as based on a somewhat uneasy bargain: the books stage scenes that gratify their spectators, but the reader who succumbs to such gratification must accept exposure.

Voyeurism, then, is constructed within the Centro Habana Cycle as a stimulating but demeaning practice, and, through its contextual ties to both tourism and reading, as a general model for outsiders' engagement with special period Cuba. Even as Gutiérrez's books play to readers' desires, they also unveil the rather sordid premise on which such desires and interests are based. This is their challenge to the market for special period fiction, a challenge that is based on derision and complicity rather than explicit ethical critique. Like Valdés's *I Gave You All I Had,* the Centro Habana Cycle plays the market at its own game, supplying it with images of an intimately exposed Cuba but at the same time incorporating a figure for the demand that drives supply. Whereas in Valdés's novel, as in chapter 3's short stories, this figure is the U.S. dollar, in the Centro Habana Cycle it is the voyeur, a figure whose shared focus with the special period's market in visual images accords it particular potency. The flair for showmanship that Gutiérrez's characters and narrator demonstrate, and that ensures voyeuristic attention toward them, makes of the cycle a sustained performance of the epigraph to *El Rey de la Habana.* Manolín el Médico de la Salsa's claim that "We're what sells like hot bread"[83] stands as a manifesto not only for *El Rey* but for the five books of the cycle and, more tentatively, for special period fiction in general. Cuba watchers, and Cuba readers, are consigned to the viable but somewhat discomfiting recognition that staged insights into the miserable but vibrant life of Centro Habana's streets and *solares* are, indeed, what they like and are willing to pay for.

CHAPTER 5

The Ruined City:
Artists and Spectators of Decay

Before swooping into the *solar* where he will murder a young woman in the gory finale to Miguel Mejides's *Perversiones en el Prado* (Perversions on Prado Street), the Rocamora character—a solitary misfit metamorphosed into a bird of doom—surveys the city before him. From his perch on the fortress of El Morro, where he remembers dead soldiers of centuries past, he has hopes for the moribund city's rebirth, that it will "rise again from beneath the earth."[1] For the present, however, Havana is in ruins. The city appears as "Long-suffering Havana that had resisted attack by her own sons, now become a Caribbean Beirut, her ruins deflated in the cry of the night . . ."[2]

Rocamora has spent most of his life on the outer edge of Centro Habana, in a squalid building overpopulated like Pedro Juan Gutiérrez's *solares* and similarly described as a zoo (120). He is soon to return there, but his brief sortie has afforded him a perspective on the city—on both its long history and its present state of decay—that his neighbors rarely glimpse. These two vantage points—the ground level of the *solar,* on the one hand, and the architectural panorama, on the other—correspond to distinct ways of approaching the ruined city in the special period. For Antonio José Ponte, whose work is the principal subject of this chapter, the predicament and allure of the city lie in its living ruins, as they do for Pedro Juan Gutiérrez. But whereas Gutiérrez's fiction borders on what its critics have called "sociology," it is to architecture that Ponte, like a number of contemporary visual artists, looks for his elaboration of the ruin; and whereas Gutiérrez's lens is fixed on lives as carnal and their material needs as immediate, the scope of Ponte's is angled more broadly, encompassing the relationship of life to the structures that harbor it.

Less than of distance, the difference is one of focus: in Ponte's work, architectural ruins are viewed as part of a wounded cityscape, a text to be read—if not reconciled—as both history and art. The ruin's surface is interrogated, its flaws and cracks drawn into contemplation of structural defects in other edifices, its foundations questioned like those of collective experience writ large. Peeling, crumbling, and fading become forms of inscription, to be deciphered and parsed in an attempt to read the times. The stench of organic decay is muted as Ponte explores fleshless skeletons, structures that hang tenuously between life and death. And whereas Gutiérrez's novels meet foreign readers' expectations for an authentic portrayal of Cuban life, it is a second propeller of contemporary Cubaphilia, nostalgia, that Ponte challenges, forcing its halfhearted resuscitation of the past in the present to confront the future of ruins. These architectural explorations are founded on a suspicion that the ruin is not innocent: that there is, as one of Ponte's most important stories insinuates, "an art of making ruins."[3] Like other figures on the cultural landscape of the special period, the ruin responds to the interests of various parties both inside and outside Cuba, whose surprising complicity emerges as fiction and art trace the construction of a city in ruins.

Havana's ruinous architecture was mined for its metaphoric potential before the special period, perhaps most meticulously in Alejo Carpentier's essay *La ciudad de las columnas* (The city of columns). Tracing the constants of the city's colonial design in later "days of evident architectural decadence,"[4] Carpentier finds in its elaborate windows, wrought ironwork, and columns the baroque style that he claims elsewhere for Cuban history, culture, and geography. As Odette Casamayor has demonstrated, Carpentier's fiction, like that of José Lezama Lima, lingers on the crumbling majesty of the old city as a way of both locating the true character that newer, U.S.-styled neighborhoods had eclipsed, and imagining Havana as ultimately transcendent. Neither author laments the physical condition of the ruin nor even considers it an inhabited space; Lezama

Lima, in particular, exalts it as a vault for the continuity, permanence, and futurity of Cubanness ("¿Cómo vivir las ruinas?" 69). Against the turmoil of the immediate prerevolutionary years, writes Casamayor, ruins stand as a refuge for these earlier authors (66).

But as the condition of the city's colonial ruins deteriorated and their number proliferated, and as they were joined by the equally precarious shells of unfinished building projects, so did the ruin's powers of suggestion multiply. In the special period, the ruin provides a constant framework for fiction. Casamayor reads its presence in the novels of Abilio Estévez, Pedro Juan Gutiérrez, and Ena Lucía Portela as a muted expression of Cuba's social and ethical crisis that corresponds to characters' needs for secrecy (Estévez), absurdist resignation (Gutiérrez), and ideological inertia (Portela).[5] For these characters, the occupation of ruins is a matter of course, there being no other environment either more reflective of their state of mind or, quite simply, available to them. Occupation in this sense, however, stands quite in contrast to that of vocation, and specifically the vocation of "ruinologist," that Ponte claims in several essays. Engaged in both the cataloging and the artistic representation of ruins, the "ruinologist" brings the retrospection of the archaeologist to the methodological vision of the architect and forms a critical and imaginative language with which to both excavate the cause and foresee the effects of the ruin. A field formed from both circumstances and affinity, ruinology's principal practitioners in Cuba are Ponte, whose essays and fiction explore the moral dilemma of loving ruins, and the visual artist Carlos Garaicoa, whose projects and accompanying texts have since the early 1990s drawn upon decayed and abandoned buildings. With other sometime ruinologists, notably artist Tania Bruguera, who in 1993 directed the project *Memoria de la postguerra* (Memory of the postwar), they assemble a nuanced archive of Havana's crumbling architecture.

From this archive there emerge two powerful transformations of the city's ruins, each of which reveals not only their physical state but also the purpose they serve in the political, economic, and cultural context of the special period. The first is the transformation of Havana's crumbling colonial-era buildings from the victims of time and the elements into victims of warfare. Havana is cast as a bomb site through a rhetoric of "postwar," initiated in the early 1990s as artists' response to the sudden changes around them and further elaborated, in order to indict further culprits, in Ponte's novel *Contrabando de sombras* (Smuggled shadows) and his essays "What Am I Doing Here?," "Carta de la Habana: La maqueta de la ciudad" (A letter from Havana: The city's scale model), and *La fiesta vigilada*. A related displacement of ruins is that envisaged by Mejides's Rocamora as he sees below him "a Caribbean Beirut." To give the "postwar" a logical cause, in several special period representations the Cuban capital becomes Lebanon's, in the aftermath of a brutal civil war that razed to the ground many of that city's buildings. And yet, like Rocamora, who believes that the city will rise from its ashes—as the Lebanese believed during their war, according to Hashim Sarkis (285–86)—Havana's ruinologists look also to a Beirut rebuilt in the wake of destruction. The displacement from one capital to another, like the concretizing rhetoric of a war that never was, serves to show how different agents—foreign Cubaphiles, government officials, writers, and artists—draw both meaning and hope from a Havana in ruins.

RUINS OF TIME AND WAR

Ruins have long spurred their contemplators' imagination. For the baroque playwrights of Walter Benjamin's *The Origin of German Tragic Drama*, "the highly significant fragment" invokes the impermanence of history relative to an overripe and decaying nature (179). "The word 'history,'" Benjamin observes, "stands written on the countenance of nature in the characters of transience," an allegorical physiognomy that "is present in reality in the form of the ruin" (177). English Romantic poets appreciated the formal similarities between poetry and architectural fragmentation and, as Anne Janowitz argues, they used the broken but common past of a newly imagined British community to authorize the nation's imperial project. Indeed, as Christopher Woodward demonstrates, it is partly through their lack—or, rather, their loss—of completeness that ruins appeal, as "each spectator is forced to supply the missing pieces from his or her own imagination" (15).

Fragmentation may be primarily a spatial property but it occurs over time, and it is in their temporal dimensions that ruins are most powerful. Viewed through a baroque or Romantic lens, the ruin occupies space so as to evoke the passage of time. It perpetuates the past in the present but also reminds that present and its inhabitants of their impermanence and looks to a future without them. "When we contemplate ruins," writes Woodward, "we contemplate our own future" (2). Ruins imply a triple temporality—past, present, and future—so vividly that time, or "Time," comes to appear as their perpetrator. The human hands that initiated a structure are in fact rarely innocent in its decline: the ruinous Rome of the eighteenth and nineteenth centuries, for example, had been plundered in AD 410 by the Visigoths and misused as a quarry by Christian builders a thousand years later (Woodward 6–7), and the shells that inspired poets of the English landscape were monasteries destroyed centuries earlier during Reformation (108–9). And yet, when ruins are beheld, the human act that caused them is often eclipsed by the ravages of time. Rather than endurance, it is transience that has been seen in the ruin; dilapidation and the encroachment of vegetation are measured as gradual, protracted over slow centuries. The victims of abandonment thus morph into the "ruins of time," human violence vanquished by the inevitability that years will pass.

These "ruins of time" in turn become synonymous with the triumph of nature over human endeavor. It is as a material testament to nature's triumph over humanity that Benjamin casts the ruin, as does Georg Simmel in his essay "The Ruin." The decline of a building, claims Simmel, "means nothing else than that merely natural forces begin to become master over the work of man"; every ruin, consequently, is "an object infused with our nostalgia, for now the decay appears as nature's revenge for the spirit's having violated it by making a form in its own image" (259). The "act of violence" (260) here is not the destruction or abandonment of an edifice but art itself, a human act that dared to impose itself upon the natural world. Indeed, ruins bearing signs of willful destruction, as Rome's do, are uninteresting to Simmel (ibid.), as are those whose inhabitants' neglect is tantamount to complicity with nature (261). Only in the encounter between human endeavor and natural forces—or between an upward impetus and a downward impulse, as Ponte, an attentive reader of Simmel, Woodward, and many other ruin theorists, sketches it in *La fiesta vigilada*—can one glimpse a salutatory and interminable moral process (264).

It is precisely the question of imputed agency that forced a reassessment of ruins, or a new way of contemplating them, in the wake of the human and architectural disasters that were the great wars of the twentieth century. Vastly broader in their reach and more technologically advanced in their weaponry than previous wars, for their contemporary beholders they compelled a distinction between the complacently ill-defined "ruins of time" and the razed victims of more recent devastation. These newer ruins had identifiable perpetrators who were faster-acting than nature and whose continuing zeal for destruction discouraged thoughtful musing. It is precisely the proximity of World War II and its still fresh spoils that impels Dame Rose Macauley, at the end of her loving, "pleasurist's" (xv) meditation on the charm of ruins, to insist that now "ruin pleasure must be at one remove" (454) for, despite a certain beauty, "the bombed churches and cathedrals of Europe give us, on the whole, nothing but resentful sadness, like the bombed cities" (ibid.). "New ruins," Macauley implies, are less oxymoronic than they are subversive of the category and effect of ruins themselves. As Ponte comments, Simmel might have reassessed the potential of human destruction had he lived to see an air raid (*La fiesta vigilada*, 113–14).

The devastation of the twentieth century's wars, then, forces the question of agency that the "ruins of time" obscure. It coincides, moreover, with a transformation of ruins' currency and location. Whereas in previous centuries classical ruins had been a destination for the traveler and a penchant for the artist, the advances in both photography and reportage that accompanied later wars brought ruins home, into the offices and living rooms of viewers far from the front lines. Susan Sontag describes Virginia Woolf's response to photographs from the Spanish civil war, the first in which photojournalists were present during military action. Photography affords Woolf an extreme proximity to "ruin(s) of flesh and stone" so thorough in their destruction that their individual components are no longer identifiable (Sontag 4, 21). War photographs, writes Sontag, give proof that "war *ruins*" (8), and in admitting "ruins" as both verb and noun they bring new power to the process of destruction. These ruins moved to the living room are relocated further as, unlike those to which the English Romantics, for example, paid homage, they are no longer set in the countryside. Cities were the prime targets of wartime ruination and, still unclaimed by the vegetal world to which Macauley insists they are vulnerable (453), their vast expanses of depopulated rubble render quaintly archaic the moss-covered stones admired by ruins' "pleasurists."

Havana's Nostalgic Ruins

The ruin today, then, has two principal forms. It is either what we might think of as a historical ruin, a physical structure in a protracted but inevitably losing battle against the forces of time and nature that Ponte, quoting Jean Cocteau, calls "an accident in slow motion" ("What Am I Doing Here?" 15); or it is a site shelled more quickly and purposefully, razed by human hands wielding superhuman weapons. Alongside these two paradigms, however, Havana's ruins stand as a strange exception; for, despite being portrayed as such in literary and visual representations of the special period city, strictly speaking they are not ruins at all. The dilapidating structures and peeling facades that compose much of Cuba's capital are not the remains of a distant past and a departed civilization: as Ponte insists in "What Am I Doing Here?" and *La fiesta vigilada,* their sad distinction is that they are inhabited. Nor are they the debris of war, the bulk of Havana's housing stock—and the greater number of its current architectural casualties—having been built during Cuba's Republican period (1902–59), since the beginning of which there have been no major battles on national territory. Rather, Havana's "ruins" fall into the category of "urban decay," which Janowitz advances as late-twentieth-century cities' version of ruination.[6] Instead of ruins, they might more accurately be described as relatively new buildings on which routine maintenance has not been performed for decades and which are consequently in a state of terminal disrepair. As Jill Hamberg traces, Havana's neoclassical inner city was already dilapidated by the beginning of the revolutionary period, and the new regime's focus on construction in rural areas came at the expense of Havana. It was not until the 1970s that attention was turned once again to Havana, but in many cases it was too late; by 1980, the deterioration and collapse of buildings in Havana's old quarters meant that 8,180 families were in supposedly temporary shelters (Hamberg 18).

Not only, then, are Havana's ruins always, as José Quiroga states, made to stand "as a metaphor for *something*" (82); they are also, in a sense, made to stand as ruins. During the special period they have been consistently cast in this way, albeit from different places and positions and motivated by the distinct interests of outside viewers, on the one hand, and their inhabitants, on the other. Perpetuating the romantic fantasy and borrowing the nostalgic temporality of the "ruins of time" are the "ruins" represented in the global cultural industries—principally music, film, and photography produced either wholly or partly outside Cuba and spearheaded by the vastly successful *Buena Vista Social Club* project. For Ponte and others working amid the rubble of Old Havana, however, it is the war ruin that has the greatest currency; and it is their readings of Havana's cityscape as a bomb site that most interest me in this chapter, for both their implicit response to the global cultural industries and their conceptualization of warfare. Against the bland postcardization of the city's ruins that marked the special period and its tourist industry, they make searing new claims. They disallow nostalgia by redirecting ruins' temporality: not only formerly grand structures slide into decay but also new building projects whose very completion lies at a later date. Havana, some suggest, must be strewn with ruins of war because this is the only logical cause of the city's devastated physical and social environment: without this explanation, the city and its recent history do not make sense. Implicit here is an indictment that Ponte's work advances most forcefully, namely, that cities do not fall into disrepair but are condemned to it, that "ruin" is a transitive rather than an intransitive verb, and that the "benign neglect" to which Jill Hamberg attributes the state of Havana's housing stock is anything but well intentioned. Neglect thus becomes a form of violence and, in thoughtful exposés that confront Cuba's political context more rigorously than do more widespread images of the special period, agency is restored to ruination.

The predominant visual images of Havana that circulated outside Cuba during the special period presented its ruins as reminders of the past glory of the revolution, as well as of its present precariousness and its presumably doomed future. Ana María Dopico, whose analysis of photography books published in Europe between 1997 and 1999 identifies recurring tropes in their representations of Cuba, sees "the crumbling beauty of buildings" (456) as one of the most prevalent, and potentially ominous, of these. "Images of decay," she writes, are "made picturesque for those who like to visit ruins" (452) as part of a broader impulse to "promise clarity, transparency, and visibility at a moment of obscurity" (ibid.). Such images, claims Dopico, render comprehensible the complexities of recent Cuban history by appealing to their foreign viewers as familiar—a familiarity, I would suggest, that is at least partly based on the long-standing appeal of places ruined by natural causes. When Cuba is represented in these photographs "as a modern and 'ordinary' place where time and politics both pass" (488n1), then the passage of time must be particularly conducive to recognition.

Giuliana Bruno reiterates elements of this same visual code by opening her reading of how Havana's museums fashion cultural memory with an affective response to the city's ruins. "Transports of joy carry you away in Havana," claims Bruno with a sentiment much repeated by tourists and travel writers from the 1990s on, "for the city is intense, and intensely ruinous" (305). Ruins, she implies, inspire joy by recalling and juxtaposing distinct moments in time: "Peeling architectural layers present themselves largely unpolished, majestically redolent of historical patina" (ibid.). Bruno's description coincides with José Quiroga's Cuban "palimpsests," in which "the sheer historical density of the present can only be captured by its temporal effects on walls and structures where history is peeled off like onion skin" (82); but Quiroga's chapter titled "A Cuban Love Affair with the Image" subjects the ruin, as it is represented in photography of the special period, to further scrutiny. Turning, like Dopico, to photographers whose work circulates principally outside Cuba, Quiroga addresses the "extraordinary aesthetic effect" that their images of ruins produce. "Collapse," he writes, "somehow allows the city to levitate in pictures" (81); and while, on the one hand, this levitation becomes a symbol of the city's resilience, it also facilitates the rendering of Havana's poverty "in aesthetic terms" (ibid.). The aestheticization of what might otherwise be a political issue allows ruins to tell a story, giving "the illusion that poverty itself could be narrated" (82). Although Quiroga implies several possibilities for this narrative, among them is surely the most artistically inspiring version, namely, the well-worn tale of the city's surrender to time. As they are cast in photographers' and visitors' accounts, Havana's ruins revive a centuries-old passion for evidence of a civilization's past glory, coupled with the reminder that human greatness will decline, and will submit like all else to the ravages of time. As Rafael Rojas notes, however, in contrast to the decline of empire that Woodward's painters and writers glimpsed in ruins, it is "the collapse of the symbolic construction that propped up the imperial fantasy of a small Caribbean country" that Havana's ruins imply.[7] They tell the story of a revolutionary project whose triumph and idealism were once, like the buildings themselves, intact, a story that overlooks the detail that neither the buildings' pristine state nor their descent into decay in fact coincides with the rise and fall of revolution.

Wim Wenders's *Buena Vista Social Club*, the film released in 1999 to wide international acclaim and based on the making of the 1997 Grammy award-winning album, also spotlights Havana's ruined buildings so that they might tell the city's story. The film's story is again one of glory fallen into decay, although its subjects are somewhat different from those of contemporary photography. The principal ruins of this film are its musicians, whose prerevolutionary grandeur was long buried only to be reconstructed in their twilight hour as they tour the world singing traditional Cuban songs. Against a backdrop of architectural ruins the film invokes the heyday not of the revolution, but of a period preceding it, when musicians pursued their own ambitions rather than those of a collective project and when, as Michael Chanan puts it, there could still exist (at least from the perspective of people's present recollections) "the idea of a music before politics and social angst" (153). Although, as Román de la Campa has noted, the film's own setting is strangely atemporal, implicit in it nevertheless is a critique of the revolution's trajectory, not only in the crass parallelism staged toward the end of the film between the slogan "the revolution is eternal" and the peeling, fading paint in which it is written, but also in the absence of revolutionary references in the musicians' speech and lives. The missing "r" in the sign for the "Karl Marx" theater, the focus of another shot, emphasizes this absence: not only is "Marx" inoperative, but it is the "r" of "revolution" that has gone. Other pointed contrasts, that especially within Cuba furthered charges of an antirevolutionary agenda, show the glittering stores of New York after the most decrepit parts of Havana, and the American rescuer Ry Cooder with his grateful Cuban dependents (Caballero 134–39). While the country and its socialist project are crumbling, the film seems to imply, octogenarian musicians can enjoy a new lease of life by reviving an earlier epoch. Although this contrast between architectural and systemic ruin, on the one hand, and human vitality, on the other, is a mainstay of special period chronicles of Cuba—particularly those of Pedro Juan Gutiérrez, as my preceding chapter discussed—its articulation in *Buena Vista Social Club,* where the recipe for revival is the recovery of prerevolutionary tradition, is especially damning.

Despite their diverging reference points, however, the ruins captured by both visiting photographers and *Buena Vista Social Club* share a perspective that is deeply nostalgic. Nostalgia here as elsewhere, as Svetlana Boym has shown by unmasking longing for a place as a longing for a time (xv), is a fundamentally temporal mood; and, indeed, it is the temporal implications of Havana's ruins—their relationship to past, present, and future, and to Cuban revolutionary history in a more political sense—that has most distinguished their representations during the special period. Quiroga insists that photography books, like other forms and processes of memorialization that took shape during the special period, are based on changing perceptions, within and around Cuba, of the country's relationship to time (4–5), and that the nostalgia staged and recorded by these books has its utopian dreams registered in ruins (104). Similarly, many of the *Buena Vista Social Club*'s critics have commented on the time, or times, at which it directs its nostalgic lens. Alan West, participating in the debate hosted by the journal *Temas* that was a barometer of the film's reception in Cuba, comments on its privileging of a particularly North American nostalgia for a "fun-loving" Cuba over the Cuban American, exilic longing for a time of lost plenitude (*"Buena Vista Social Club* y cultura musical cubana," 168–69). Michael Chanan, comparing *Buena Vista Social Club* to the Dutch film *Lágrimas negras* that also records elderly Cuban musicians' success in Europe, locates the former's nostalgic thrust in its images rather than its music and in the reminders of an "age of innocence" long lost to capitalist countries (152–53). Ariana Hernández-Reguant comments on the extreme expansiveness of the film's nostalgic time that directs its appeal to "universal values of responsibility toward disappearing cultures, which were presented not as the patrimony of a particular group, but as the patrimony of Mankind" ("Radio Taino," 229).

What is identified by each of these critical commentaries—and by others, for to call *Buena Vista Social Club* nostalgic is hardly to go against the grain—is the film's allusion to a time whose location in the past is somewhat vague and whose value lies in a perfection that was never fully realized. As the perfect tense, this nostalgia's past is specious. As Ponte has commented, both the narrative of a glorious revolutionary past that is implicit in images of its present ruins and that of a prerevolutionary idyll presented in *Buena Vista Social Club* invoke a past unity that did not in fact exist. On the one hand, the revolution's fervent rhetoric harks back to the moment of its triumph, but also to promises that remain to be made good ("What Am I Doing Here?" 15); and, on the other, Ry Cooder's Buena Vista project attempts to restore a group that never actually sang together, falsely re-creating "the sound of a 1960s Cuban band that had never existed."[8] This longing for an ideal that appears to have no place in time contributes to the broader currency of Cuba in the special period when, through the primarily temporal image of the ruin, the island was advertised as lost or suspended in time.

Central to the nostalgia generated by representations of Havana's ruins is that the vague past to which it is directed is one whose recuperation for, and reconstruction in, the present is neither feasible nor desirable. The cultural nostalgia that de la Campa reads in *Buena Vista Social Club,* and that the special period saw directed at Cuba more broadly, has as its object of desire a history whose relationship to the present has become incommensurable (131–32). Reliving this time in the present, or making it a model for current practice, is simply out of the question, epistemologically rather than merely practically. This incommensurability allows nostalgia to be a politically neutral, or nonactionable, response and to inspire, as it did increasingly in Cuba's special period, a mood rather than an agenda. It is consistent with the "reflective nostalgia" that Boym distinguishes from the "restorative" form. While the latter, which in the Cuban context might be attributed to political groups in exile, "attempts a transhistorical reconstruction of the lost home" (xviii), the latter "thrives in *algia*, the longing itself, and delays the homecoming—wistfully, ironically, desperately" (ibid.). Thriving on relics of a time that they would not reinstate, *Buena Vista Social Club* and the image industry that it fueled added to restorative nostalgia the morbid pleasure in watching Cuba decline that is proper to the contemplation of "ruins of time." Stimulating the rush that Rose Macauley feels when visiting ancient ruins—"ruins change so fast that one cannot keep pace" (xvii)—this industry catalyzed interest in Cuba by playing the newness of the country's exposure against the imminence of its extinction as a socialist regime. Although Havana's buildings might not, strictly speaking, be "ruins of time," then, it was as such that they became an iconic image of the special period, their structure and surface speaking the inevitability that all human achievement—including that proclaimed and promised at the beginning of the Cuban Revolution—will come to dust.

THE SPOILS OF WAR

The portrayal of Havana's buildings as "ruins of time," and the nostalgia that such a portrayal breeds, is disrupted by artists and writers working in Havana—many of whose relationship to the market for images of special period Cuba is, as previous chapters have discussed, deeply ambivalent. Nevertheless, the exploration of ruins' human, rather than merely natural, causes, and the consequent implication that Havana's ruins are more appropriately cast as victims of warfare than of time, begins with an interrogation of their temporal dimension. Disrupting the continuum of progressive decline, from past glory to present poverty to eventual extinction, projects by visual artists Carlos Garaicoa and Manuel Piña, for example, mine the relationship between ruins and the future. Much of Garaicoa's work has architecture as both its impulse and its method. The works in his exhibition *La ruina, la utopía* (Ruin, utopia) took Havana's colonial ruins as the departure point for a fantastic reinvention of the city, one that rather than tracing the decline of one utopian project—the revolution's—instead replaced it with a new, more personal, and fantastic version. *The First Field of Hallucinogenic Mushrooms in Havana* (1996) juxtaposes the photograph of a building's exposed foundations with a drawing in which those foundations become neat rows of mushrooms, lining the path to the still intact building behind. Others—*About the Construction of the Real Tower of Babel* (1994–95), *Project about Triumph* (1994–99)—make Havana's rubble a building block for the great projects of past civilizations. Beginning from what might otherwise be considered "the end of a specific story" (Garaicoa, "Interview with Holly Block," 24), the photographs in this project superimpose rebirth on the decayed facades of old buildings, thus reversing their narrative of decline and, effectively, rewriting nostalgia as hope.

In a subsequent project, *Continuity of Somebody's Architecture*, Garaicoa photographs buildings that were initiated but never completed during the tenure of the revolutionary government and takes their architects' original plans as the basis for his own completed models. These pieces, he states, "take off from a ground zero in history, or better yet, from the rhetoric of history, from the thwarting of a political and social project" (ibid., 24–25). In reducing the temporal span of ruins—in compressing their conception and their decay into two decades rather than ten or more—Garaicoa's project denies nature a role in Havana's ruination, attributing this instead to human negligence. Moreover, in adding these more recently unfinished buildings to Havana's inventory, it opposes the ruins of past eras to a new class that he calls "ruins of the future": "an architecture that has never been completed, poor in its incompletion, proclaimed Ruin before its existence" (*Continuity*, 9). The permanent incompleteness in which his photographs capture their subject foregrounds the disproportionate weight that the revolution, architect of these buildings, accorded the future in its glorification of the present. Both this incompleteness and the project's title question what is essentially a discontinuity between lived present and promised future. *Continuity of Somebody's Architecture* implicitly calls, then, for a restoration of the future to its proper place: a place, on the one hand, aligned with the imagination, hence the artist's completion in his own style of an abandoned collective project; and, on the other, continuous with, rather than always deferred from, the present.

The buildings documented in *Continuity of Somebody's Architecture* are the "Microbrigades," which both implement the revolutionary government's ideas about collective property and account for much of the new housing built under its command. Devised by Fidel Castro in the early 1970s as a way to augment the country's housing stock and reemploy construction workers, the Microbrigade program subsidized groups of workers to construct low-rent homes for themselves and each other

(Scarpacci, Segre, and Coyula 141–42). Built largely of prefabricated materials, the poor quality of these homes and their high cost to the government made the Microbrigades program short-lived: although the late 1980s were to see the revival of a modified version of the program, by the late 1970s it had largely come to a standstill in its original form, and many of its projects had been abandoned (Mathey 251–54). In their various states of incompletion, the Microbrigades are also the subject of Manuel Piña's installation *(De)Constructing Utopias (Tribute to Eduardo Muñoz)* (1996). Although some of the buildings in the installation are more intact than others, the technique with which they are photographed guarantees their deterioration: they are not chemically fixed so that, in the words of René Morales, "over time they have darkened, like the luster of the utopian schemes they represent" (31). This casting of incomplete construction projects as ruins recurs in John A. Loomis's essay and photographs of the National Art Schools, perhaps the first architectural ruins of the revolutionary era and described by Ponte as particularly beautiful (*La fiesta vigilada*, 184). As Loomis chronicles, the schools were commissioned in 1961. Their construction began shortly thereafter but was halted when their design was deemed too sensuous and indulgent to represent the young revolution. The schools were inaugurated in 1965, but their buildings were never completed. Although the Microbrigades were meant to stand as the ideological opposite of the Art Schools, both were conceived and then abandoned during the revolutionary period and, in the temporal distortion that Garaicoa and Piña expose, their ruin precedes their completion.

The attempt to reinstate continuity between the present and the future is inherent in invoking Havana as a "postwar" landscape, whose "post" reiterates the concern with what comes next. Inscribed as a "postwar" in Tania Bruguera's project *Memoria de la postguerra* (1993–94), the image of Havana as a bomb site recurs in subsequent literature and art and maps the special period as the scene of real battles. The narrator of Pedro Juan Gutiérrez's *Dirty Havana Trilogy*, for example, looks out from his rooftop onto a city that "Semeja una ciudad bombardeada y deshabitada" (206) ("It looked bombed out and deserted," 224). One of the principal impressions of the city that the character Victorio, in Abilio Estévez's *Los palacios distantes* (The distant palaces), retains is "that of having been bombed, that of a city awaiting only the lightest rain shower, the lightest gust of wind to collapse in a heap of stones."[9] Analyzing the pictures of Cuba that predominated in international markets during this period, Quiroga notes that "in the moving diorama of Latin American history of the past several decades, photographic images of Cuba are striking because they seem to note the absence of conflict" (82); instead of the tragedy of war, they show "the melodrama of crumbling buildings" (ibid.). For Cuba's "postwar" artists and writers, however, Havana's resemblance to a bomb site overrides the absence of war: war's absence is translated as war's aftermath.

Memoria de la postguerra is a collective project in the form of a magazine, coordinated by the artist Tania Bruguera and published in two issues in November 1993 and June 1994. Its participants were principally visual artists, some of whom had recently left Cuba, and their wry articles and illustrations—among these a sketch for Garacoia's *About the Construction of the Real Tower of Babel*—address the intellectual and social prospects for artists on the island. An early marker of what Sujatha Fernandes terms Cuba's "artistic public spheres," which "represent new kinds of negotiation within and against the limits of state power and cultural markets" (14), *Memoria* subjects to mockery both revolutionary propaganda and the international market, as well as the notion of an authentically national art to which both subscribe. The magazine was not permitted to proceed beyond its first two issues, nor was it necessarily conceived as an ongoing publication. As Eugenio Valdés Figueroa observes, "Bruguera, a performance artist, had never been very interested in objects and their permanence" (19). *Memoria de la postguerra* nevertheless became "a testament and definition of its epoch" (ibid.).

Many of the project's participants address the "postwar" of its title, alluding to two "wars" that are quite distinct in their scope. The first is the period in the 1980s during which Cuban art, in a climate of relative tolerance, became both experimental and increasingly willing to engage social questions publicly (Navarro 359–60). In 1989 and 1990, however, as the Soviet Union disassembled and the Cuban regime appeared increasingly precarious, a number of artistic interventions deemed too radical were shut down, silencing the art world's challenge to the status quo and culminating in the emigration of some of its most prominent figures (Valdés Figueroa 17). This sequence of events accounts for the sustained reflections on diaspora in the second issue of *Memoria de la postguerra,* as well as for the project's references to the time of "postwar" in which the Cuban art world currently stood. The spoof article by Rafael López Ramos in the November 1993 issue, titled "La guerra ha terminado, Afirma jóven artista cubano" (The war is over, affirms young

Cuban artist), is peppered with military terms for the war formerly waged by artists, the conclusion being that there is little likelihood of "a possible regrouping of forces on the part of the army formerly known as Young Visual Artists."[10] In another piece in the same issue, Nelson Herrera Ysla repeats the phrase "the war is over" in a meditation on what art has done and will do for people (12).

Coming so soon after the fall of the Berlin Wall and the disintegration of the Soviet Union, however, the war of *Memoria de la postguerra* is also the Cold War, and one of the project's driving questions is how this war's aftermath is to be experienced in Cuba. That the project's recourse to a "postwar" temporality represents a search for cognitive tools to navigate unfamiliar territory and times is clear in the question that closes Jacqueline Brito Jorge's contribution: "What can do the most for us, the memory of the past or the uncertainty of the present?"[11] The usefulness—indeed, the inevitability—of the "postwar," however, is addressed most succinctly in Tania Bruguera's introductory note to the first issue. She deploys the term "postwar" because so much of the city—its architecture, its residents' state of mind, the attitude of its artists—resembles a silenced battlefield: "postwar for its similarity to the city at a physical level, for what is inside people, for the social character of art."[12] Although this deployment of the term renders physical a war named for having confronted ideologies rather than armies, it is the very coldness of the Cold War—the very fact that it involved little combat—that makes it an inadequate explanation for the appearance and experience of Havana. Only a war of bodies and machines rather than merely of minds, Bruguera implies, can account for the architectural surface of the city and the life within it. These correspond to each other as scenes of devastation, and art responds as a social act. In its search for a logical explanation, Bruguera's "postwar" moves from simile to identity: because Havana looks like a postwar scene, it must *be* such a scene. The "postwar," then, is what makes sense of Havana's ruinous landscape; and when Luis Camnitzer claims in his 1995 review that "*Memoria* has not only assembled ideas but has helped maintain a sense of coherence" (29), it is striking that this coherence should be founded on inventing for Havana's recent history a clash of armed forces, or a war that never was.

PONTE'S WAR ON RUINS

The war that never was returns as a theme and an accusation in Ponte's essays, for it is one of the bases on which he identifies the Cuban government as an agent of Havana's ruins. Although to cast Havana's ruins as casualties of war is to imply a human perpetrator for them, *Memoria de la postguerra* stops short of naming one. Rather, the project explores the postwar in its visual and affective dimensions, lingering on the city's resemblance to, and therefore logical explanation as, a bomb site. For Ponte, however, the simile itself is suspect. Not because the city does not look like a battlefield: indeed, it does, as he affirms in telling an interviewer that "here no war has existed but it's a city that seems to have been through a war."[13] But the simile should be scrutinized because there are interests beyond its residents' need for logic in endowing Havana with war ruins. The image of Havana as a bombed city, that is, might itself be manipulated in bad faith. What Ponte's work adds to others' visualizations of a devastated cityscape is an insistence on establishing a causal relationship between architectural ruins and a bellicose rhetoric crafted to convince Cubans that their country is perpetually at war.

Ponte's ruined city, sketched in a number of essays and elaborated more fantastically in his fiction, has two defining traits: it is inhabited, and its occupants are survivors. That Havana's ruins are inhabited, claims Ponte, is of central importance to his work, for it sets his own mediations on ruins apart from those of the predominantly European writers whom he engages in his essays (Interview with Anna Solana and Mercedes Serna, 131). Inhabitants emerge from the city's ruins as survivors of a devastation that leaves them haunting the rubble like the protagonists of Mary Shelley's *The Last Man* and David Markson's *Wittgenstein's Mistress* (*La fiesta vigilada*, 166), with the difference that, in the aftermath of war, lone figures proliferate oxymoronically: only war can produce "so many last men on Earth."[14] The couple who people Ponte's story "Heart of Skitalietz" are war survivors in this sense. Scorpio is an out-of-work historian and his companion Veranda an ailing astrologist: faltering between his lost past and her fading future, like the disinherited Russian wanderers from whom the story takes its name, they drift through the unlit streets of an almost empty Havana until the city they have mapped for themselves can no longer be their refuge. Scorpio and Veranda share their need to relearn the contours of their once familiar surroundings with the participants in *Memoria de la postguerra*: the end of the Cold War has left their world in a bewildering silence.

Ponte's wanderings among Havana's inhabited ruins and their shell-shocked survivors draw his work toward the ultimately political question of ruins' authorship. For there to be ruins in Havana today, there have to have been agents of destruction; for there to be survivors, there has to have been prior violence. From the series of essays that deal most directly with ruin, three suspects emerge as possibly complicit in causing and perpetuating the ruination of Havana. These are their survivor-inhabitants themselves; the writer, also a survivor and inhabitant, but one particularly predisposed to find ruins beautiful; and the revolutionary regime, which ultimately emerges as perpetrator rather than mere accomplice and is charged with masterminding the dilapidation of much of the city while it simultaneously oversees the reconstruction of the colonial core.

In *La fiesta vigilada*, Georg Simmel's essay "The Ruin" is the basis on which Ponte elaborates the role of the ruin's inhabitant. For Simmel, the people whom he saw living in Roman ruins were unambiguously agents of those ruins' destruction, parasites who could only weaken their host's structure and power to charm. Their very presence broke the spell of silence that surrounds a ruin, proving them to be complicit with, as Ponte puts it, "one of the two adversaries," the one charged with destruction.[15] In Simmel's formulation of a ruin as scenario for the struggle between nature and spirit, wherein the first drives downward and the second toward the skies, the squatters had to be nature's accomplices. And yet, to what Simmel laments as the dilapidation of an aesthetic effect, Ponte opposes a hope that the buildings, and thence the life within them, will remain standing against the odds. After the war—specifically World War II, but others by implication—the persistence of survivors unwilling to stop living rendered Simmel's conclusions untenable (167). Rather than mere accomplices in the destruction of their dwellings, Ponte suggests, might not these survivors be double agents, in the service of both decay and hope? In Havana, particularly in densely populated and perilously ruined Centro Habana, these double agents militate in an ongoing battle between "tugurization," the overpopulation of poorly maintained buildings owing to a severe housing deficit (174), and "miraculous statics," the phenomenon wherein a building remains standing despite structural calculations that would render this impossible (173).

With survivors exonerated to a degree, writers and admirers are charged with advancing ruins' decline. "What Am I Doing Here?" is in part its author's mea culpa for deriving from Havana's ruins the aesthetic gratification familiar to previous generations of "pleasurists," in Rose Macauley's phrase. In this essay Ponte suggests that it is unseemly—indeed, unethical—to appreciate ruins for their form when from their inhabitants' perspective they are a shelter and lifeline: "Sometimes," he

writes, "I must have considered the collapse of a building as an opportunity, a new perspective opened to the eye. And my concern for those
who may have lost their homes or met their deaths would have been secondary compared to my interest in the newly opened vein" (16). Ponte
reiterates this unease with the merely aesthetic appreciation of ruins
(Interview with Teresa Basile, 35), but rather than renounce it he returns to it insistently, exploring its relationship to the political realities
of Cuba.

La fiesta vigilada uses a comparison from World War II to develop the
all-important figure of the "ruinologist," whose impassioned vocation is
closely aligned with Ponte's own. This vocation involves the scientific
study of ruins but at the same time admits a more sentient response.
While Woodward, for example, distinguishes between the archaeologist's interest in determining a ruin's historical cause and the artist's
more imaginative response to its present form (30), the "ruinology" the-
orized and practiced by Ponte takes both approaches simultaneously. As
an archaeologist, his ruinologist mines the reasons, both historical and
hypothetical, for Havana's dilapidation while, as an artist, he traces the
contours and surfaces of those ruins with an affection born of both familiarity and "urbanistic despair" (181). In *La fiesta vigilada,* Ponte puts
the ruinologist's relationship to ruins to the test. To Simmel's interest in
ruins, he contrasts that of John Piper, an English artist in the service of
the War Artists Advisory Committee whose task Woodward describes
as documenting the destruction of his country's churches during World
War II (Woodward 212–19). Woodward's account of Piper painting a
still-smoldering Coventry Cathedral tells of an initial apprehension that
later gave way to a penchant for other ruins, victims of time as well as
of war, in whose horrors he unashamedly found beauty. Ponte admits
more affinity with Piper's obsession with beautiful atrocities than with
Simmel's contained critique of Roman ruins: just as Piper was implicated in the ruins (171–72), so, then, is Ponte, as his city's self-appointed
ruinologist, implicated in the ruins of Havana. His innocence is compromised by his finding beauty in ruins and even—in the context of
Cuba's, rather than Coventry's, postwar—by his alignment with an industry that has thrived on casting Havana as beautiful in its decay.

There is necessarily, however, a limit to how much Ponte's ruinologist can be held accountable for Havana's ruins, and his mea culpa
comes with a degree of irony; for the aesthetic valorization of Havana's
ruins is merely one element in a broad and deeply nuanced examination

of the city, its representations, and the interests therein—a point Teresa Basile makes in distinguishing in Ponte's work a "cognitive perspective" on, and "intellectual exploration" of, ruins (5). Admiring ruins for their appearance but deploring their cause, the writer as ruinologist is at most an ambivalent accomplice in the perpetuation of Havana's decay. This is particularly the case for the postwar writer whose love of ruins stems from the strangely comforting familiarity of a shelled city. Based on the German writers Heinrich Böll and W. G. Sebald, who in the wake of World War II preferred the comfort and paradoxical hopefulness of ruined cities to the lifelessness of intact ones (Interview with Teresa Basile, 35), this ruinologist seeks not only beauty but a correspondence between physical surroundings and historical experience. He thus resembles the artists of *Memoria de la postguerra,* who look to Havana's "war" ruins for a similar coherence, and the character of the Spanish photographer in Ponte's novel *Contrabando de sombras.* Having spent much of his life in war zones, this photographer prefers ruins and rubble to "the excessive unreality of a perfect row of facades,"[16] and this is precisely why he feels at home in Havana. "I see all these buildings on the verge of collapse," he confesses, "the absence of color on house fronts all the way down to the sea, and you can have no idea how well I understand the beauty of this city."[17]

Responsibility for the perpetuation of ruins is an especially harsh charge for such figures. They are complicit, and one of the distinctive gestures of Ponte's essays is to take this complicity seriously even while testing its limits. These figures may be less hedonistic in their appreciation of ruins than is the admiring flaneur of "What Am I Doing Here?"—but if Havana is cast as a postwar zone, then even its most starry-eyed lovers of ruins are battle survivors, too. Even more than to see ruins as beautiful, to see them as the confirmation of personal and social experience may indeed entail a desire that they persist; but it does not make these beholders accountable for the condition of the city. This accountability, in fact, is reserved for an agent both more sinister and more powerful, whose role in the city's ruination is exposed diffusely but categorically in Ponte's work. It is the relationship between ruin (as both metaphor and physical structure) and revolution (as act and process) that indicts this culprit beginning, as in the work of Garaicoa and Piña, with reflections on the notion of revolutionary time. "What Am I Doing Here?" claims that every revolution's "attack on the fortress of the temporal very soon brings about its own immurement" (15), and the wall that best serves this "immuring" purpose, it emerges, is a bombed and crumbling one.

In this conspiracy theory, the revolution defines itself through "a celebration of the past, a campaign of self-praising remembrances" (ibid.); and the image of a war-destroyed Havana is the one that best commemorates the revolution's most urgent and thus most legitimizing moment: the October 1962 confrontation between the United States and the USSR–Cuba alliance that brought the world to the brink of war. Commemoration and perpetuation being closely aligned, it is in the interests of the government to maintain the appearance of the capital city as the scene of a conflict because, Ponte suggests, "that way it can revisit the period when, thanks to the deployment of Soviet arms on Cuban territory, the island could fancy itself a great power."[18] For Ponte, this engineering of the physical surface of the city to reflect a past event that did not in fact occur recalls Ry Cooder's nostalgia in reviving a group that never existed ("Carta de la Habana," 255). In contrast to Cooder, however, the perpetrators of Havana's ruins keep alive nonevents in the present and the future, as well as in the past. The city's ruined landscape serves to concretize a threefold conflict: the threatened U.S. invasion during the 1962 Missile Crisis, so a past war that never materialized; the present and ongoing attack that is the U.S. embargo; and the full-scale war with the imperialist enemy, of proportions unimaginable, that is always imminent. Dilapidating Havana is thus not merely a monument to but an instrument of the revolution: it is the visual dimension of the rhetoric of militarization that has permeated Cuban public speech from the early campaigns and battles against vice and illiteracy to the "special period in times of peace." The ruinologist's investigations, then, point to the revolutionary regime as the chief architect of the city's ruins. Although reconstruction, specifically of the city's colonial core, was the government's most heavily advertised building project during the special period, Ponte's work implies that this activity is merely a front for a more sinister, subterranean program of sustained neglect. Ever scathing about rehabilitation plans for the colonial city—that empty a vital area of its inhabitants and replace them with museums to simultaneously attract tourists and moralize against leisure (*La fiesta vigilada,* 180–81)— it is the perpetuation of warlike ruins, he charges, that best serves the interests of the revolution.

Charting the way for Ponte's meditations on Havana's ruins is his short story "A Knack for Making Ruins." Just as it is positioned centrally in the collection *Tales from the Cuban Empire* because its themes are fundamental to the hypothetical Cuban empire ("Un arte de hacer ruinas: Entrevista," 184), so too does this story provide an important interpretative framework for Ponte's subsequent essays. It is set in a Havana afflicted by two contemporary urban problems, overcrowding and the frequent collapse of its buildings, and it tells of a student attempting to write his thesis on the creation of space where none exists. The student's preliminary investigations lead him to unexpected and inexplicable encounters: with an elusive figure who counterfeits money and with two professors whose work on the city's overcrowding leads first to their ostracism from the university and then to death at the hands of the very tribe that has set out to destroy the city. This is the tribe of "Tugures"— zealous practitioners of "tugurization," the urban phenomenon that, here as in *La fiesta vigilada*, Ponte opposes to the "miraculous statics" of Centro Habana's buildings. In "A Knack for Making Ruins" the struggle between tugurization and miraculous statics is a catalyst for the fantastic exploits of the Tugures, who thrive on causing, but escaping, the collapse of still-standing buildings. Because of their determination to house all their relatives in one-family homes, dividing single rooms into two, Havana is a city growing inward. And yet it is also a city growing downward: as the student finds in his final and most nightmarish discovery, a further level of surreptitiously practiced tugurization undermines the city's structural miracle. At the end of the story, he stumbles upon a strange underground city to which the inscription on a pilfered counterfeit coin is the surprising key. Beneath Havana is a parasitic replica of the city being reconstructed with materials stolen from above, which perpetuates the illusion of a sustainable structure aboveground while in fact rendering it ever more precarious. This city is Tuguria, "where everything is preserved as in memory" (43),[19] and it provides proof of tugurization's victory over miraculous statics. When the narrator reaches the subterranean hideout of the Tugures, he has no doubt that the missing wall of a partly reconstructed building will soon disappear from its present aboveground location.

The title of this story, also the title of Ponte's collected fiction, insists that ruins do not merely happen as time takes its course; rather, they are created purposively. Havana's collapse is the result of a paradoxically constructive act—an act, moreover, that presupposes a certain art, or skill. The story thus lends itself to allegorical readings that might establish who are the agents and accomplices of Havana's ruination. The question becomes: who, or what, are the "Tugures," for whom destruction is both a pleasure and a mission and who ruin the visible city in order to re-create an intact one underground? As in Ponte's discussion of Simmel in *La fiesta vigilada,* the city's inhabitant-survivors invite immediate suspicion. Caricatures of Simmel's parasitic Roman ruin-dwellers, they occupy fragile buildings knowing—and indeed, hoping—that their presence there will be detrimental to that building's stability. The Tugures arrive from the countryside daily and in droves, stretching the physical limits of their new dwelling until it finally surrenders beneath their weight. Survivors of many devastations, it is their explicit endeavor—at least, in Professor D.'s necessarily clandestine analysis of them—to create destruction.

That making ruins is an art, however, cannot be overlooked and, prefiguring the concerns of "What Am I Doing Here?" and *La fiesta vigilada,* the artist is implicated in ruins' construction. As the essays explore, admirers of ruins' beauty harbor a desire, albeit a conflicted one, for the persistence of that beauty. Furthermore, the story's title suggests that contemplation, admiration, and representation are not innocent acts, and that to represent ruins is to construct and perpetuate them. Although the narrator of this story has a surname that means "builder," one can build ruins as well as complete structures. Professor D.'s account of the Tugures burrowing inward because their island is too constricted a space to travel outward—that "if you can't get out, you go in" (35)[20]—leads Teresa Basile to read the Tugures as Cuban essayists of the 1990s, Ponte among them. These essayists' constrained physical and intellectual mobility, Basile suggests, spurred them to question the foundations of Cuban nationalism and the "miraculous statics" that had kept the revolutionary regime in place after the demise of the Eastern bloc states, despite its widely predicted collapse (3–4). They would then be deconstructors of state-sponsored nationalism and its attendant social manifestations. But the essayist in the story who had planned to write a book called *An Art of Making Ruins,* namely, Professor D., prefers to die rather than become a Tugur (70), leaving the role of Tugur open for other actors in contemporary Cuba. It is to the subterranean city that we might look to unmask the Tugures, for their activities there dramatize the commemorative practices through which, according to Ponte's essays and interviews, the revolutionary regime establishes both its own legitimacy and the imminence of war. Tuguria, the subterranean city, has been built to preserve a memory; and if this is the memory of Cuba's global protagonism in the Missile Crisis to which Ponte refers in "Carta de Habana," then it follows that the city aboveground should be crafted and maintained as a ruin. The Tugures, in this scenario, represent the builders of the revolution, and it is their covert interest in preserving a memory of greatness and perpetuating the fear of war that destroys the aboveground city. Consistent with Ponte's subsequent essays, "A Knack for Making Ruins" casts Cuba's regime builders as the primary artists of postwar ruins.

HAVANA AS BEIRUT

Ponte's Tuguria lies directly beneath Havana in order to erode the city's architectural foundations and cement the ambitions of its political leaders. Tuguria is not Havana's only alter ego, however, for other "postwar" writing takes Havana somewhere else: to Beirut. This displacement endows Havana's dilapidating landscape with an identifiable cause, namely, the civil war that razed large tracts of the Lebanese capital between 1975 and 1990. At the same time, however, to invoke Havana as Beirut, whose postwar years saw large-scale reconstruction efforts, offers a sliver of hope for architectural, but emphatically nonideological, rebirth. It is as "a Caribbean Beirut" that Mejides's Rocamora sees his ruined city, in the scene that opened this chapter. Havana again appears as Beirut for the Spanish photographer in Ponte's *Contrabando de sombras,* who sees a close resemblance between these two ruined cities. "The streets of Beirut, devastated by the war, would belong perfectly in this city," he observes as he looks out on Havana, where he has come in order to supplement his collection of "images of empty streets, buildings propped up or reduced to rubble."[21] This is an observation a reader of a 1998 issue of *El caimán barbudo* (The bearded caiman), the cultural supplement to the Union of Young Communists' newspaper *Juventud rebelde* (Rebellious youth), might also have made; for, accompanying a poem titled "Fotógrafo en posguerra" (A photographer in the postwar) by Yamil Díaz Gómez, author of three collections of poems about war, are two photographs of crumbling buildings in rubble-strewn streets. Neither this poem nor Díaz Gómez's later collection of the same title is expressly about Havana, but the reiteration of the term "postwar" from Bruguera's project, the final line "they say that we are the survivors," and the photographs themselves suggest this particular context.[22] Indeed, so familiar do these images seem in the wake of the photography boom that disseminated Havana's ruins far and wide that it is surprising to see, stamped in small print, the photograph's actual subject. It is Beirut, and it was taken by the Italian Gabriele Basilico in 1991 as part of a six-artist project to document the scars of war known as "the Beirut photographic mission."

The mistake toward which this photograph in *El caimán barbudo* might push its readers—that is, to take Beirut for Havana—is testament first to the intensely visual presence that the Lebanese civil war had worldwide. As historian and journalist Samir Kassir commented, this war was almost incessantly broadcast on television sets internationally, so that viewers could tune in for "death, and more death, at prime time."[23] Although in raw numbers the Lebanese civil war claimed fewer lives than other concurrent conflicts—in Cambodia, for example—it was Beirut, nevertheless, that became synonymous with war for a generation of television watchers (24). Kassir attributes the intense filming of this war to technological advances of the time, specifically in satellite communications and video, but also to the Lebanese people's bilingualism, which made interviews easier and more immediate (25). Although not the first war to be fully televised—this, according to Susan Sontag, was the Vietnam War—the Lebanese civil war was covered extensively and vividly, in Cuba as elsewhere.

Scenes of a war-ruined Beirut are familiar enough to Cubans like Mejides and Ponte, then, for them to compare the Lebanese capital to the tumbledown streets of special period Havana. The two cities invite comparison to each other because they are or have been in a similar physical condition. Because Beirut's ruins are the result of documented, televised war, while Cuba's so-called war is far more insidious, Beirut serves to further illuminate Havana's predicament, just as Gabriele's photographs illustrate Díaz Gómez's poem. In other words, bombed Beirut concretizes Bruguera's "postwar" with an image that makes sense. The physical state of the city and the inner experience of its people, both of which for Bruguera justify considering Havana a postwar city, suggest, by extension, an event like Beirut's. A real war is what Havana needs to explain its appearance and experience; and, in the absence of such a war, Beirut supplies the history. As a referent for the Cuban capital it facilitates the shift from simile to identity, from a Havana that looks like the scene of a postwar to a Havana that *is* the scene of a postwar, that is central to the projects of both Bruguera and Ponte. Beirut allows the rescue of Havana's ruins for contemporary politics, specifically for the notion of war waged from within, that Ponte's work explores as a government conspiracy and that Mejides's Rocamora implies in his lament for a "long-suffering Havana that has resisted attack by her own sons."[24]

Rocamora's bird's-eye view over the city is not limited to its recent devastation, however; rather, he sees beyond its present to a future rebirth. It is Beirut, precisely, that enables him and other Cubans to envisage their city reborn, for rebirth is both a powerful myth and a more moderate reality for the Lebanese capital. As Rocamora watches Havana become a "Caribbean Beirut," he thinks he sees it rise again in hope: "it seemed to him that he saw a hopeful city, ready to rise again in a new calendar."[25] The rebirth of the ruined city is also on the mind of Díaz Gómez's postwar photographer. This technician of the visual, whose words unfold beneath an image of Beirut, can affirm that, despite the destruction, "something will be reborn."[26] Both dreams of rebirth recall the myth of self-renewal that, Harshim Sarkis writes, was especially potent during the Lebanese civil war. The counterpoint to Beirut's other defining myth, of self-consumption and necessary destruction, the myth that this city that had already been destroyed and rebuilt six times would rise yet again, sustained shelter-bound residents through the war years (285–86).

Rebirth, in the more scripted form of architectural reconstruction, was also a rallying cry when the civil war was over, particularly for the Beirut Central District (BCD). The BCD harbored important historical and residential sites but bore the scars of war deeply: among its many problems, in the words of urban planner Angus Gavin, were "the destruction beyond salvage of two thirds of the urban fabric and public spaces," "the rubble of destroyed buildings," and "the detritus of war" (218). In order to address these, the Lebanese government in 1991 charged a private real estate company, known as Solidère, with forming and implementing a master plan to reconstruct the district. During the decade after the war ended, much of the BCD was cleared in order to be rebuilt. The city's cautious rebirth was heavily advertised abroad, replacing images of ruins with new ones of prosperity and laissez-faire, but it was always controversial. Rodolphe el-Khoury observes that Solidère's plans were never greeted with unanimous admiration (184) and that the BCD's "reconstruction" was celebrated as too superficial an allegory for Lebanese peace and prosperity (183).

In some respects, the BCD's "master plan" recalls Old Havana's, which also had economic revitalization as one of its main motives (Leal Spengler 11). That the reconstruction of Beirut's Central District should have prioritized the development of new residential buildings as well as the restoration of historical landmarks is important, however, in distinguishing it as a repository of hopes for Havana's rebirth as a city and not just as a tourist attraction; for the criticisms advanced by Ponte and by architectural critic Paul Goldberger that Habana Vieja (Old Havana) has been reduced to a series of moralizing museums (Ponte, *La fiesta vigilada*, 180–81) or to an "Old Havanaland" (Goldberger 60) are based on evictions of local inhabitants to accommodate visitors. This is not so clearly the case for Beirut's Central District, which included (admittedly expensive) new homes and was planned, at least, as an integrative reconstruction, responsive to the present and ongoing needs of the city's inhabitants (Rowe and Sarkis 16).

Unlike Havana, then, ruined Beirut did undergo a large-scale reconstruction project in its postwar—representing a fractious, partial, and difficult rebirth but a rebirth nevertheless. Most important, it did so during Cuba's special period. The end of the Lebanese war coincides with the end of the Cold War, so that both Beirut and Havana begin their "postwar" years simultaneously. While Beirut experiences these as times of architectural renewal and development, for Havana they are years of accelerated urban ruin. Images of Beirut stand in for Havana not only to materialize and provide a historical logic for the devastation of war but also to serve as a model for postwar reconstruction, for what the aftermath could look like. In this regard, Cubans' recourse to images of Beirut to represent Havana is both descriptive and anticipatory. It is descriptive because Havana looks like Beirut during and immediately after its civil war, and anticipatory because of what the future might hold for Cuba's postwar landscape if Beirut's can be reconstructed. It is, Ponte observes, for this very promise of renewal that Heinrich Böll was drawn only to war-ruined cities. Böll found in devastation itself the promise of renewal, of something born outside the influence of the war: "only ruins awoke in him a sense of rebirth, of a possible futurity."[27] It is for this reason that Beirut can stand simultaneously as a postwar city, whose fractured surface corresponds to its recent history in a way that Havana's does not, and as a repository of necessary renewal.

Garaicoa's work with ruins offers a similar narrative of rebirth, although Beirut is not their specific referent. The projects collected in both *La ruina, la utopía* and *Continuity of Somebody's Architecture* attempt to give new life to decayed and abandoned projects, but to do so in a cumulative way, building on existing structures and with modest but inhabitable results. Garaicoa insists in an interview with Thomas Loeb that *Continuity of Somebody's Architecture* was not, as critics had insisted, about either critiquing or reinstating utopian visions. His interest, rather, was in "the real constructive possibility that these buildings have."[28] Garaicoa's collaboration with experienced architects produced solutions practicable in the immediate future, as all the plans and cost estimates they drew up for the unfinished Microbrigades were ready for implementation, and the buildings could be constructed if money were available (8).

Restoring continuity between present and future means doing away with the future as utopia and embracing instead a gradual, small-scale process of rebuilding, and in this cautious vision Garaicoa and Ponte coincide. Ponte's sympathy with the "sense of rebirth, of a possible futurity" that ruined cities inspired in Heinrich Böll is implicit in interviews (Interview with Teresa Basile, 35; Interview with Anna Solana and Mercedes Serna, 131–32), and his essays elaborate on the limited ambitions with which reconstruction should proceed. If "What Am I Doing Here?" warns against the stagnating effects of revolutionary utopianism, then references to families assembling their shelters from fragments and keeping them cleanly swept present an alternative, making building a much more measured activity (*La fiesta vigilada*, 166–67). Even the architects of Tuguria, who are simultaneously destroyers, rebuild their city in slow steps, dismantling the aboveground city and reassembling it below piece by piece. Reconstruction is envisaged as neither dramatic nor expansive but rather as a sequence of modest labors. As Ponte suggests, his own hopes for the city are very small in scale. Others might dream of great political upheaval in the post-Castro era, but he is concerned merely with "the fate of a few streets."[29]

To the extent that Ponte's work, like Garaicoa's, admits the possibility of reconstructing ruins, it does so quite differently from, and in opposition to, the grand promises of the early revolution. Although the revolution's rhetoric promised renewal on a national scale, and writers such as Carpentier and Lezama Lima shared an "apocalyptic vision" of a lasting city (Casamayor 68), hopes for rebirth are vastly reduced during the special period and are directed at the repair and maintenance of parts rather than an overnight rebuilding of the whole. That hopes should be so diminished is a consequence, perhaps, of their having grown out of the ruins of war—ruins salvaged from the nostalgic abuses of an international image industry and, in Ponte's reading, of the government itself. Reclaiming ruins for a Beirut-inspired postwar, and cognizant of the precariousness of the special period's future, Havana's ruinologists advance the possibility of brick-by-brick reconstruction rather than the constantly deferred rewards of an idealist dream.

Afterword

As I revised the early chapters of this manuscript, the U.S. dollar was withdrawn from circulation in Cuba. Some months later, Fidel Castro suggested that the special period had ended. And in case these reminders of the precariousness of my project were not enough, as I completed it in the summer of 2006 an unwell Castro transferred the leadership of Cuba to his brother Raúl and raised to fever pitch the anticipation that neither he nor his revolution was much longer for this world.

Faced with the prospect of immediate irrelevance—or, as Carlos Garaicoa describes Havana's Microbrigade projects, of this book's ruination preceding its completion—I prefer instead to take the rapidity of change as an opportunity. An opportunity to put my verbs in the past tense and consider the last sixteen years as a bygone era rather than a present to keep pace with. An opportunity to reflect and assess what was special about the "special period" in terms that are not those of the government that invented the epithet. To consider, that is, how the interim period of legal dollars, high-volume tourism, and booming cultural exports might have altered the place of Cuban literature at home and in the world.

Speculation about the future of Cuba these days is an international pastime and at the same time an impossibility; the question "what comes next?" is one I avoid at all costs. But, like Ponte's ruinologist, who, while others guess at how the future might look in the big picture, limits his own concerns to "the fate of a few streets," I will venture to suggest that the changes of the special period will prove significant when these years come to be recorded in Cuban literary history. Just as a reversion to their unruined state would make of Ponte's streets the lifeless anachronism that he sees in Old Havana, so it is difficult to imagine that Cuban literary production might revert to a pre–special period "norm." The markets that this period opened, the new readers it presented, and the intense interest that it witnessed in all things Cuban seem likely to persist at least until whatever comes next is no longer news. The same might be said of writers' ambivalence toward such changes and their challenges to how both Cuba and its literature are valued. The special period deinstitutionalized— perhaps even revolutionized by unrevolutionizing—literary production not fully, but at least irreversibly; and, although the U.S. dollar has been usurped in Cuba's domestic economy, it will not, I think, be so readily erased from fiction.

Acknowledgments

Over the years that this book has been brewing, I have benefited from the advice and brilliance of many friends. I would like to thank in particular Doris Sommer and Jorge I. Domínguez for their mentorship in the early days and ever since. I am thankful, too, for the continued interest and encouragement of my colleagues in Brown University's Department of Comparative Literature, especially Stephanie Merrim.

Rey Chow, Dore Levy, Karen Newman, Nancy Armstrong, Leonard Tennenhouse, Daniel Kim, Daniel Frost, and Susan Amatangelo commented on versions of the proposal for this book, for which I am very grateful, and conversations with Ariana Hernández-Reguant, Elliott Colla, Anke Birkenmaier, Jesús Jambrina, and many others have helped me along the way. Juan Flores responded warmly to my project, and I thank him, Jean Franco, George Yúdice, and Richard Morrison for the opportunity to publish in the Cultural Studies of the Americas series. José Quiroga read and recommended my manuscript with the generosity toward junior colleagues for which he is by now well known. And in a category all her own, as colleague, draft reader, and ready listener, is my great friend Jacqueline Loss.

This book is in many ways a collaborative project, even though my collaborators might not approve of its conclusions. It could not have been completed without the kindness and perspicacity of Caridad Tamayo Fernández and Víctor Fowler Calzada, nor could it have been started without the patience of Jorge Fornet, who suggested that I narrow the dizzying scope of my dissertation and opened the doors that would help me do so. I value greatly the friendships of Antonio José Ponte and Pedro Juan Gutiérrez, each of whom has taken kindly and seriously my engagement with his work. Also in Havana, Anna Lidia Vega Serova, Francisco García, Vilma Vidal, Amir Valle, Reina María Rodríguez, Jorge Miralles, and Claudia Lightfoot have always welcomed and guided me.

Closer to home, my deepest thanks go to my parents, for decades of confidence in me and hours of unpaid proofreading, and to my husband, Jeff. My son, Ellis, timed his arrival to coincide with the completion of a first draft—just one of the ways in which he has brought immense joy.

Lastly, a word of appreciation for the cultural attaché at the Cuban Embassy in London who, fifteen years ago, was the only Latin American diplomat to respond to my no doubt misdirected request to study literature in his country. When he sent me to Santiago de Cuba during one of the hardest years of the special period, little did he—or I—know what he had set in motion.

Notes

1. Selling Like Hot Bread

1. "Somos lo que hay/Lo que se vende como pan caliente . . . somos lo máximo" (Manolín, el médico de la salsa, "Somos lo que hay").

2. Ariana Hernández-Reguant traces the ambivalent implications and uses of "Somos lo que hay." Calling it "a minimalist song of nationalist defiance" ("Radio Taino," 320), she notes that it lent itself to appropriation by Cuba's Unión de Jóvenes Comunistas (Union of Young Communists). UJC made the refrain its radio jingle and "somos lo máximo" its slogan when, following the dismantling of Cuba's Eastern bloc support structure, the reconsolidation of national identity became a priority of the Cuban state's cultural apparatus (355–90).

3. By mid-2007, *Trilogía sucia de la Habana* had been published in eighteen countries

4. In a speech on Women's Day, March 8, 2005, Fidel Castro made reference to "the extremely hard special period, that we are now leaving behind" ("el período especial durísimo, que vamos dejando atrás," Calzadilla and Ríos 1). By this time many in Cuba agreed that the special period was over, but pointed to the end of the very worst years rather than of hardship per se.

5. Rafael Rojas has taken issue with linking contemporary literature, specifically that of Antonio José Ponte, to the "special period"—which he claims is not only to admit that this period "decisively marks the Island's cultural

production" ("marca decisivamente la producción cultural de la Isla") but also, more gravely, to "excessively date the Island's literary production, to subordinate the dialectic of tradition to the capricious historical periodizations of the State" ("fechar excesivamente la producción literaria de la Isla, subordinar la dialéctica de la tradición a las caprichosas periodizaciones históricas del Estado," "Partes del imperio," 253). My project, however, is not to condone the state's demarcation of this period nor the measures it undertook accordingly; and nor is it to merely record the ways in which these years mark Cuban literary production. Rather, I trace the challenges writers mounted, within their work, to the material and ideological difficulties of this period, writers whose work is (with reference to the terms Rojas opposes to one another) both "of" *and* "against" the special period.

6. James Buckwalter-Arias, for example, identifies a different trend in narrative written during the special period and also positioned between the directives of the Cuban state and the international market, namely, the reemergence of aesthetic, "extrarevolutionary" concerns. Through the fictional and autobiographical writings of Jesús Díaz, Eliseo Alberto, Leonardo Padura, and Senel Paz, he traces "an intense nostalgia for pre-revolutionary Cuban culture, a reassertion of a brand of aesthetic discourse the socialist government emphatically rejected, a will to free art from political exigencies, and a reinscription of a romantic idea of artistic genius that the revolution disavowed" (364). As my third chapter discusses further, Buckwalter-Arias regards writers' attempts to restore an artistic space "beyond contingencies" as deeply compromised by the political climate in which they write, as well as by an undertheorization of the aesthetic category itself (370–72).

7. In a speech on January 28, 1990, Castro introduced the "special period" in these terms: "How great is the vision of our Party; how useful have been all the energies spent over the years, working from the conception that the entire people participates in this struggle. However, we might be faced with other possibilities, for which we have to prepare ourselves. We called the period of total blockade a special period in wartime; but now we must prepare ourselves for all these problems, and make plans for a special period in times of peace" ("Qué visión tan grande la de nuestro Partido; qué útiles han sido todas las energías gastadas en estos años, trabajando con esa concepción que parte de la participación de todo el pueblo en esa lucha. Sin embargo, pueden venir otras variantes para las cuales tenemos que prepararnos. Nosotros llamamos a ese período de bloqueo total, período especial en tiempo de guerra; pero ahora tenemos que prepararnos por todos estos problemas, e incluso hacer planes para período especial en tiempo de paz," "Discurso 28 de enero").

8. "hoy la vida, la realidad, la dramática situación que está viviendo el mundo, este mundo unipolar, nos obliga a hacer lo que de otra forma no habríamos hecho nunca si hubiésemos tenido capital y si hubiésemos tenido tecnología para hacerlo" (Castro, "Discurso por el XL aniversario," 14).

9. Resolution no. 80/2004 of the Cuban Central Bank came in the wake of

U.S. President George W. Bush's restrictions on dollar remittances and travel to Cuba, announced in June 2004. Its preamble is translated in *Granma International* as "Whereas in the last few months the U.S. government has intensified its economic war on the people of Cuba by dictating new measures aimed at systematically hindering the external financial flows of our country, thus causing serious damage and creating grave risks for the exercise of our normal international financial activity . . ."

10. "si se acepta la divisa tal como es, del mismo color que trae, el mismo billete" (Castro, "Discurso por el XL aniversario," 8).

11. As Lorena Barberia states, "From the early 1960s until 1993, Cuba prohibited the circulation of foreign currency and limited receipt of remittances to in-kind transfers." The U.S. government legalized remittances from Cuban Americans to family members in 1978 but subsequently put these regulations to political use (Barberia 354).

12. Following on from Monreal's reading, Susan Eckstein argues that remittances have redrawn transnational borders along the family lines that map other migrant economies and have dramatically transformed the norms and values of Cuban society (Eckstein 333–43).

13. The restrictions on economic interaction between U.S. and Cuban residents announced by President George W. Bush in June 2004 eliminated the authorization of a quarterly remittance of three hundred dollars sent from any person subject to U.S. jurisdiction to any Cuban household, allowing remittances to be sent only by a spouse, child, grandchild, parent, grandparent, or sibling and prohibiting the transfer of funds to government officials and certain members of the Communist Party (Department of the Treasury 33770).

14. "si tuviéramos el petróleo de Kuwait o de otros países, nosotros habríamos desarrollado el turismo casi exclusivamente para el disfrute de los nacionales del país, pero las circunstancias actuales nos obligan a desarrollar el turismo, fundamentalmente para disfrute de los turistas extranjeros" ("Discurso en el XL aniversario," 14).

15. "Fidel affirmed that we have not renounced the idea of constructing socialism, that we are adhering to the circumstances in which we currently live, and that our objectives are to defend the Fatherland, the Revolution, and socialism's conquests" ("Fidel ratificó que nosotros no hemos renunciado a la idea de construir el socialismo, que nos atenemos a las circunstancias actuales que vivimos, y que nuestros objetivos son defender la Patria, la Revolución y las conquistas del socialismo," Calzadilla 1).

16. "La explosión literaria de la Habana."

17. In that same year Rubén Cortés wrote in Mexico's *Crónica* newspaper that "after four decades publishing within and almost exclusively for the island, Cuban writers are storming Spanish and Latin American bookstores to unleash a Boom in Cuban literature" ("luego de cuatro décadas publicando dentro y casi exclusivamente para la isla, los escritores cubanos asaltan las librerías de España y América Latina para destapar un Boom de la literatura

cubana"). In June 2000 the Spanish monthly book review *Leer* published an article titled "The new Cuban *boom* in Spain" ("El nuevo *boom* de la narrativa cubana en España"), in which Raúl Cremades and Ángel Esteban traced the increasing popularity and visibility of Cuban literature in Spain; and the on-line U.S.-based Spanish-language bookstore Exodusltd.com introduced a section titled "El boom cubano" where it proclaimed, "Throughout the world of Spanish-language books, the word has spread that there's a new Cuban boom" ("Se ha empezado a colar la frase por el mundo del libro en español de que ha surgido un 'boom' cubano"). The term was taken up in Cuban newspapers, too, particularly in marketing the country's literary successes to foreign readers (see Edel Morales; Perdomo).

18. Among the significant European prizes awarded to Cuban authors during this period are the Spanish Premio Azorín to *El hombre, la hembra y el hambre* (Man, woman, and hunger) by the Miami-based Cuban Daína Chaviano in 1998; Spain's Premio Alfaguara to Eliseo Alberto's *Caracol Beach* in 1998; Radio France International's Premio Juan Rulfo to Ena Lucía Portela's story "El viejo, el asesino y yo" in 1999; the French prize for Best Foreign Book to Abilio Estévez's *Thine Is the Kingdom* in 1999; the Spanish Lengua de Trapo prize shared in 1999 between the Cubans Ronaldo Menéndez Plasencia for *La piel de Inesa* (Inesa's skin) and Karla Suárez for *Silencios* (Silences); and the 1995 Premio Café Gijón for Leonardo Padura Fuentes's *Máscaras* (Masks), as well as the Premio Hammett for both this novel in 1998 and Padura's *Paisaje de otoño* (Autumn landscape) in 1999.

19. The cult of the new came to a head in Cuba in the early 1990s as Salvador Redonet's term *los novísimos* ("the newest"), to which I turn in chapter 3, spawned a genealogy of *posnovísimos* and *pos-posnovísimos*. Writers best known in an earlier period whose work was republished in Spain in the 1990s include José Lezama Lima (*Poesía completa;* Alianza, 1999), Reinaldo Arenas (*El color del verano;* Tusquets, 1999), and Virgilio Piñera (*Cuentos completos;* Alfaguara, 1999).

20. As Alejandro Herrero-Olaizola has indicated, "Boom" competes as a commercial denominator with the more aesthetically geared "la nueva novela" ("the new novel"), the term of choice for Carlos Fuentes in his analysis of this period in Latin American literature, *La nueva novela hispanoamericana* (The new Spanish American novel). Reading these two terms as revising the coexistence of Pierre Bourdieu's two fields of restricted and large-scale production, Herrero-Olaizola argues that "both terms, Boom and *nueva novela,* can be reconciled without discarding their complementary nature" (330). Regarding the Boom "as a distinct—and yet concurrent—manifestation of the *nueva novela* helps to understand how this literary period oscillates from elitist to popular, from restricted to large-scale production, from the politically-committed author to the *autor-superestrella*" (337).

21. The looseness of this idea of "cultural perspective" is evidently problematic, as the Boom writers themselves were conspicuously well traveled and

often lived in exile, adding a further dimension to the internationalization of their literature. Mario Santana observes that during the years of the Boom, "not only did many Latin American writers live, write and publish in Spain, but some of them were even more influential and widely read than several Spanish authors normally included in studies and courses on the period" (19). Donoso notes: "Obviously, we cannot talk of a mere coincidence if Cortázar, García Márquez, Vargas Llosa, Cabrera Infante, Severo Sarduy, Salvador Garmendia, Jorge Edwards, Roa Bastos, Augusto Monterroso, Carpentier, Carlos Fuentes, and Mario Benedetti are living or have lived for so long outside their countries . . . In any case, it cannot be denied that exile, cosmopolitanism, internationalization, all more or less connected, have shaped a very considerable part of the Latin American narrative of the 1960s" (*The Boom,* 68). He argues, however, that a common history and predicament among Latin American writers produced in them "a cohesiveness of origin and development" (89) that formed for them "a continental parish" (ibid.).

22. From a national perspective, Mario Santana argues that Spain's dominion over the Latin American Boom forced a reciprocal reconsideration of Spanish-born writers' claims to "Spanish" literature. Mayder Dravasa and Alejandro Herrero-Olaizola focus particularly on Barcelona, for which, as Carlos Barral explores in his memoir of the period, publishing Latin American literature during the later years of the Franco regime was an act of decentering the cultural authority of Madrid.

23. In "Boceto de mercado" (A sketch of the market), the Cuban writer Pedro Marqués de Armas describes the strangeness of his experience in Havana's hard-currency bookstores, where "a Bernhard at $15 and a Broch at $27—not to mention medical books and scientific literature in general—are beyond anyone's means, except in very long installments" ("un Bernhard en 15 y un Broch en 27 dólares—para no hablar de libros de medicina y de literatura científica en general—son incomprables, salvo a muy largo plazo," 7). Nevertheless, he notes, "here the best sellers have their outlet, as does the yoga-cookery-self-help-esoteric package that, by the way, promotes Cuban sociability" ("encuentran salida los *best-sellers* y el paquete yoga-cocina-autoauyda-esoterismo, que, dicho sea de paso, fermenta la socialidad cubana," ibid.).

24. The Cuban authors Abilio Estévez, Ena Lucía Portela, Jorge Ángel Pérez, Anna Lidia Vega Serova, Arturo Arango, and Pedro Juan Gutiérrez, for example, published books in two editions—foreign and Cuban—between 1994 and 2004.

25. "sus lectores naturales" (Morales 7; Campa 8).

26. "Cuba . . . comienza a depender tanto de los extranjeros, de los dólares y de la industria del libro español como el resto de Latinoamérica" (357).

27. Law Decree No. 145 of November 17, 1993, on the conditions of labor for creators of literary works, acknowledges the status of workers as creators whose artistic work is not linked to an institution and at the same time establishes a Ministry of Culture registry for such works. Law Decrees No. 105

(August 5, 1988) and No. 144 (November 19, 1993) established these same rights for visual artists and musicians, respectively. February 17, 2005. http://www.cubagob.cu/des_soc/cultura/legis.html.

28. Heberto Padilla was censored for his collection *Sent off the Field,* which the Cuban Writers' Union in its 1968 edition of the book criticized for defending individualism over the needs of society. In 1971, Padilla was arrested, and released after signing and reciting to gathered members of the Writers' Union a document in which he admitted to having harbored antirevolutionary thoughts. The documents from these episodes are gathered in Ediciones Universal's 1998 commemorative edition of *Fuera del juego.*

29. A central argument of García Canclini's *Hybrid Cultures: Strategies for Entering and Leaving Modernity,* revisited in *Consumers and Citizens* and *La globalización imaginada* (Globalization imagined), is that Latin American cultural producers' entry into "modern" global markets has spurred adaptive creativity. Appadurai's insistence in *Modernity at Large* that "globalization is not the story of cultural homogenization" (11) and that consumption is not "the end of the road for goods and services" (66) leads him to prioritize the relationship between consumption, the imagination, and agency (7; 66–85).

30. Donoso remarks, "I think that if the Boom had nearly complete unity in anything—accepting the variety of shadings—it was in faith in the cause of the Cuban Revolution; I think the disillusionment produced by the Padilla case destroyed that faith and destroyed the unity of the Boom" (*The Boom,* 50). As Ángel Rama recalls, Boom literature was heavily marketed at university campuses, whose bourgeois frequenters "during the 1960s assumed a contestatory stance along the lines of revolutionary Castroism, lending their support to guerrilla groups and assaults on the power of conformity via the 'foco' concepts that Régis Debray formulated from Havana" ("asumieron una posición contestaria durante los años sesenta en la línea del castrismo revolucionario, promoviendo los grupos guerrilleros y el asalto al poder de conformidad con las concepciones foquistas que teorizó desde la Habana Régis Debray," 62).

31. Martin's assessment is based on "works like Cortázar's *Hopscotch* (1963), Cabrera Infante's *Three Trapped Tigers* (1967), Vargas Llosa's *The Green House* (1966), Lezama Lima's *Paradiso* (1967), García Márquez's *One Hundred Years of Solitude* (1967) and Fuentes's *Terra nostra* (1975)" (60); and it contributes to his argument that in the 1960s Latin America reached its "Joycean" moment, both politically and culturally.

32. "Gracias a la paciencia y los esfuerzos de un conjunto de especialistas en distintas ramas, a partir del local más tumultuosamente habitado se obtiene un sitio lo menos habitable" ("De 'Un paréntesis de ruinas,'" 123).

33. "Para algunos, como el diseñador italiano Luciano Benetton, se trata de una cuestión sobre todo estética: es la luz pastel que se filtra a través de los soportales a las siete de la tarde y colorea el rostro de los cubanos y de las fachadas desconchadas de La Habana, convirtiéndolos en una misma cosa. Para otros, el morbo está en la contradicción política, en el contraste del uniforme

verde oliva de Fidel Castro mientras la ciudad se llena de coches japoneses. En los cadillacs desvencijados y las consignas políticas de los años sesenta— '¡Patria o muerte, venceremos!'—que dan la sensación de tiempo detenido. En los mojitos de la Bodeguita del Medio, que a uno le hacen sentirse joven. En la forma de mirar que tiene la gente. En el sexo fácil, que se mezcla con la estética de Numancia. '¡Hay que ir a Cuba; pero ahora, luego ya no será lo mismo', dicen algunos. También en esta condición de parque ideológico, de última reserva del socialismo, está la magia de Cuba. Y en la libido que generan en los empresarios las oportunidades de negocios que vendrán después" (5).

34. Patullo's analysis of the social and economic costs of tourism to the Caribbean addresses tourists' expectations of island residents in the following terms: "The Caribbean person, from the Amerindians whom Columbus met in that initial encounter to the twentieth-century taxi driver whom tourists meet at the airport, is expected to satisfy those images associated with paradise and Eden. The images are crude: of happy, carefree, fun-loving men and women, colourful in behaviour, whose life is one of daytime indolence beneath the palms and a night-time of pleasure through music, dance and sex" (142).

35. "se ha convertido en el actor de un parque temático llamado Cuba, el habitante oportuno de ese abrevadero de nostalgias—de izquierdas y derechas, del son primigenio y del Ché Guevara, del Cabaret y la Sierra Maestra, del *Paradiso* de Lezama Lima y de la masa de puerco en los paladares—en que se ha convertido la isla" (167).

36. Davies's analysis of postmodernism in post-Soviet Cuban intellectual discourse identifies two distinct currents of thought. In the more nationalist of the two, the postmodern is figured as a resurgence of the heterogeneity that has long been seen as characterizing Cuban culture. In the other, principally the domain of performance and iconography, the postmodern is mapped more directly onto disenchantment with revolutionary historicism.

37. Daphne Berdahl describes how the mid- and late 1990s "have witnessed the birth and boom of a nostalgia industry in the former East Germany that has entailed the revival, reproduction, and commercialization of GDR products as well as the 'museumification' of GDR everyday life" (193).

38. A tourist attraction, in MacCannell's formulation, is only constituted as such if it is encompassed by trappings that affirm its status (109–33). Frow proposes that the distinction between a tourist sight and its marker is really that between a real object and its representation, "and it therefore holds open the possibility of a sight's being either represented truly or misrepresented" (131).

39. "escenas de las casas deterioradas, de los carros deteriorados, de toda la miseria que ha causado el bloqueo" (*"Buena Vista Social Club* y la cultura musical cubana," 165).

40. In the late 1990s, particularly following Pope John Paul II's visit to Cuba in January 1998, President Bill Clinton's administration promoted a "people-to-people" policy of limited, low-level engagement with Cuba. Despite the restrictions of the Helms-Burton Act of 1996, U.S. citizens were permitted

to travel to Cuba under general licenses for educational and humanitarian purposes. The rationale behind this policy was to promote democracy through contact between individual Cubans and low-spending Americans (Morley and McGillion 146–58). It was largely reversed by President George W. Bush in June 2004.

2. DOLLAR TROUBLE

1. Juan Carlos Rodríguez, of the Spanish newspaper *La razón*, reported in November 2000 that Prieto, who was visiting Madrid to promote his own novel *The Flight of the Cat*, claimed that Cuban publishers were not interested in Valdés's work because "hace un pésimo subproducto literario, no por cuestiones políticas" ("it is a terrible literary subproduct, not for political reasons").

2. In 1996, few "new" Cuban authors were available in English translation, with the exception of those in Ruth Behar's *Bridges to Cuba/Puentes a Cuba* (1995) that unites texts by Cuban and Cuban American authors in both English and Spanish. This situation was soon to change as the Cuba boom gathered force, with anthologized collections leading the way. Peter Bush's *The Voice of the Turtle* (1997) showcased young authors alongside greats from earlier in the twentieth century; and Mirta Yáñez's *Cubana* (1998) includes women from several generations of the revolution. Translations of longer-established authors living outside Cuba, such as Guillermo Cabrera Infante and Antonio Benítez Rojo, were more readily available at this time.

3. "una isla que quiso construir el paraíso" (*Te di la vida entera*, 15).

4. In the special period, the word *inventar* acquired this specific meaning, drawing it back to its etymology in *in-venire*, to come across or discover. Jorge Pérez-López defines *inventar* as "figure out a way to solve a problem arising from shortage of goods or services"; and *resolver* as "make ends meet; do whatever needs to be done. In the case of consumers, relates to steps to put food on the table and obtain consumer goods. For enterprises, it might entail barter of commodities and the like" (187–88). Carlos Paz Pérez locates *resolver*, and by implication *inventar*, in the lexicon of an underworld economy that, I would argue, expanded its sphere dramatically in the special period. Of *resolver* he writes: "It is often used euphemistically for *to steal*, e.g., 'Yesterday I procured [*resolver*] three pounds of flour from my workplace'" ("Muchas veces se utiliza eufemísticamente por robar, 'Ayer resolví tres libras de harina en mi centro trabajo,'" 234).

5. "¡Ah, mamey, cuánta añoranza, eres sólo una palabra para saborear en la literatura!" (73).

6. "Intenta acordarse de lo que comió ayer. No, no comió. Ingirió tajada de aire y fritura de viento" (178).

7. Critics who focus primarily on *I Gave You All I Had* include Carmen Faccini, who traces the evolution of an ironic discourse of revolution in *Yocandra in*

the Paradise of Nada to a discourse of the absurd in *I Gave You All I Had;* Cristina Ortiz Ceberio, who reads Valdés's work as constructing a space for narratives excluded by the official and totalizing discourse of the Cuban Revolution; Miguel González-Abellás, who sees Valdés's "narrative universe" as mapping Cuban experience both on the island and in exile (González-Abellás, "'Aquella isla'"), and *I Gave You All I Had,* in particular, as exploring the Cuban government's complicity in "commercializing" Cuban women (González-Abellás, "Sexo transnacional"); Lidia Santos, who reads *I Gave You All I Had* in terms of Latin American melodrama; and René Prieto, who argues that this novel, in contrast to Pedro Juan Gutiérrez's *Dirty Havana Trilogy,* is parodic rather than erotic. Perla Rozencvaig reads *Yocandra in the Paradise of Nada* as creating a language that withstands that of political containment; Madeline Cámara, in her study of baroque and postmodern elements in *Yocandra,* draws an explicit analogy between the role of hunger in this novel and in the Spanish picaresque (78–79).

8. "Ella abrió la mano. En la palma lisa, joven, descansaba cuidadosamente dobladito, un dólar del año 1935. Así fue su bautismo con un billete americano, al cual no dio tanta importancia. Al fin y al cabo, no era tan diferente del peso nacional, era sólo un papel en otro idioma. Pensó que, de todas formas, debía encontrar un sitio seguro para esconderlo, y lo sembró en la maceta de malanga. Él regresaría, como siempre, desbordante de dinero, de orgullo y de amor. Y se sentó en un sillón. A esperar" (96).

9. "Cuca Martínez se da cuenta de que es un papel raro, y a trasluz logra leer en letras grandes y armoniosas, centradas y adornadas con otros signos que impiden comprender el idioma al cual pertence la palabra: ONE. Claro, ella es vieja, aunque no tanto, pero se siente casi como un Matusalén, pero no tiene ni un pelo de boba. Escudriña rápidamente hacia ambos lados, hacia atrás, y engancha a toda velocidad el billete verde de un dólar en el hueso que otrora fue el entreseno. ¡Un dólar! ¡Cristo! ¡Viejito Lázaro milagros, ¿qué se comprará, qué se comprará?!" (181–82).

10. "un chupa-chups, no, no, no, una coca-cola, qué va, qué va, qué diría el XXL de mí, loca por el refresco del enemigo!" (182).

11. *Te di la vida entera,* 288–90.

12. McLaughlin continues: "What comes to the surface with paper in the nineteenth century, then, is an alternative understanding of value, one with important, and complex, affiliations to a widespread discourse of virtuality that, as several historians have shown, emerged in nineteenth-century natural and social sciences in the wake of Kant and *Naturphilosophie*" (964).

13. Coins, of course, enact this same dissociation; but theorists of money discerned a qualitative difference between their relationship to value and that of the banknote. Both Marx and Wittgenstein, as Shell explores, distinguish "the dissociation of symbol from commodity that seems to occur in the minting of metal ingots into coin, from the less apparent and ideologically more subversive disassociation of symbol from commodity that occurs in printing money" (Shell 19).

14. Shell discusses how "The Gold Bug" is written "on gold" by "a poor author who could only wish to exchange his literary papers for money" at a time when "financiers were turning paper into gold by means of the newly widespread institution of paper money" (8).

15. "Además, pasaba billetes falsos" (160). The sleepy-eyed general, "el General con los ojos dormidos," is General Francisco Vicente Aguilera. He was the face on the one-hundred-peso bill of both the Certificados de Plata, certificates issued between 1934 and 1948 and guaranteed by silver coins deposited in the Treasury, and the currency issued by the newly established Cuban National Bank in 1948 (*Numismática Cubana*, 31–33). He is described in a further history of Cuban money as "one of the principal organizers of the 1868 war. Military chief of Oriente province and vice president of the Republic of Cuba in Arms" ("uno de los principales organizadores de la Guerra del 1868. Jefe militar de la provincia de Oriente y vicepresidente de la República de Cuba en Armas" (*Cuba: Emisiones de monedas y billetes, 1915–1980*, 94).

16. "'Démelo,' dijo el policía, viendo que era bueno. 'Se hará constar en el acta'" (160).

17. Lorraine Elena Roses reads "La noche de Ramón Buendía," written in 1933 although first published in 1942, as a story that "demythifies the concept of engaged literature: that the individual must commit himself politically and that the writer too must align with the Revolution through words" (78).

18. "se precipitaba, furiosamente, en zigzag, al tiempo que arrojaba puñados de billetes a sus perseguidores" (84).

19. "pasaban por encima de los billetes sin recogerlos, disparando" (ibid.).

20. "moneda nacional de buena ley" (78).

21. As minister of industries from 1961 to 1965, Guevara sought to centralize Cuba's economy and implement a comprehensive program of labor incentives that would phase out the need for money. This did not happen, but the system of labor incentives and food subsidies was to continue into the special period.

22. "Yo había perdido la noción del dinero, apenas veíamos grandes billetes, había olvidado la ley del valor, de la oferta y la demanda" (123).

23. "es inaplazable eliminar la inseguridad y el riesgo resultante del hecho de que los billetes cubanos actualmente en circulación vengan imprimiéndose en empresas extranjeras que están fuera del control efectivo del Gobierno Revolucionario" (*Numismática cubana*, 45).

24. Prior to the establishment of the U.S.-brokered Cuban republic, various currencies had circulated in Cuba, prevalent among them the Spanish peseta. When the United States occupied Cuba following the 1898 Treaty of Paris, the Spanish and French currencies were devalued and the U.S. dollar became the official currency. Cuba minted its first coins in 1914, but a law decreed at the same time made both the Cuban peso and the U.S. dollar legal tender. The first Cuban banknotes were issued in 1934 and circulated alongside the dollar (*Numismática cubana*, 25–33). The creation of the Banco Nacional

de Cuba in 1948 marked the end of the dollar's official status, although it continued in circulation, particularly as the currency in which people hoarded money, for some time thereafter (Rowe and Yanes Faya).

25. "esa normalidad tan anormal a la cual estamos habituados" (189).

26. This is how the same pun appears in Daína Chaviano's *El hombre, la hembra y el hambre,* for example. "Las jineteras sólo se acuestan por *dolores*" (265) ("*jineteras* only get into bed for *dolores*"), says a character about women who consort with foreigners, affirming the woeful consequences of such behavior. The pun is also the subject of Nelsón Domínguez's mixed-media illustration "¿Dolorización?" (2002) ("Dolorization?") on the back cover of the journal *Temas* 30 (July–September 2002).

27. That *Tres tristes tigres* is a "novel of language" (Merrim) in which neither Fidel Castro nor the Cuban Revolution are directly mentioned, does not preclude it from being "a bitter social novel, marked deeply by the Cuban Revolution" (González Echevarría, *Voice of the Masters,* 140). Stephanie Merrim looks to *TTT*'s *choteo,* or "low" humor, for the novel's political basis because, "though not always political in content, *choteo* is none the less political in its motivation, stemming from a hatred of authority, a chafing impotence or inability to act" (Merrim 49). In Philip Christian Sutton's words, "Castro is little talked about in TTT; but a novel set in 1958 and published in 1967, and concerned with flux and change seen as an ideological threat, needs to be read with Castro's revolution as a referent" (Sutton 553).

28. *Te di la vida entera,* 102; *I Gave You All I Had,* 62.

29. *Te di la vida entera,* 189; the direct reference to "plan jeba" is omitted in Benabid's translation of *I Gave You All I Had.* Of the "plan jaba" (shopping-bag plan), Elizabeth Stone writes that it "gave working women priority for service in the stores and allowed women to leave their shopping bags, with lists of items wanted, at the grocery store on the way to work and pick up the filled bags on the way home" (17).

30. "Ahí es donde, de verdad, literalmente, el dólar alivia el dolor. Y es cuando aparece el nuevo síndrome: el dolor del dólar" (179).

31. "—Uan, ¿qué has hecho de nuestro amor?—preguntó Cuca Martínez, semejante a la bandera de Bonifacio Byrne, *deshecha en menudos pedazos. /*—¿Y tú, Cuquita, qué hiciste del dólar? / Por supuesto, con las orejas apretuncadas debido al abrazo, y por culpa del empecinamiento que padecemos las mujeres de idealizar más allá de lo máximo a los tipos, ella entiende dolor en lugar de dólar" (238).

32. "¿Tú Habana, capitulada?/¿tú en llanto? ¿tú en exterminio?/¿Tú ya en extraño dominio?/¡Qué dolor! ¡Oh Patria amada!" (362). The reference within Valdés's novel is to Manuel Moreno Fraginals, *Cuba/España, España/Cuba: Historia común.* Moreno Fraginals quotes these same lines from Beatriz de Jústiz y Zayas, marquesa de Jústiz y Santa Ana, as the epigraph to his chapter on the English occupation of Cuba, which lasted for eleven months of the year 1762 (128–36).

33. "Su serie es el número correspondiente a la mayor cuenta que poseemos

en Suiza. No hemos podido tocarla en treinta y seis años, porque el billete contiene en su fabricación, nueve hilos de oro, y cada uno de quilates diferentes. Es la clave que nos exigen para poder tocar la cuenta" (160–61). Benabid's translation does not make clear that the different karats (i.e., presumably their different numerical values) themselves constitute the code.

34. The current edition of the one-dollar bill has been in circulation, with changes in only the signatures of the treasurer and secretary of the treasury, since the 1950s. Like the Cuban banknotes introduced a year earlier, the 1935 dollar bill is a silver certificate, promising "one dollar in silver payable to the bearer on demand," rather than the current Federal Reserve Notice.

35. "*—Cuídalo como oro. De él depende nuestro futuro*" (146).

36. Alejandro Herrero-Olaizola distinguishes between the terms *boom* and *nueva novela* by arguing that the latter allowed authors and critics to skirt the question of the market.

37. "Cuba se resiste a dejar de ser un punto de referencia de importancia para los españoles. Continúa como objeto de nostalgia familiar, real o en cierta manera románticamente inventada . . . En un mundo complejo, la isla es un escenario geográfico de dimensiones asequibles para el empresario español. Al mismo tiempo ofrece una cierta dosis de exotismo por su diversidad racial y su ubicación caribeña" (Roy 167).

38. *Panorámica de la edición española de libros* listed Planeta as the fifteenth-largest publisher of fiction in 2000. This is a lower ranking than in previous years: in 1999 Planeta was number six, in 1998 number four, in 1997 number five, and in 1996 number five.

39. Valdés's Web site, http://www.zoevaldes.com, lists the editions of her books in Spanish and other languages.

40. *Te di la vida entera*, 296–97.

41. "(la) recomposición de un mito que incluye el hecho de que esté gastado."

42. "nada comparable al boom de treinta años atrás." Claude Durand, literary director of Le Seuil publishers from 1965 to 1978 and president of Arthème Fayard publishers since 1980, cited in Hasson.

43. "'Por cierto,' afirma Alzira Martins, 'esa moda o manía provocó un exceso de productos culturales cubanos, en detrimento de la calidad . . . Unas normas 'cariturescas' llegan a perjudicar a los escritores más valiosos que no coinciden con cierta estética folklorista, tal como la entiende en Francia algunos medios culturales'" (Alzira Martins, of Actes Sud, in ibid.).

44. "No cabe duda de que existe el interés por lo cubano, a lo cual el éxito de Zoé Valdés en Francia ha contribuido en gran parte" (Annie Morvan, of Le Seuil Éditeurs, in ibid.).

45. "Elle écrit beaucoup, trop sans doute. Ses récits partent dans toutes les directions. Ils changent brusquement de tempo, de forme, de ton, comme si un génie ou un rêve la tirait par le main . . . Il ne faut pas y chercher le bon goût, la perfection, l'unité de ton. Zoé Valdés prend tout ce qui remonte, désirs et frustrations, puis le jette sur la page comme si le temps brûlait" (8).

46. "un lugar de encuentro democrático, donde sean al fin superados los antagonismos: no sólo aquellos que oponen la Habana a Miami, sino también los que existen en el interior del exilio y en el interior de la Isla" (Díaz, *"Encuentro,"* 102).

47. "El éxito comercial de Zoé Valdés proviene de que ella escribe lo que cierta parte del público europeo desea leer: una dosis de feminismo, una dosis de sexo, una dosis de desarraigo, una pizca de Lezama Lima. Es una forma de turismo literario, en el momento en que Cuba se convierte en un paraíso del sexo barato. Se ha comercializado la tragedia cubana. La literatura, la verdadera, es el lugar imposible donde tratan de expresarse la tragedia y la comedia, el abismo y la ambigüedad entre los que se mueve este siglo; toda la complejidad del destino humano. Son necesarias la lucidez y la locura y no una fuga hacia unos personajes que no son otra cosa que marionetas ideológicas" (103).

48. "¿No te da pena hacer eso, siendo hijo de una Revolución tan grande, no te avergüenzas de manchichar (por mancillar) la memoria del Che?" "Tengo que comer. ¡Muérte, vieja roja!" (294).

3. COVERING FOR BANKNOTES

1. Following rioting in the Centro Habana section of the Cuban capital that began on August 5, 1994, Fidel Castro lifted the border guard on August 12. In the following twelve-day period, 14,066 Cubans left the country on makeshift rafts, and a total of 32,385 departed in August and September of that year (Ackerman and Clark 22 and 39). As Richard Gott recounts, economic conditions in the country—which the legalization of the dollar had not yet succeeded in alleviating—were a major factor in this civil unrest (298–300).

2. Of the 143 literary titles published in 1993, only 83 were books, the remainder being slimmer brochures *(folletos).* This represented a 75 percent drop in the Insituto Cubano del Libro's production. In previous decades, the ICL's share of total titles published had ranged from a quarter to a third of Cuba's total book production (Más Zabala 49). In her paper "Writing and Publishing in Cuba during the Special Period," Patricia Catoira discusses in more depth the production and distribution of books, as well as the changes in thematic emphasis and readership during these years.

3. "La crisis de papel en Cuba ha reducido a límites antes insospechados lo que, hasta hace poco, era su importante industria editorial" (9); "una actividad que continúa produciéndose aunque, por el momento, no reciba su justa respuesta editorial" (9).

4. *Anuario Narrativo* summarizes the situation as follows: "Today, the production of books in our country is limited to meeting the requirements of the education system. As a consequence, fiction has been limited by the circumstances to the few literary magazines that still come out and, especially, to what has gradually become a vast national movement of leaflets and booklets sustained by the scraps of paper printing presses throw away" ("Hoy día, la

producción de libros en nuestro país, se contrae, en lo fundamental, a cubrir los requerimientos des los distintos niveles educacionales. Por consiguiente, la literatura de ficción ha sido confinada por las circunstancias a las contadas revistas literarias que continúan apareciendo y, sobre todo, a lo que, poco a poco, ha ido configurando un vasto movimiento nacional de publicación de folletería y *plaquettes* que se sustenta aprovechando recortes y deshechos de algunas impresoras," 9).

5. Gerardo Soler Cedre describes the Colección Pinos Nuevos, conceived as an act of solidarity between Argentina and Cuba, as "one of the most important projects in the history of the book in our country" ("unos de los proyectos más importantes en la historia del libro en nuestro país," 20). Its first two lists, released in 1994 and 1996, each included the unpublished work of one hundred authors, divided between six different genres.

6. "centros de estudio y laboratorios literarios . . . donde prima el concepto de la creación literaria, como práctica, como labor consciente y sostenida" (Smorkaloff, *Literatura y edición de libros,* 283).

7. In her introduction to the Brazilian anthology of Cuban stories, *Nós que ficamos,* Jacqueline Shor, for example, states: "I have no intention other than to invite the reader to watch and hear, through reading, this small selection of the work of authors born and raised in the controversial world of the 'children of the revolution'" ("Não tenho outro intencão senão a de convidar o leitor a olhar e escutar, lendo, esta pequena parcela da obra de autores nascidos e criados no controvertido mundo dos 'filhos de Revolucão,'" 9).

8. Redonet's generational classifications are but one example of the many subcategories to which young writers were subjected, beginning with Arturo Arango's 1988 division of them into "the violent ones" ("los violentos") and "the exquisite ones" ("los exquisitos") (Arango, "Los violentos," 9–16).

9. "trajeron temas inéditos o postergados hasta entonces: la relación traumática con la realidad y las instituciones, el mundo marginal (con sus rockeros, frikis y otras formas de 'alienación'), la homosexualidad, el lado angustiado de la guerra" (Alonso Estenoz 4).

10. "revitalizaron la escritura, al subvertir la estructura tradicional del relato e incluir elementos reconocidos como posmodernos (intertextualidad, diversidad de voces, fragmentación, ironía, pastiche, relativización de centros y periferias)" (ibid.). Margarita Mateo's *Ella escribía poscrítica* examines the *novísimos'* relationship to postmodernism, arguing that, although they are its most sophisticated practitioners, they nevertheless draw from precursors in the Cuban literary canon.

11. "la drogadicción, la sexualidad como alucinógeno, la inadaptación, el *heavy rock* y la alienación" (125).

12. "¿hasta dónde puede el cuento, sin perder su naturaleza distintiva, dejar de narrar, hacer trizas su anécdota, despreciar la construcción, al menos, de un personaje?" ("Paisajes," 50).

13. "tienen una actitud marginal dentro del límite que puede ser marginal en un país como éste" ("Ruptura," 71).

14. "¿Es marginalidad o inadaptación su sustancia?" ("Para días de menos entusiasmo," 35).

15. "que abarca la precariedad material pero también incluiría cambios notables en nuestras formas de vida, en la proyección (y valor material) de la literatura y en las maneras de relacionarse la política con las artes" ("Paisajes," 52). Arango is reluctant to identify these new thematic preoccupations too closely with the special period, "porque entonces, inevitablemente, estaría aludiendo a carencias y mortificaciones cotidianas, y se trata de un fenómeno mucho mayor" (52) ("because then, inevitably, it would be alluding to shortages and daily challenges, when the phenomenon is in fact much bigger"). Nevertheless, the preoccupations he lists—changes in lifestyle, in the distribution and material value of literature, and in ways of relating to both literature and art—are all intimately connected with the economic changes of the special period.

16. In their introductory essay to the inaugural issue of *Rockstalgia,* dated February 2005, Raúl Aguiar and Yoss present rock music and its history in distinctly non-Cuban terms, positioning the genre in opposition to a broadly defined "establishment" (3).

17. Anke Birkenmaier notes that although Gutiérrez's work has in common with that of the *novísimos* the theme of marginality, the latter prolong a revolutionary narrative of incorporating the margins, whereas Gutiérrez's character stands resolutely outside this effort ("Más allá del realismo sucio," 41–42). She concludes that "Gutiérrez thus positions himself in a literary space that is not that of a marginal literature, but one in which the place of enunciation, Cuba, is circumstantial to his purpose" ("Gutiérrez se coloca de esta manera en un espacio literario que no es el de la literatura marginal, sino uno donde el lugar de enunciación, Cuba, es circunstancial para su propósito," 42). For reasons elaborated in my next chapter, I disagree with this assessment of Cuba's merely circumstantial place in Gutiérrez's fiction: the Havana that gives his first two books their title is, I think, crucial to their establishment of a particular narrator–reader dynamic.

18. Ena Lucía Portela attributes the proliferation of marginal themes in Cuban fiction of the 1990s in part to the demands of the foreign market, to "what in the literary metropolis of the Spanish language, that is, in Madrid or Barcelona, far away, is expected of a Cuban author" ("lo que en la metrópolis literaria de la lengua española, o sea, en Madrid o Barcelona, allá lejos, se espera de un narrador cubano" ["Con nombre y sin dinero," 64]). As I discuss further in chapter 4, however, Portela's exoneration of Pedro Juan Gutiérrez from the charge of pandering to the market on the grounds that his characters are authentic, unlike those of writers who did not experience the special period so harshly, establishes somewhat problematic criteria for the claim to marginality.

19. "emigrantes frustrados" (75).

20. "El dinero, éste que ahora se ha convertido de mil cien en mil setenta, lo han ahorrado—el diablo sabe cómo—durante un año; y no para convertirlo, en mágica multiplicación de papeles, en su formidable equivalente en moneda local, sino para metamorfosearlos en dos pasajes a México" (64).

21. "la amante a horcajadas, pantalón a la altura de las rodillas, alfombra verde y dinero verde, pantalón azul *blue jean,* amiga verde . . ." (68).

22. "tras nombrar el libro ambos se derrumban como si acabaran de comprobar el resultado positivo de un análisis sobre el SIDA" (ibid.).

23. "se resignan antes que anochezca definitivamente y puedan dormir" (ibid.).

24. Jacqueline Loss addresses Arenas's place in the recent cultural memory of Cubans, listing as examples the inclusion of his short story "El cometa Halley" in a 1999 anthology; the "Celestino" prize, named after Arenas's first novel, awarded by the Asociación Hermanos Saiz of Holguín; and the critiques of Julien Schnabel's film, *Before Night Falls,* posted on the Cuban electronic journal *La jiribilla* ("Global Arenas," 337–39).

25. "es un *best seller* por el que me darán los treinta dólares" (75).

26. "Saca el libro de Reinaldo Arenas y lo manosea como quien manosea un fajo de billetes" (ibid.).

27. "en lugar de rebuscar algún pretexto extremo y convincente, se abandona a la imagen del libro que se hunde de repente por la inercia de la caída, y luego, aunque parece que va a flotar, se vuelve invisible bajo el gris turbio del desagüe" (76).

28. "la preeminencia que la moneda extranjera tiene hoy en nuestras vidas" (*Historias del cuerpo,* 343).

29. Araújo bases her reading of a "narrative of enclosure" ("narrativa de encierro") partly on the women's stories in Redonet's anthology *Los últimos serán los primeros,* but she expands the corpus of *novísima* writing to include work published in national journals, as well as unpublished stories (213–16).

30. "le daba una vergüenza terrible que alguien viera lo que come" (16).

31. "era un desconocido y, además, era extranjero" (ibid.).

32. "se sentó en el piso y puso el dinero delante, en fila . . . Los agrupó en bulticos de a cien, los puso uno encima de otro en abanico" (17).

33. "Hizo un bolsito y guardó el sobre dentro. Se lo ajustó en el bloomer y lo prendió con un alfiler" (20).

34. "la fuerza que se coloca en oposicíon a las capacidades del dinero es el amor" (*Historias del cuerpo,* 344).

35. "la utopía implícita el final" (ibid.).

36. Arturo Arango characterizes the critical attack on musicians' success as targeted initially at the vulgarity and alleged misogyny of their lyrics and then at the ostentation of their lifestyles compared with those of the general populace ("Escribir en Cuba hoy [1997]," 14).

37. "el exceso de la frivolidad que se manifiesta hoy en en determinados sectores de nuestra cultura" ("La hoguera de las vanidades," 2).

38. "¿frivolidad, mediocridad o marketing?" (ibid.).

39. "tras esta apertura, o tras la inevitabilidad de la apertura, hay mucha gente que se aprovecha para simplificar el conocimiento serio, para banalizar la cultura" (ibid.).

40. "las aperturas no tienen que implicar necesariamente esa frivolización" (ibid.).

41. "debemos partir de la base de que el mercado no es, necesariamente, el enemigo de la cultura" (ibid.).

42. "¿mercado o protección del arte? ¿mercado o desarrollo de una política dirigida a los más jóvenes?" (4).

43. "equivalía a querer tapar el sol con un dedo" (26).

44. "todo el mundo trata de hacer dos cosas: no apartarse de las exigencies del mercado y ser fieles a una poética personal" (Alonso Estenoz 6).

45. "una frikie jinetera drogadicta de padres balseros y hermano con sadismo anal" (3).

46. Manuel Ávila González (Manín)'s response singles out de Águila's failure to realize that "las temáticas no hacen la literatura" (28) ("themes don't make literature"); to take into account the presence of violent themes in pre–special period literature; and to acknowledge that, despite their aspirations, only a small percentage of young Cuban writers publish abroad. He recognizes that some authors write for economic motives but insists that in the case of most stories, "the motives for which the narrator wrote them are of secondary importance" ("las motivaciones que llevaron al narrador a escribirlo pasan a un segundo plano," 28).

47. In an essay published in Stockholm in 1999, Portela describes her inability to produce the stereotyped portrait of "Cuban reality" that foreign editors demand.

48. "La literatura, la verdadera, es el lugar imposible donde tratan de expresarse la tragedia y la comedia, el abismo y la ambigüedad entre los que se mueve este siglo; toda la complejidad del destino humano. Son necesarias la lucidez y la locura y no una fuga hacia unos personajes que no son otra cosa que marionetas ideológicas" (103).

49. As I discuss in further detail in chapter 2, the judgment immediately preceding this appeal is as follows: "Zoé Valdés's commercial success comes from her having written what a certain sector of the European public wants to read: a dose of feminism, a dose of sex, a dose of uprootedness, a dash of Lezama Lima. It's a form of literary tourism, in a moment when Cuba is becoming a paradise for cheap sex. The Cuban tragedy has been commercialized" ("El éxito comercial de Zoé Valdés proviene de que ella escribe lo que cierta parte del público europeo desea leer: una dosis de feminismo, una dosis de sexo, una dosis de desarraigo, una pizca de Lezama Lima. Es una forma de turismo literario, en el momento en que Cuba se convierte en un paraíso del sexo barato. Se ha comercializado la tragedia cubana," ibid.).

50. "les frontières entre la vraie et la fausse littérature, entre le roman, la

nouvelle et le simple témoignage, dans un présent chaotique comme tous les présents, ne sont pas toujours délimitées avec précision" ("Méditations," 221).

51. "qui cultivent la banalité et la vulgarité" (ibid.).

52. "ces étranges caprices de la mode et du marché" (ibid.).

53. "aquella que se produce siempre al margen de la moda, los negocios, o las coyunturas políticas" (López Sacha, "Literatura Cuban y fin de siglo," 160).

54. "las trampas de los mercaderes y de los malos políticos" (8).

55. "lo que hasta ahora hemos venido considerando como valores de lo literario" (5).

56. Desiderio Navarro describes how "in the 1970s the image of the intellectual in mass culture (in songs, soap operas, comic shows) became increasingly ridiculous and unsympathetic. The intellectual was presented not only as unpopular but, in general, as someone lacking 'cubanía' (that is, an aristocratic, pompous, and pedantic person out of touch with social reality, the people, and hard work)" (367). Navarro provides this account in his discussion of the artistic intelligentsia's place in the public sphere in revolutionary Cuba, a place he reads as primarily one of exclusion. Successive attempts at critical intervention on the part of intellectuals, he argues, were confronted by a discourse that legitimized administrative measures against them on the grounds that they undermined the tenets of the revolution.

57. "Los medios culturales no pueden servir de marco a la proliferación de falsos intelectuales que pretenden convertir el esnobismo, la extravagancia, el homosexualismo y demás aberraciones sociales, en expresiones del arte revolucionario, alejados de las masas y del espíritu de nuestra Revolución" ("Fragmento de la Declaración," 52).

58. Subsequent assessments of this period have seen Fornet as both euphemistic in his term and generous in his calculation. Desiderio Navarro, for example, calls this a "euphemistic denomination" for "the authoritarian and dogmatic period that, on the one hand, in fact lasted for about fifteen years (approximately from 1968 until 1983) and, on the other, was in fact not gray but black for many intellectual lives and works" (366).

59. "The revolution frees art and literature from the rigid mechanisms of supply and demand that govern bourgeois society. Art and literature cease to be merchandise and possibilities are opened for expression and aesthetic experimentation in their most diverse manifestations, based on ideological rigor and high technical expertise" ("La Revolución libera el arte y la literatura de los férreos mecanismos de la oferta y la demanda imperantes en la sociedad burguesa. El arte y la literatura dejan de ser mercancías y se crean todas las posibilidades para la expresión y experimentación estética en sus más diversas manifestaciones sobre la base del rigor ideológico y la alta calificación técnica," "Fragmento de la Declaración," 59).

60. "Fragmento del Informe" makes reference to "valores culturales" (67), "valores consagrados del arte" (70), and "valores nacionales" (75).

61. "Se estimulaban el sensacionalismo, el entretenimiento fácil y un arte

de evasión. Los recursos eran utilizados para desvirtuar los valores culturales de nuestro pueblo y falsear la historia" (67).

62. "Only socialism recognizes the real value of art and literature, restores their social role, and gives the artist the freedom and stability, both professional and material, that assure him the decent life to which he has a right" ("Sólo el socialismo reconoce al arte y la literatura sus reales valores, reivindica su papel social y da al artista libertad y estabilidad laboral y material que aseguran la vida decorosa a que tiene derecho," "Tesis y resolución," 87).

63. "los nuevos valores de la revolución" (ibid., 96).

64. "debe estimular la aparición de nuevas obras capaces de expresar en su rica y multifacética variedad y con clara concepción humanista, los múltiples aspectos de la vida cubana" (ibid., 99).

65. "el aislamento, el localismo, las normativas, los errores de la política cultural" ("La pelea cubana," 7).

66. "un programa estético e ideológico que postulaba como verdades supremas el reflejo directo, el personaje positivo, la tendencia evidente, el final optimista" (6).

67. In the narratives by Jesús Díaz, Eliseo Alberto, and Leonardo Padura that are the focus of Buckwalter-Arias's article "Reinscribing the Aesthetic," "the most explicit, strident critique, in all three novels, is leveled at the regime" (365); this is much less clearly the case in the short stories I discuss in this chapter.

68. "the revived extrarevolutionary aesthetic is thrust into a narrative environment so profoundly dialogic, politically charged, and historically specific that the generally ahistorical, universalizing discourse bumps up against its own limitations, as it were" (364).

69. Pamela Smorkaloff notes, however, that these incentives were not intended as a means of professionalizing writing, to the exclusion of other social activities, and that authors' income did not derive exclusively from their creative work (*Literatura y edición de libros*, 259–60). Nevertheless, prior to the special period, the broader sphere of literary activities within Cuba often provided full material support for writers. As Arturo Arango puts it, "Even though we Cuban writers had never been able to support ourselves exclusively from our literary labor (unlike the rest of the artistic community, writers were not officially recognized as independent workers until 1994), it had been possible since the mid-80s for a few of us to become freelancers because our income gradually increased from the sales of the rights to our books and especially from articles sold to magazines, as well as scripts for radio, television, or movies—all better remunerated than literature proper" ("To Write in Cuba, Today," 120).

70. Más Zabala does not define "books for tourists" in his article but he clarified in a personal interview in February 2005 that this designation includes bilingual editions, high-quality books of photography, Cuban literary classics, and works on Cuban historical figures, particularly Fidel Castro and

Che Guevara. These are books both sold in hard-currency bookstores in Cuba and exported via international book fairs.

71. Despite these accommodations of international visitors and traders (which also included its relocation from a large exhibition pavilion to the Spanish fort at La Cabaña), the Feria del Libro continued to be a popular event. Moreover, its yields to individual Cuban writers soon disappointed as, except during the very height of the Cuban boom, foreign exhibitors were more intent on selling their wares than on contracting new authors. Indeed, as the costs of exhibiting at the Feria became prohibitive to all but the most commercially successful of foreign publishers, and as these in turn were alienated by restrictions on selling the work of exiled Cuban authors, the international character of the fair diminished (personal interview with Amir Valle Ojeda, formerly of El Instituto Cubano del Libro, February 2005).

72. The socialist-realist imperative was shorter lived and less institutionalized in Cuba than in the USSR, where, for a time, as Katerina Clark explores, formulaic socialist-realist novels were held up as models of popular literature. Nevertheless, Desiderio Navarro's comments on Cuban socialist-realist literature suggest that its thematic aspects are its most important. He refers to "the fallacious Socialist Realist requirement that the totality of a society be reflected not by the whole body of the works of a culture but by the individual literary, artistic, or social-scientific work. The work must be a microcosmos in which nothing can be left out" (364). Seymour Menton, in his early and comprehensive survey of post-1959 Cuban fiction, quotes Juan Marinello on the centrality of theme and the support role of formal clarity in revolutionary literature: "if literature is to be an important part of our revolution . . . it should make an effort to incorporate in its trajectory, regardless of the style or the manner of presentation the authors may prefer, the powerful anxieties, the untiring efforts, and the energetic colors that are woven into today's heroic life of our people. In order to achieve this, the writer should wisely adopt a clarity accessible to everyone" (Menton 113, quoting Juan Marinello, "Sobre nuestra crítica literaria," *Vida Universitaria* 21, no. 219 [May–June 1970]: 48).

73. The items on Arturo Arango's list of "sociological" demands are the following: "that the works should reflect, explicitly, contemporary Cuban reality; and that with this in mind they should feature material difficulties and their absurd or crazy or ridiculous solutions; that they should also include some of the figures who characterize the crisis: the *pícaro,* the *jinetera,* the tourist, the corrupt official; that they should deal with issues that, either supposedly or really, would invite censorship in Cuba (which demonstrates, by the way, the author's personal bravery and his objection to the country's situation, and rules out his being a spokesperson for the regime); that they should not lack humor and eroticism; that there should be some fantasy" ("que las obras reflejen, explícitamente, la realidad cubana contemporánea; por tanto, que aparezcan las dificultades materiales y sus soluciones absurdas o enloquecidas o ridículas; que estén también algunos de los personajes que caracterizan

la crisis: el pícaro, la jinetera, el turista, el funcionario corrupto, que se traten aspectos que, supuesta o realmente, serían motivo de censura en Cuba [lo que demostraría, de paso, la valentía personal del autor, su inconformidad con la situación del país y dejaría fuera de dudas que sea un vocero del régimen]; que no falten el humor y el erotismo; que haya algo de fantasía" ["Escribir en Cuba hoy (1997)," 18]).

74. Víctor Fowler Calzada referred to the frequent use of the phrase "hago social" in a personal interview in July 1999.

75. Arango's view that Cuban fiction was being shaped by outside demand is a revision of his more optimistic insistence, in a 1995 version of the same essay, that this fiction remained unaffected by its market. There he claimed that "Internationally . . . Cuban literature is making an increasingly greater impact. It is doing so, moreover, without changing in any way that would imply concessions, including the abandonment of its characteristic passion for local matters that might be difficult to comprehend outside of Cuba" ("To Write in Cuba, Today," 127) ("Hacia el exterior . . . está ocupando un espacio cada vez mayor y, al menos hasta el presente, sin que el posible cambio de interlocutor implique concesiones de alguna índole, e incluso sin que cierta zona de la literatura abandone un apego desmedido por asuntos de carácter local, de difícil comprensión fuera de Cuba" ["Escribir en Cuba hoy (1995)," 93–94]).

76. ";es verdaderamente literario o tiene una base política o, incluso, sociológica? ¿Se quiere saber cómo se escribe en Cuba o cómo se vive en Cuba? ¿Qué escriben los jóvenes cubanos o cómo piensan?" ("Escribir en Cuba hoy [1997]," 17).

77. "hay un abismo que sólo puede entenderse desde la literatura, pero jamás si se mira con curiosidad sociológica" (ibid., 18).

78. "la realidad cotidiana del país" (ibid., 19).

79. From the mid-1970s on, Arango argues, Cuban fiction was in obsessive dialogue with "immediate reality" (ibid.). Around 1984 he notices a turn away from this obsession toward a more abstract, absurd practice; but the 1990s demands of international publishers threatened to turn the tide again. Reflecting on this, Arango maintains that "fiction . . . should aspire to do much more than denounce: more than *bear witness*" ("la ficción . . . debe proponerse mucho más que denunciar: más que *dar testimonio*," 22).

80. The pseudonymous Julián B. Sorel (exiled Cuban journalist Miguel Sales) traces a form of "revolutionary nationalism" from the nineteenth-century independence hero José Martí to Fidel Castro's post-Soviet discourse, a genealogy that Rafael Rojas accepts in *Isla sin fin*.

81. "As new political and economic conditions arose, this official discourse on political nationalism increasingly coexisted with another one that strategically emphasized culture rather than ideology as the basis for community" ("Radio Taíno," 111). Hernández-Reguant traces the beginning of this strategic cultural nationalism to the 1978 dialogues between Cubans and exiles, during which Castro invoked a shared heritage despite political differences (119–31).

82. Hernández-Reguant cites Radio Rebelde's 1999 propaganda efforts that "unlike typical propaganda messages . . . did not emphasize the need for political action, they merely stated the uncontestable 'facts' of being Cuban—which resulted from culture, historical legacy, and collective rights" (ibid.). The appropriation of Manolín el Médico de la Salsa's song "Somos lo que hay" by the Union of Young Communists (UJC) is a further example of such state-directed displays of national pride (ibid., 381–91).

83. Hernández-Reguant attributes the failure of the cultural-nationalist project among young people to the fact that, like earlier discourse on political community, it was "deployed as [an] ideological argument against foreign cultural flows" (ibid., 27) and identified its constituency as "the masses" rather than as individuals. Writers and other cultural producers' suspicion toward the project has similar grounds, I believe.

84. Rojas states that from the end of the 1980s, "The values, symbols, ideas, practices, and institutions of revolutionary nationalism experience a fatal exhaustion . . . and the essay has been, since the founding texts of Montaigne and Bacon, the auspicious genre for conscience searching, for the reflective construction that bears witness to the transition from one image of the times to another. For this reason, one of the most eloquent testimonies of the island's cultural change is that articulated by essayists" ("Los valores, los símbolos, las ideas, las prácticas y las instituciones del nacionalismo revolucionario experimentan un agotamiento fatal . . . Y el ensayo ha sido, desde los textos fundadores de Montaigne y Bacon, ese género propicio para el examen de consciencia, esa construcción reflexiva que de fe del tránsito entre una y otra imagen del tiempo. Por eso uno de los testimonios más elocuentes del cambio cultural de la isla es el que articulan los ensayistas" [*Isla sin fin*, 217]).

85. Fowler's essay first addresses the duo sexuality/money, and then a further pairing of the body and writing. His closing reading of Vega Serova's "Billetes falsos" draws together these two pairs to both demonstrate "the contraction of the national" ("[la] contracción de lo nacional" [*Historias del cuerpo*, 318]) and "enjoy the ways in which an entire generation of women writers reclaims the right to assume, as women, their representation on the literary scene" ("gozar los modos en los que toda una promoción de escritoras reivindica el derecho a asumir ellas, como mujeres, su representación en el escenario de la literatura"). The overarching idea of this essay, that reads fifteen stories on the sexuality/money or body/writing pair, is stated as follows: "the founding idea of this text is that the dominated one always preserves an ungraspable essence, a zone resistant to any kind of domestication" ("La idea de base de este texto es que el dominado conserva siempre una esencia inapresable, una zona renuente a cualquier domesticación," 346). The final chapter of Jorge Fornet's *Los nuevos paradigmas* also traces the circulation, or itinerary, of money through Cuban literature, beginning with the autobiography of the slave Juan Francisco Manzano. Subsequent coins and banknotes, he shows, appear at moments of particular intensity in Cuban history (125–38).

86. "por más que el dinero trata de transformar en objetos a los cuerpos, la clave de los intercambios está en manos de quien mantiene control de la representación y, en consecuencia, hace de la identidad un acto performativo de la libertad interior" (345).

87. "Si en Cuba hubiera cosas y se acaban los apagones sería un país mil veces mejor que este Tulús, lleno de gente egoísta y mala, que lo miran a uno por lo que tiene y no por lo que vale" (258).

88. "¡Qué tonta fui al pensar que tenía la vida resuelta, que había encontrado estabilidad y que con el dinero terminarían mis angustias!" (68).

89. "mujer increíblemente gorda, fea, con el pelo teñido de rubio" (6).

90. Mary Berg translates "Erre con erre" as "Peter Piper Picked a Peck" because it comes from the tongue twister "Erre con erre cigarro, erre con erre barril."

91. "en mis facciones está el peligro, el delicado riesgo del robo o la enfermedad venérea, pero también la dulzura de la caña, la sincera amistad, el buen salvaje de Rousseau" (91).

92. "Yo te absuelvo y te dejo suficiente culpa para que regreses pronto" (94).

4. MARKETS IN THE MARGINS

1. In a personal interview in July 2004, Gutiérrez assured me that he was not consulted about the Polish cover illustration and considered it disrespectful.

2. By mid-2007, *Trilogía sucia de la Habana* had been published in eighteen countries, *El Rey de la Habana* in six, *Animal tropical* in thirteen, *El insaciable hombre araña* in six, and *Carne de perro*, the last in the cycle, in three. Gutiérrez had also published a "prequel" to these five books, *El nido de la serpiente: Memorias del hijo del heladero* (The serpent's nest: Memories of the ice-cream seller's son), in Spanish, Brazilian, Italian, and French editions.

3. Prior to the publication in Spain of *Trilogía sucia de la Habana*, Gutiérrez's Cuban publications included two books of poetry, *Poesía* (Poetry) and *La realidad rugiendo* (Reality roaring), published in small print runs in Pinar del Río province; a book on space travel, *Vivir en el espacio: Del sueño a la realidad* (Living in space: From dream to reality); and a collection of short stories in a series honoring the writer Onelio Jorge Cardoso. Gutiérrez elaborates on his pre-*Trilogy* career as a writer in his interview with Marilyn Bobes (36–37).

4. In a footnote to her article on *El Rey de la Habana*, Ena Lucía Portela expresses bemusement at why that novel remains unpublished in Cuba while there is a Letras Cubanas edition of *Animal tropical*: "I would love to prepare a Cuban edition of *El Rey* . . . I've been trying for some time. I am told that there is no money and that, after all, the book in question is 'absolutely filthy' and unrevolutionary, although it barely mentions politics. Curiously, Letras Cubanas has just published Pedro Juan's second novel, *Animal tropical*, which shares the 'defects' of *El Rey* . . . without sharing its virtues. Does anyone understand anything?" ("Me encantaría preparar la edición cubana de *El*

Rey . . . llevo tiempo en eso. Me dicen que no hay dinero y que, a fin de cuentas, el librito en cuestión es 'tremenda cochiná' y poco revolucionario, aunque apenas hable de política. Curiosamente, Letras Cubanas acaba de publicar la segunda novela de Pedro Juan, *Animal tropical,* que comparte los 'defectos' de *El Rey* . . . sin compartir las virtudes. ¿Alguien entiende algo?" 72). I would suggest, as Víctor Fowler Calzada does to some extent ("Innovación," 4), that the setting of *Animal tropical,* partly in Sweden and partly in Centro Havana, on the one hand minimizes its portrayal of special period Cuba and, on the other, establishes an ultimately favorable comparison of life in Cuba versus life abroad. With regard to *Melancolía de los leones* (2000), the first of Gutiérrez's books to be published in Cuba in the wake of *Trilogía*'s success elsewhere, Marilyn Bobes offers an interpretation of Cuban critics' interest in its short stories. That Ediciones Unión should have chosen to publish *Melancolía,* she suggests, "showed that Pedro Juan can also produce literature for the fine tastes of those who prefer a more lyrical and gentle tone" ("demostró que Pedro Juan también puede hacer literatura para los gustos exquisitos de quienes prefieren un tono más lírico y reposado," 36).

5. "en verdad una novela de tesis" ("Literatura cubana y fin de siglo," 159). López Sacha writes of *Trilogía sucia de la Habana* that "more than a novel, it is a handful of chronicles, stories, and vignettes about the Havana underworld during the special period. In this book the influence of Miller and Bukowski is too visible, the sketches are very clumsy, and you can see the narrator's efforts to give continuity to material that, in reality, is neither ductile nor elaborated" ("más que una novela, es un puñado de crónicas, relatos y viñetas del bajomundo habanero durante el Período especial. En este libro es demasiado visible la influencia de Miller y Bukowski, los trazos son muy burdos y se nota el esfuerzo del narrador por dar continuidad a un material poco dúctil, en realidad, poco elaborado," ibid.). Of the second book in the cycle he writes: "In contrast, in *El Rey de la Habana,* published a year later, we truly have a novel with a thesis constructed from the brutal and anodyne life of a marginal character. Beyond the horror that he relates, and that at times appears excessive, there is here a willful style and an effect that emerges from the development of the plot itself, from the almost microscopic and naturalist dissection of a character situated in nothingness" ("En cambio, en *El Rey de la Habana,* publicada un año después, hay en verdad una novela de tesis construida con la vida brutal y anodina de un personaje marginal. Más allá del horror que relata, y que por momentos resulta excesivo, hay aquí una voluntad de estilo y un resultado que emerge del propio desarrollo de la trama, de la disección casi microscópica y naturalista de un personaje situado en el vacío," ibid.). Similar responses are echoed in the reception of Gutiérrez's work after his first public reading in Havana of *Animal tropical.* The reading was hosted by the Centro Cultural de España, which, before its closure in early 2002, was an important alternative to Cuban institutions as a forum for cultural events. *Letras en Cuba* (Letters in Cuba), a weekly e-mail bulletin distributed principally outside Cuba by the

writer and critic Amir Valle throughout 2000, reported that "those attending the reading commented on the low level of drama and of dialogue in this last novel, even though the chosen topic is attractive and lends itself to human tensions" ("los asistentes a la lectura comentaron el bajo nivel dramático y de realización de diálogos en esta última novela, aún cuando el tema escogido es atractivo y de gran tensión humana" [*Letras en Cuba* 17, April 12, 2000]).

6. "¡Ni que yo estuviera loca! . . . [tiene] un millón de negros fajaos, y policías, y viejas locas y viejos cochinos, y cucarachas y ratones y las fosas botando mierda" (*Animal tropical,* 50).

7. "[L]os turistas no entran en las profundidades del infierno. Prefieren tomar las fotos desde el Malecón. Es una gran aventura observar el terremoto desde la periferia y evitar el epicentro" (*El insaciable hombre arena,* 104).

8. "La literatura cubana produce, así, otro discurso turístico: aquel que entrelaza el venero exótico de la ciudad con el peligro, la miseria y la violencia" (*Tumbas sin sosiego,* 373).

9. "maricones, ligues, pajeros, las muchachitas rayadoras de pajas" (*El Rey,* 181).

10. Carlos Venegas Fornias describes the *solar* as "a multi-family residential building with one main entrance and rooms giving onto a central courtyard or a main hallway, with common areas for cooking, bathing and washing clothes" and indicates that *solar* is the term used in Havana for what was elsewhere more commonly known as *ciudadela* (22). Scarpacci, Segre, and Coyula distinguish between the terms for the *solar* on the basis of size: "Of the many variables that go into classifying the collective housing for the poor in Cuba, the number of rooms per structure is perhaps the least controversial. A *casa de vecindad* consists of homes or buildings with twelve rooms; the *solar* held about twenty to thirty rooms, and *ciudadelas* more than one hundred" (76n3). Kosta Mathey is more specific about the architectural origins of the *solar*: "Ciudadelas (also: *solares, casas de vecindad*) are a modified version of the former servants' quarters in the rear part of colonial mansions" (248).

11. "la dolorosa tragedia del caserón sombrío, donde se debaten hombres y mujeres acorralados por la miseria, la humedad y la pestilencia, en la penumbra de sus estrechos albergues" (Chailloux Cardona 19). More recently, Pedro Marqués de Armas has explored the association of the *solar* with crime and lack of hygiene, in sociological and literary texts ("Ficción y realidad del solar habanero").

12. "hace cuarenta años o más que no lo reparan, ni siquiera lo pintan. Está demasiado arruinado. Hay cartones y tablas en el lugar donde irían los vidrios de las ventanas" (*Animal tropical,* 267).

13. "Cuando caían aguaceros fuertes todo el mundo temblaba porque aquel edificio era tan antiguo que las paredes estaban construidos con ladrillos, arena y cal. Sin cemento" (*Trilogía,* 49).

14. "Desde aquí arriba se ve toda la ciudad a oscuras . . . Semeja una ciudad bombardeada y deshabitada. Se cae a pedazos, pero es hermosa esta cabrona ciudad donde he amado y he odiado tanto" (ibid., 206).

15. "Más que un simple telón de fondo, este paisaje derruido es expresión de un modo de vida y de una opción existencial" ("¿Cómo vivir las ruinas habaneras de los años noventa?" 82).

16. "una ética del absurdo" (Casamayor 88).

17. "el protagonista persigue otra cosa: paz y reflexión" (19).

18. "un laberinto construido con tablas podridas y pedazos de ladrillos" (*Trilogía*, 293); "la gente se asfixia de calor entre la mierda y el hambre" (ibid.).

19. "[El solar] es como un monstruo enorme y torpe, que se revuelca, escupe fuego y provoca terremotos durante seis días y al séptimo descansa y recupera energía" (ibid., 160).

20. "En Centro Habana . . . te acostumbras a vivir con los colmillos y las garras afiladas, listo para destrozar al primero que te mire mal" (109). In the Spanish texts the references to "la fauna" are on page 102 of *Trilogía* and 257 of *Animal tropical*. In the latter instance, Peter Lownds translates "fauna" as "menagerie."

21. "Se cagan a escondidas en la escalera. Mean en todos los rincones" (*Trilogía*, 133).

22. The page references for these episodes in the Spanish text are 295–303, 159–61, and 324–31 respectively.

23. It is precisely this play-off between animal and cerebral, or nature and culture, that Guillermina de Ferrari addresses in "Aesthetics under Siege: Dirty Realism and Pedro Juan Gutiérrez's *Trilogía sucia de la Habana*." De Ferrari proposes that "The political value of *Trilogía sucia de la Habana* resides in its abolition of the distinctions between nature and culture" (40) and that this novel unveils "a human truth that transcends the local circumstances of contemporary Cuba" (39). She concludes that postmodernist readings are likely to be more appreciative of this aim than "ethnographic" ones that focus narrowly on *Trilogía* as a document of life in special period Havana. Although I agree that to privilege the local in Gutiérrez's work is to eclipse other aspects of it, it is exactly the "ethnographic" reader, the markets from which this reader consumes, and the effects of these on Cuban cultural production more broadly that are my concerns here.

24. The title of "Salíamos de las jaulas" is rendered in Natasha Wimmer's translation as "Breaking Out" (145).

25. "Loca a la pinga" (*Trilogía*, 74 and 187).

26. "Vivir en el cuartucho de Olga era como estar metido dentro de una película pornográfica" (ibid., 58).

27. "El sexo es un intercambio de líquidos, de fluidos, saliva, aliento y olores fuertes, orina, semen, mierda, sudor, microbios, bacterias. O no es" (ibid., 11).

28. "nos olfateamos" (ibid., 54).

29. "A ninguno le molestaba la suciedad del otro. Ella tenía un chocho un poco agrio y el culo apestoso a mierda. Él tenía una nata blanca y fétida entre la cabeza del rabo y el pellejo que la rodeaba. Ambos olían a grajo en las axilas, a ratas muertas en los pies, y sudaban. Todo eso los excitaba" (55).

30. "pinchar un poco y obligar a otros a oler la mierda" (85).

31. "Ese es mi oficio: revolcador de mierda" (*Trilogía,* 104); "un artista convierte esa mierda en materia prima. Material de construcción" (*Animal tropical,* 138).

32. "una fauna de bichos raros para ver en un parque zoológico, al otro lado de las rejas" ("Con hambre y sin dinero," 71); "cubanos de la calle, nada extraordinarios en ningún sentido" (70).

33. "una configuración biológica y territorial fundamental que se transforma en un modo de ser históricamente determinado (el período especial)" (365).

34. "la basura y los escombros" (*Animal tropical,* 38).

35. Introducing his coedited collection of essays *Out There: Marginalization and Contemporary Cultures,* Russell Ferguson acknowledges the problematic relativity of the marginal position, or the difficulty of answering the question "marginal to what?" Nevertheless, he has recourse to Audre Lourde's term "the mythical norm," defined as "white, thin, male, young, heterosexual, Christian and financially secure" (Ferguson et al. 9). As the remainder of his introduction makes clear, the primary context for marginality thus defined is the United States, and, although some features of "the mythical norm" might pertain to the Cuban margins, they do not all do so easily.

36. "ajenos a toda práctica asocial que no sea la tendencia a la autodestrucción" ("Para días de menos entusiasmo," 35).

37. "grupos casi siempre de estudiantes, receptores y practicantes de modelos culturales extranjeros (la cultura del rock), poseedores de limpios historiales delictivos y rebeldes, en lo primordial, ante sus padres" ("Innovación," 3).

38. "una limpieza semántica que era, a la vez, mentira social y purga étnica" (ibid.).

39. "la marginalidad, por increíble que parezca, se vuelve centro o, cuando menos, obligada referencia" ("Con hambre y sin dinero," 63).

40. These are the terms of Jesús Díaz, Francisco López Sacha, Abilio Estévez, and Edel Morales for whom, as I discuss at length in chapter 3, the thematic repertoire that the special period and its market's demands brought to fiction represented a threat to a fundamentally aesthetic notion of literary value, and pitted "false" against "true" literature.

41. "no dominan el tema, idealizan o condenan, reproducen estereotipos, a menudo no saben una papa de lo que están hablando" ("Con hambre y sin dinero," 65).

42. "rigurosamente fiel a los detalles" (ibid.).

43. "el fenómeno de marginalidad es cultural y política" ("¿Entendemos las marginalidad?" 73).

44. "una marginalidad muy vinculada el racismo, a la discriminación y al prejuicio racial" (ibid., 79). Alejandro de la Fuente's chapter on conceptions of race during the special period discusses several Cuban studies that address the revolution's success, or lack thereof, in overcoming discrimination (322–29).

During this period, Cuba's research institutions, notably the Fundación Fernando Ortiz and the UNEAC, directed attention to this question, resulting in roundtable discussions and publications such as *La Gaceta de Cuba*'s special issue on race in February 2005. Outside Cuba this period also saw a renewed interest in, and abundant publications on, race relations in Cuba.

45. Fowler comments on the *novísimos'* turn away from the working classes toward more cerebral figures. He writes, "I hope that it will be easy to see the inversion strategy: the intellectual is opposed to the worker, the ascension of thought (note the abundance of metatextual reflection) to the mythification of action, the absence of a secure future to its presence" ("Espero que con facilidad se note la estrategia de inversión especular: a lo obrero se opone lo intelectual, a la mitificación de la acción la ascensión del pensamiento [atiéndase a la abundancia de reflexión metatextual], a la seguridad del futuro la ausencia de él" ["Para días de menos entusiasmo," 35]). In relation to this inversion, Gutiérrez's recuperation of socioeconomic marginality represents something of a return to the revolution's aims in the early 1960s, although, crucially, without the "secure future" ("seguridad del futuro") that underpinned the earlier period. Portela explains her term as follows: "an 'enlightened leftist' would be someone who in some way is interested in the most humble . . . but without idealizing them, without attributing to them particular virtues nor a revolutionary vocation nor a political culture nor class consciousness nor anything of the sort" ("un 'izquierdista lúcido' vendría siendo alguien que de algún modo se interesa por los más humildes . . . pero sin idealizarlos, sin atribuirles particulares virtudes ni vocación revolucionaria ni cultura política ni conciencia de clase ni nada"["Con hambre y sin dinero," 77]).

46. "una novela veraz, incisiva, certera" (ibid., 67).

47. "[el] valor literario, muy en función del valor commercial, de todos estos libros está determinado . . . por el vínculo más o menos evidente que se establezca entre ellas y la vida real en la Cuba de ahora mismo, por la noción de 'autenticidad'" (ibid., 65).

48. "por su verismo, su ritmo y colorido tan auténticos, su fidelidad a los detalles de la jerga habanera" (ibid., 72).

49. "no aportaría ninguna garantía de autenticidad" (ibid., 67).

50. In *Foundational Fictions,* Sommer reads nineteenth-century Latin American novels as nation-building projects, romances of "star-crossed lovers who represent particular regions, races, parties, economic interests and the like" and whose "passion for conjugal and sexual union spills over to a sentimental readership in a move that hopes to win partisan minds along with hearts" (5). *Cecilia Valdés* is a more hesitant example of this genre than is Gertrudis Gómez de Avellaneda's *Sab,* but it nevertheless implies a harmony that the racial hierarchies of slavery prove impossible (124–31).

51. Delgado's lyrics begin: "Walking down 23rd Street, relaxing / You think it's Madrid, but it's Vedado" and continue: "If you want to know what Havana is like / walk through Havana, Centro Havana, the true Havana"

("Andar por Veintitrés, muy relajado / Te piensas que es Madrid, y es el Vedado . . . Si quieres conocer cómo es La Habana / andar La Habana, Centro Habana, la verdadera Habana").

52. Odette Casamayor notes that, in *Dirty Havana Trilogy*, it is precisely as Pedro Juan rejects his respectable life as a journalist, embracing instead misery and abjection, that he takes black women as sexual partners—thus associating these women firmly with his social decline: "Everything is described as though making love to these women didn't just represent an act very different from making love to white Cuban women, but as though it were also a sign of the character's social decline" ("Todo es descrito como si hacer el amor con estas mujeres no solamente representase un acto muy diferente a hacerlo con cubanas blancas, sino que constituye además un signo de la decadencia social del personaje" ["Negros, marginalidad y ética," 67]).

53. "porque son mentirosos, vagos, inútiles, cochinos, tienen la pinga muy larga y dan inflamación pélvica" (*Animal tropical*, 283).

54. Pedro Juan states: "I'm new in the building, and people don't trust me. I don't trust them either" (*Tropical Animal*, 166) ("Yo soy nuevo en el solar. Y la gente no me tiene confianza. Ni yo le tengo confianza a la gente" [*Animal tropical*, 155]).

55. "Esta novela es una obra de ficción. Cualquier parecido con circunstancias o personas reales es una casualidad."

56. "ese Pedro Juan es excesivamente autobiográfico, tanto que no he vuelto a leerlo jamás porque me resulta muy doloroso" ("Animal literario," 37).

57. "I realize that my life had been marked by a series of circumstances and that, in an unconscious way, all this started to appear in *Trilogía sucia de la Habana*. For the first time I put myself inside a character to whom I deliberately gave my name. And he is even the same age as me. I changed very little in him. The book was almost an act of revenge against myself" ("Me doy cuenta de que mi vida estuvo marcada por una serie de circunstancias y que, de manera inconsciente, todo eso empezó a aparecer en *Trilogía sucia de la Habana*. Por primera vez me meto dentro de un personaje al que, con toda idea, le puse mi nombre. Y hasta tiene mi edad. Cambié en él lo mínimo. El libro fue casi un acto de venganza contra mi mismo" [ibid.]).

58. "autobiográfico y descarnado de forma desafiante." This claim to autobiography is made in the jacket copy of Anagrama's first edition of *Carne de perro*.

59. By mid-2007, *El Rey de la Habana* had been published in Spain, Germany, Brazil, France, Italy, and Portugal. Commenting on English-language publishers' lack of interest in the book, Gutiérrez speculated, in a personal interview in January 2003, that its ending (in which Rey murders Magda and is then himself devoured by rats) is too violent. The explanation I find more plausible is that this novel's third-person narration is less appealing than the first-person narration of *Dirty Havana Trilogy* and *Tropical Animal*, each of which has been published in both the United Kingdom and the United States.

60. "Escribir en primera persona es como desnudarse en público" (*Animal tropical,* 56).

61. "Me gusta masturbar oliéndome las axilas. El olor a sudor me excita" (*Trilogía,* 133).

62. "pinchar un poco y obligar a otros a oler la mierda" (ibid., 85).

63. This understanding of the book industry draws in part from Pierre Bourdieu's theorization of the field of literary production as both a system whose institutions include "academies, journals, magazines, galleries, publishers etc." (32) and as a site of position takings and conflicts (29–37).

64. The "paratext," in Genette's formulation, has two principal components; the "peritext," or all markings on a book other than the body of the text (including title, preface, jacket copy, etc.), and the "epitext," or "those messages that, at least originally, are located outside the book, generally with the help of the media (interviews, conversations) or under cover of private communications (letters, diaries, and others)" (5).

65. "nos revelan a un escritor de pura raza, a un implacable cronista de un país y unos tiempos contradictorios, terribles, fascinantes."

66. "Una voz desgarrada, cruel, auténtica."

67. To a question from Álvaro Matús of the Chilean magazine *¿Qué pasa?,* for example, Gutiérrez answers: "forgive me, but I don't like to answer political questions. I turn my back on politics. I'm not with the Indians or the cowboys. I'm the lone ranger" ("tú me perdonas, pero a mí no me gusta responder a preguntas políticas. Le doy la espalda a la política. No estoy ni con los indios ni con los cowboys. Soy el llanero solitario" (2). And yet the absence of explicit references to Fidel Castro clearly does not preclude an implicit criticism in the books' scenes of despair, and the dissonance between the abject misery of the *solar* dwellers and the social aspirations of the revolution is glaringly obvious.

68. "el mexicano" (*Trilogía,* 71), "la alemana" (*Trilogía,* 154–58), "arquitectos alemanes, españoles, italianos, franceses" (*Animal tropical,* 277).

69. "un turista que exhibía su oro en un país donde la gente pasa hambre" (ibid., 209).

70. "evidentemente no entendía ni cojones" (*El Rey,* 170).

71. In the Spanish text, this character appears on pages 157–58.

72. *Animal tropical,* 37–38.

73. *El insaciable hombre arena,* 104.

74. A brief roster of special period voyeurs might include Ildelisa, whose surreptitious peeping through an eye-shaped hole in her front door opens Miguel Mejides's novel *Perversiones en el Prado* (Perversions on Prado Street); Vido, the adolescent voyeur in Abilio Estévez's *Thine Is the Kingdom*; and Ena Lucía Portela's *El pájaro: Pincel y tinta china* (The bird: Brush and Chinese ink), in which watching is a basis for sadomasochism. Andrés Jorge, writing in Mexico, titles his 2001 novel *Voyeurs,* while the act of watching is further explored in a number of short stories by Ena Lucía Portela, Aida Bahr, Francisco García González, and others (Loss and Whitfield, Introduction to *New Short Fiction from Cuba*).

75. *Trilogía*, 178.

76. Ibid., 116.

77. *Animal Tropical*, 69.

78. Doris Sommer takes Barthes to task on precisely this point. In framing the relationship between text and reader as one of mutual desire, and insisting that the text "must prove to me *that it desires me*" (Barthes 27), he fails "to notice and name the ways a text's desire for the reader is punctuated by apparent deaths of intimacy" (*Proceed with Caution*, 12). Barthes fails, that is, to recognize the strategies writers deploy to exclude, rather than embrace, their reader.

79. "loca a los pajeros, a vacilarlos con sus caras frescas a veces y asustados en otras ocasiones, escurridizos, alejados, siempre moviéndosela" (*El Rey*, 60).

80. *Animal tropical*, 69, 22.

81. Ibid., 286–87.

82. Knowing that he and his girlfriend are being watched by an elderly couple, Pedro Juan states, "A todos nos gusta hacer de voyeur. Era evidente que los viejos se divertían. Es muy bueno hacer el bien a los demás" (*Animal tropical*, 206). Peter Lownds omits the last sentence, "it's very good to do something worthwhile for others," from his English translation: "We all enjoy playing the voyeur. Evidently the old folks were having fun" (*Tropical Animal*, 212).

83. "Somos lo que se vende como pan caliente."

5. THE RUINED CITY

1. "resurgir desde el subsuelo" (118).

2. "Sufrida Habana que había resistido el ataque de sus mismos hijos, ahora convertida en un Beirut caribeño, sus ruinas desinfladas en el grito de la noche . . ." (118).

3. In Spanish, Ponte's story is titled "Un arte de hacer ruinas," literally, "an art of making ruins." The title is translated by Cola Franzen and referred to in this chapter as "A Knack for Making Ruins."

4. "días de decadencia arquitectónica evidente" (8).

5. Specifically, Casamayor proposes that the characters in Estévez's *Los palacios distantes* (The distant palaces) find solace in secrecy, in abandoned spaces of the ruined city, while Gutiérrez's narrator casts the dilapidation around him as a projection of his own existential ruin and survives each moment by adopting an ethics of absurdity and resignation. In *Cien botellas en una pared* (One hundred bottles on a wall), Portela's protagonists retreat inward from the crumbling mansions of Vedado as they do from their social context more broadly, with a de-ideologized inertia that Casamayor reads as characteristic of a younger generation of Cubans (96).

6. In keeping with her broader discussion of the relationship between ruins and the British Empire, Janowitz describes urban decay in the London of late-twentieth-century stage and film directors as "physical ruin associated

with both poverty and the racism inextricable from and remaining as a legacy of British imperialism" (2).

7. "el desplome de la construcción simbólica que apuntalaba la fantasía imperial de un pequeño país caribeño" (*Tumbas sin sosiego,* 374).

8. "el sonido de una orquesta cubana de los años sesenta que nunca había existido" ("Carta de la Habana: La maqueta de la ciudad," 255).

9. "la de haber sido bombardeada, la de una ciudad que espera el más leve aguacero, la más ligera ráfaga para deshacerse en montón de piedras" (21).

10. "un posible reagrupamiento de fuerzas por parte del ejército conocido antaño como *Plástica Joven*" (5).

11. "¿Qué puede más para nosotros, la memoria del pasado o la incertidumbre del presente?" (1:1, 2).

12. "postguerra por la similitud a nivel físico de la ciudad, por el interior de la gente, por lo social del arte" (1).

13. "aquí no ha existido una guerra pero es una ciudad que parece haber pasado una guerra" (Interview with Anna Solana and Mercedes Serna, 131).

14. "tantos últimos hombres sobre la tierra" (*La fiesta vigilada,* 166).

15. "una de las partes en pugna" (165).

16. "lo demasiado irreal de una hilera perfecta de fachadas" (36).

17. "[V]eo todas estos edificios a punto del derrumbe, la ausencia de color en todas las fachadas hasta el mar, y comprendo la belleza de esta ciudad como ustedes no pueden tener idea" (37).

18. "así logra revisitar aquella temporada en que, gracias al emplazamiento de armas soviéticas en territorio cubano la isla pudo darse aires de grandísima potencia" ("Carta de la Habana," 255).

19. "donde todo se conserva como en la memoria" (73).

20. "si no vas a salir, entonces entra" (66).

21. "Las calles de Beirut, devastadas por la guerra, podían perfectamente pertenecer a esa misma ciudad" (23); "imágenes de calles vacías, de edificios apuntalados o convertidos en escombros" (22).

22. "dicen que somos los sobrevivientes" (11).

23. "la mort, encore la mort, en prime-time" (24).

24. "sufrida Habana que había resistido el ataque de sus mismos hijos" (*Perversiones,* 118).

25. "le pareció ver una ciudad esperanzada en un nuevo calendario para resurgir desde el subsuelo" (ibid.).

26. "algo va a renacer" (11).

27. "las ruinas eran las únicas que le despertaban un sentido del renacer, de futuridad posible" (Interview with Teresa Basile, 35).

28. "la posibilidad constructiva real que tienen los edificios" (8).

29. "la suerte de unas calles" (181).

Works Cited

Ackerman, Holly, and Juan M. Clark. *The Cuban Balseros: Voyage of Uncertainty*. Miami: Policy Center of the Cuban American National Council, 1995.

Aguiar, Raúl, and Yoss. "El tema prohibido (o casi): El Rock, su reflejo en la narrativa cubana." *Rockstalgia* 1 (February 2005): 1–4.

Alberto, Eliseo. *Caracol Beach*. Madrid: Alfaguara, 1998.

Alonso Estenoz, Alfredo. "Joven narrativa cubana: El deseo de perdurar." *La revista del libro cubano* 1:4 (1997): 4–7.

Álvarez, José B. *Contestatory Short Story of the Cuban Revolution*. Lanham, Md.: University Press of America, 2002.

Álvarez-Borland, Isabel. *Cuban-American Literature of Exile: From Person to Persona*. Charlottesville: University of Virginia Press, 1998.

Álvarez-Tabío Albo, Emma. *La invención de la Habana*. Barcelona: Casiopea, 2000.

Appadurai, Arjun. *Modernity at Large*. Minneapolis: University of Minnesota Press, 1996.

Arandia Covarrubia, Gisela. "Concha Mocoyu: Center for Yoruba Studies in the Solar 'La California,' Havana." http://www.afrocubaweb.com/mocoyu.htm (accessed May 30, 2005).

Arango, Arturo. *El libro de la realidad*. Barcelona: Tusquets, 2001; Havana: Letras Cubanas, 2002.

―――. "Escribir en Cuba hoy (1995)." In *Segundas reincidencias (Escribir en Cuba ayer),* 80–94. Santa Clara, Cuba: Editorial Capiro, 2002. Trans. Nancy Westrate. "To Write in Cuba, Today." In "Bridging Enigma: Cubans on Cuba," ed. Ambrosio Fornet, special issue, *South Atlantic Quarterly* 96:1 (winter 1997): 117–27.

―――. "Escribir en Cuba hoy (1997)." In *Segundas reincidencias (Escribir en Cuba ayer),* 9–25. Santa Clara, Cuba: Editorial Capiro, 2002.

―――. "Los violentos y los exquisitos." *Letras Cubanas* (July–September 1988): 9–13.

―――. "Paisajes después de la lectura." *La gaceta de Cuba* (May–June 1995): 50–52.

Araújo, Nara. "El espacio otro en la escritura de las (novísimas) narradoras cubanas." *Temas* 16–17 (October 1998–June 1999): 212–17.

Arenas, Reinaldo. *Antes que anochezca* (1992). Trans. Dolores M. Koch. *Before Night Falls.* New York: Viking, 1993.

―――. *Celestino antes del alba.* Havana: Ediciones Unión, 1967. Trans. Andrew Hurley. *Singing from the Well.* New York: Viking, 1987.

―――. *El color del verano.* Barcelona: Tusquets, 1999.

Ávila González, Manuel (Manín). "Narrativa cubana de los noventa. ¿Pathos?, ¿Marketing?" *El caimán barbudo* 32:295 (1999): 28–29.

Baker, Christopher P. *Mi moto Fidel: Motorcycling through Castro's Cuba.* Washington, D.C.: National Geographic Society, 2002.

Barbería, Lorena. "Remittances to Cuba: An Evaluation of Cuban and U.S. Government Policy Measures." In *The Cuban Economy at the Start of the Twenty-first Century,* ed. Jorge I. Domínguez, Omar Everleny Pérez Villanueva, and Lorena Barbería, 353–412. Cambridge: Harvard University and David Rockefeller Center for Latin American Studies, 2004.

Barnet, Miguel. *Biografía de un cimarrón.* Havana: Instituto de Etnología y Folklore, 1966. Trans. Jocasta Innes. *Autobiography of a Runaway Slave.* New York: World, 1969.

―――. "Miosvatis." In *Anuario 1994/Narrativa,* 79–85. Havana: Ediciones Unión, 1994.

Barral, Carlos. *Los años sin excusa.* Madrid: Alianza, 1982.

Barthes, Roland. *The Pleasure of the Text.* Trans. Richard Miller. New York: Noonday Press, 1975.

Basile, Teresa. "Incursiones en el imaginario nacional cubano: Las relecturas del orden revolucionario en los textos de Antonio José Ponte." Paper delivered at the Latin American Studies Association Congress. San Juan, Puerto Rico, March 17, 2006.

Behar, Ruth, ed. *Bridges to Cuba/Puentes a Cuba.* Ann Arbor: University of Michigan Press, 1995.

Bejel, Emilo. *Gay Cuban Nation.* Chicago: University of Chicago Press, 2001.

Benjamin, Walter. *The Origin of German Tragic Drama.* Trans. John Osborne. London and New York: Verso, 1988.

Berdahl, Daphne. "'(N)Ostalgie' for the Present: Memory, Longing and East German Things." *Ethnos* 64:2 (1999): 192–211.

Beverley, John. "The Margin at the Center: On *Testimonio*" (1989). In *The Real Thing: Testimonial Discourse and Latin America,* ed. Georg Gugelberger, 23–41. Durham, N.C.: Duke University Press, 1996.

Birkenmaier, Anke. "El realismo sucio en América Latina: Reflexiones a partir de Pedro Juan Gutiérrez." *Miradas* 6 (2004). http://www.miradas.eictv.co.cu.

———. "Más allá del realismo sucio: *El Rey de la Habana* de Pedro Juan Gutiérrez." *Cuban Studies* 32 (2001): 37–54.

Bobes, Marilyn. "Pregúntaselo a Dios." In *Estatuas de sal: Cuentistas cubanas contemporáneas,* ed. Mirta Yáñez and Marilyn Bobes, 252–59. Havana: Ediciones Unión, 1996. Trans. Amanda Hopkinson. "Ask the Good Lord." In *The Voice of the Turtle: An Anthology of Cuban Stories,* ed. Peter Bush, 337–45. New York: Grove Press, 1997.

Boldy, Stephen. "Making Sense in Carpentier's *El acoso.*" *Modern Language Review* 85:3 (July 1990): 612–22.

Bourdieu, Pierre. *The Field of Cultural Production.* New York: Columbia University Press, 1993.

Boym, Svetlana. *The Future of Nostalgia.* New York: Basic Books, 2001.

Bruguera, Tania, dir. *Memoria de la Postguerra* (Havana). November 1993 and June 1994.

Bruno, Giuliana. "Havana: Memoirs of Material Culture." *Journal of Visual Culture* 2:3 (2003): 303–24.

Buckwalter-Arias, James. "Reinscribing the Aesthetic: Cuban Narrative and Post-Soviet Cultural Politics." *PMLA* 120:2 (March 2005): 362–74.

Buena Vista Social Club. Dir. Wim Wenders, 1999.

Buena Vista Social Club. World Circuit/Nonesuch, 1997.

"*Buena Vista Social Club* y la cultura musical cubana." Roundtable debate. *Temas* (Havana) 22–23 (July–December 2000): 163–79.

Burri, René. *Cuba y Cuba.* Foreword by Marco Meier. Poetry by Miguel Barnet. Milan: Federico Motta, 1997.

Bush, Peter, ed. *The Voice of the Turtle: An Anthology of Cuban Stories.* New York: Grove Press, 1997.

Caballero, Rufo. "La excusa. Semiosis, ideología y montaje en *Buena Vista Social Club.*" *Temas* (Havana) 27 (October–December 2001): 133–40.

Cabrera Infante, Guillermo. "Include Me Out." In *Requiem for the "Boom"— Premature? A Symposium,* ed. Rose Minc and Marilyn Frankenthaler, 9–20. Montclair, N.J.: Montclair State College, 1980.

———. *Tres tristes tigres* (1967). Barcelona: Seix Barral, 1998. Trans. Donald Gardner and Suzanne Jill Levine. *Three Trapped Tigers.* New York: Harper and Row, 1971.

Calzadilla, Iraida. "Tenemos potencial turístico, pueblo preparado, alto espíritu de hospitalidad, voluntad de hacer bien las cosas." *Granma* (Havana), May 21, 1994, 1.

Calzadilla, Iraida, and Anett Ríos. "Acerca del discurso pronunciado por el Presidente de la República de Cuba, Fidel Castro Ruz, al clausurar el acto por el Día Internacional de la Mujer, efectuado en el Palacio de las Convenciones, el 8 de marzo de 2005." *Granma* (Havana), March 9 2005 (accessed March 28, 2005). http://www.cubaminrex.cu/Archivo/Presidente/2005/ FC_080305.htm.

Cámara, Madeline. "Del barroco a la postmodernidad: Parodia de la picaresca en *La nada cotidiana* de Zoé Valdés." In *La letra rebelde: Estudios de escritoras cubanas,* 57–86. Miami: Ediciones Universal, 2002.

Camnitzer, Luis. "Memoria de la Postguerra." *Art Nexus* 15 (January–March 1995): 29–30.

Campa, Homero. "Libros sin capital." *Mural* (Guadalajara, Mexico), November 30, 2002 (Hoja por hoja): 8–9.

Capello, Ernesto. "The Havana Street as Political Discourse, 1959–1975." Paper delivered at "Articulating the Urban" conference. Urban Issues Program, University of Texas at Austin, April 21, 2001.

Carpentier, Alejo. *El acoso* (1956). Barcelona: Seix Barral, 1992. Trans. Alfred MacAdam. *The Chase.* Minneapolis: University of Minnesota Press, 2001.

———. *La ciudad de las columnas.* Barcelona: Editorial Lumen, 1970.

Casamayor, Odette. "¿Cómo vivir las ruinas habaneras de los años noventa?: Respuestas disímiles desde la isla en las obras narrativas de Abilio Estévez, Pedro Juan Gutiérrez y Ena Lucía Portela." *Caribbean Studies* 32:2 (July–December 2004): 63–103.

———. "Cubanidades de un fin de siglo, o breve crónica de ciertos intentos narrativos por salvar la cubanidad." *La gaceta de Cuba* (Havana) (November–December 2002): 36–40.

———. "Negros, marginalidad y ética." *La gaceta de Cuba* (Havana) (January–February 2005): 66–68.

Castilla, Amelia and Mauricio Vicent. "La explosión literaria de la Habana." *El país* (Madrid), December 29, 1997 (Cultura): 27.

Castro Ruz, Fidel. "Discurso pronunciado por el Comandante en Jefe Fidel Castro Ruz, Primer Secretario del Comité Central del Partido Comunista de Cuba y Presidente de los Consejos de Estado y de Ministros, en la clausura del acto central por el XL aniversario del asalto a los cuarteles Moncada y 'Carlos Manuel de Céspedes,' el 26 de julio de 1993, 'Año 35 de la Revolución.'" Database "Discursos e intervenciones del Comandante en Jefe Fidel Castro Ruz, Presidente del Consejo de Estado de la República de Cuba." February 22, 2005. http://www.cuba.cu/gobierno/discursos/1993/ esp/f260793e.html.

———. "Discurso pronunciado por Fidel Castro Ruiz, Presidente de la República de Cuba, en la clausura del XVI Congreso de la CTC, celebrado en el Teatro 'Carlos Marx,' el 28 de enero de 1990, 'Año 32 de la

Revolución.'" Database "Discursos e intervenciones del Comandante en Jefe Fidel Castro Ruz, Presidente del Consejo de Estado de la República de Cuba." February 17, 2005. http://www.cuba.cu/gobierno/discursos/1990/esp/f280190e.html.

———. "Fragmento de la Declaración del Primer Congreso Nacional de Educación y Cultura, La Habana, abril de 1971." In *Política cultural de la Revolución cubana: Documentos,* 51–64. Havana: Editorial de ciencias sociales, 1977.

———. "Fragmento del Informe del Comité Central del Partido Comunista de Cuba al Primer Congreso del Partido, presentado por el Comandante en Jefe, Fidel Castro Ruz, Primer Secretario del Comité Central del PCC. Diciembre, 1975." In *Política cultural de la Revolución cubana: Documentos,* 67–77. Havana: Editorial de ciencias sociales, 1977.

———. "Palabras a los intelectuales." *Política cultural de la Revolución cubana: Documentos,* 5–47. Havana: Editorial de ciencias sociales, 1977.

Catoira, Patricia. "Writing and Publishing in Cuba during the Special Period." Paper delivered at "Cuba Today: Continuity and Change since the 'Período Especial'" conference. Cuba Project/Bildner Center at the Graduate Center of the City University of New York, October 4, 2004.

Chailloux Cardona, Juan M. *Síntesis histórica de la vivienda popular en Cuba: Los horrores del solar habanero.* Havana: Jesús Montero, 1945.

Chanan, Michael. "Play It Again, or Old-Time Cuban Music on the Screen." *New Left Review* 238 (November/December 1999): 150–56.

Chaviano, Daína. *El hombre, la hembra y el hambre.* Barcelona: Planeta, 1998.

Clark, Katerina. *The Soviet Novel: History as Ritual* (1981). 3d ed. Bloomington: Indiana University Press, 2000.

Codrescu, Andrei, and David Graham. *Ay, Cuba! A Socio-Erotic Journey.* New York: St. Martin's Press, 2001.

Comisión Económica para América Latina y el Caribe (CEPAL). *La economía cubana: Reformas estructurales y desempeño en los noventa.* Mexico City: CEPAL/Fondo de Cultura Económica, 2000.

Cortés, Rubén. "La buena salud de las letras cubanas." *Crónica* (Mexico City), February 21, 1998. *Academic Universe.* Lexis-Nexis. February 25, 2005. http://www.web.lexis-nexis.com/.

Cremades, Raúl, and Esteban, Ángel. "El nuevo *boom* de la narrativa cubana en España." *Leer* (Madrid) 16:113 (June 2000): 48–51.

Cuba: Emisiones de monedas y billetes, 1915–1980. Havana: Museo Numismático/Banco Nacional de Cuba, 1982.

Culler, Jonathan. "The Semiotics of Tourism." In *Framing the Sign: Criticism and Its Institutions,* 153–67. Norman: University of Oklahoma Press, 1988.

Daniel, Yvonne. *Rumba: Dance and Social Change in Contemporary Cuba.* Bloomington: Indiana University Press, 1995.

Davies, Catherine. "The Soup of Signs: Postmodernism, Politics and Culture in Cuba." *Latin American Perspectives* 27:4 (July 2000): 103–21.

de Águila, Rafael. "¿Pathos o marketing?" *El caimán barbudo* 31:292 (1998): 2–3.

de Ferrari, Guillermina. "Aesthetics under Siege: Dirty Realism and Pedro Juan Gutiérrez's *Trilogía Sucia de La Habana*." *Arizona Journal of Hispanic Studies* 7 (2003): 23–43.

de la Campa, Román. "El sublime encanto de la nostalgia cultural." *Temas* 27 (October–December 2001): 126–32.

de la Fuente, Alejandro. "The Special Period." In *A Nation for All: Race, Inequality, and Politics in Twentieth-Century Cuba,* 317–34. Chapel Hill: University of North Carolina Press, 2001.

de la Nuez, Iván. "De la tempestad a la intemperie: Travesías cubanas en el poscomunismo." In *Paisajes después del muro: Disidencias en el poscomunismo diez años después de la caída del muro de Berlín,* 163–75. Barcelona: Ediciones Península, 1999.

Delgado, Isaac. "Solar de la California." *La fórmula*. Ahí-namá Music, 2001.

Delany, Paul. "Who Paid for Modernism?" In *The New Economic Criticism: Studies at the Intersection of Literature and Economics,* ed. Martha Woodmansee and Mark Osteen, 335–51. London: Routledge, 1999.

dell'Amico Ciruta, Souleen. "Contradicciones." In *El ojo de la noche: Nuevas cuentistas cubanas,* ed. Amir Valle, 61–69. Havana: Letras Cubanas, 1999.

Department of the Treasury, Office of Foreign Assets Control. "Cuban Assets Control Regulations; Interim Final Rule. Revocation of OFAC Specific Licenses to Engage in Travel-Related Transactions Incident to Visiting Close Relatives in Cuba; Notice." *Federal Register* (Washington, D.C.), June 16, 2004 (31 CFR Part 515): 33768–75.

Derrida, Jacques. *Given Time I: Counterfeit Money.* Trans. Peggy Kamuf. Chicago and London: Chicago University Press, 1992.

Diana, Goffredo. "Testimonio in Cuba: Limits and Possibilities." Ph.D. diss. University of Pittsburgh, 1997.

Díaz, Jesús. "*Encuentro,* entre la isla y el exilio." Interview with François Maspéro. *Encuentro de la cultura cubana* 10 (fall 1998): 101–3.

———. *Las palabras perdidas.* Barcelona: Editorial Anagrama, 1992.

Díaz Gómez, Yamil. "Fotógrafo en posguerra." *El caimán barbudo* (Havana) 31:287 (1998): 11.

———. *Fotógrafo en posguerra.* Havana: Ediciones Unión, 2004.

Domínguez, Jorge I. *Cuba: Order and Revolution.* Cambridge: Belknap Press of Harvard University Press, 1978.

Donoso, José. *Historia personal del Boom.* Barcelona: Anagrama, 1972. Trans. Gregory Kolovakos. *The Boom in Spanish American Literature.* New York: Columbia University Press, 1977.

Dopico, Ana María. "Picturing Havana: History, Vision and the Scramble for Cuba." *Nepantla: Views from South* 3:3 (2002): 451–93.

Dravasa, Mayder. *The Boom in Barcelona: Literary Modernism in Spanish and Spanish-American Fiction (1950–1975).* New York: Peter Lang, 2004.

Eagleton, Terry. "Capitalism, Modernism, and Postmodernism." In *Modern Criticism and Theory: A Reader,* ed. David Lodge, 385–98. London: Longman, 1988.

Eckstein, Susan. "Transnational Networks and Norms, Remittances, and the Transformation of Cuba." In *The Cuban Economy at the Start of the Twenty-first Century,* ed. Jorge I. Domínguez, Omar Everleny Pérez Villanueva, and Lorena Barberia, 319–51. Cambridge: Harvard University/David Rockefeller Center for Latin American Studies, 2004.

Edinger, Claudio. *Old Havana.* Texts by Guillermo Cabrera Infante and Humberto Werneck. Stockport, U.K.: DBA, 1998.

el-Khoury, Rodolphe. "The Postwar Project." In *Projecting Beirut: Episodes in the Construction and Reconstruction of a Modern City,* ed. Peter G. Rowe and Hashim Sarkis, 183–86. Munich: Prestel, 1998.

"El rojo y el verde." Roundtable debate. *El caimán barbudo* (Havana) 30:280 (1996): 4+.

"¿Entendemos la marginalidad?" Roundtable debate. *Temas* (Havana) 27 (October–December 2001): 69–96.

Estévez, Abilio. "Cuba está de moda." *El país* (Madrid), March 15, 1999, 16.

———. *Los palacios distantes.* Barcelona: Tusquets, 2002.

———. "Méditations sur la littérature cubaine d'aujourd'hui." *Cahiers des Amériques Latines* 31–32 (1999): 211–21.

———. *Tuyo es el reino.* Barcelona: Tusquets, 1997; Havana: Ediciones Unión, 1998. Trans. David Frye. *Thine Is the Kingdom.* New York: Arcade, 1999.

Faccini, Carmen. "El discurso político de Zoé Valdés: *La nada cotidiana* y *Te di la vida entera.*" *Ciberletras* 7 (July 2002). http://www.lehman.cuny.edu/ciberletras/.

Fagen, Richard R. *The Transformation of Political Culture in Cuba.* Stanford, Calif.: Stanford University Press, 1969.

Feld, Steven. "A Sweet Lullaby for World Music." *Public Culture* 12:1 (2000): 145–71.

Ferguson, Russell, et al. *Out There: Marginalization and Contemporary Cultures.* Cambridge: MIT Press, 1990.

Fernandes, Sujatha. *Cuba Represent! Cuban Arts, State Powers, and the Making of New Revolutionary Cultures.* Durham, N.C.: Duke University Press, 2006.

Fernández, Nadine. "Back to the Future? Women, Race, and Tourism in Cuba." In *Sun, Sex, and Gold: Tourism and Sex Work in the Caribbean,* ed. Kemala Kempadoo, 81–89. Lanham, Md.: Rowman & Littlefield, 1999.

Fernández, Roberto G. *Raining Backwards.* Houston: Arte Público, 1988.

Fernández Retamar, Roberto. *Calibán: Apuntes sobre la cultura en nuestra América.* 2d ed. Mexico City: Diógenes, 1974.

Fornet, Ambrosio. "A propósito de *Las iniciales de la tierra.*" *Revista Casa de las Américas* (Havana) 164 (September–October 1987): 149–53.

Fornet, Jorge. *Los nuevos paradigmas: Prólogo narrativo al siglo XXI.* Havana: Letras Cubanas, 2006.

Fowler Calzada, Víctor. "The Day After." In *Cuba y el día después,* ed. Iván de
la Nuez, 37–49. Barcelona: Mondadori, 2001.

———. *Historias del cuerpo.* Havana: Editorial Letras Cubanas, 2001.

———. "Innovación, adaptación, repetición, influencia." May 30, 2005.
http://www.pedrojuangutierrez.com/Ensayos_ensayos_Victor-Fowler.htm.

———. "Para días de menos entusiasmo." *La gaceta de Cuba* (Havana)
(November–December 1999): 34–38.

Freud, Sigmund. *Jokes and Their Relation to the Unconscious* (1905). Trans. James
Strachey. New York: Norton, 1960.

———. "The Sexual Aberrations." In *Three Essays on the Theory of Sexuality*
(1905), trans. and ed. James Strachey, 1–38. London: Hogarth Press and the
Institute of Psychoanalysis, 1974.

Frow, John. "Tourism and the Semiotics of Nostalgia." *October* 57 (summer
1991): 123–51.

Fuentes, Carlos. *La nueva novela hispanoamericana.* Mexico City: Joaquín
Mortiz, 1969.

Fusco, Coco. "Hustling for Dollars: *Jineterismo* in Cuba." In *Global Sex Workers:
Rights, Resistance, and Redefinition,* ed. Kemala Kempadoo and Jo Doezma,
151–66. New York: Routledge, 1998.

Garaicoa, Carlos. *Continuidad de la arquitectura ajena/Continuity of Somebody's Architecture.* Project for Documenta 11, Platform 5. Kassel, Germany,
June 8–September 15, 2002.

———. Interview with Holly Block. *Bomb* 82 (winter 2002/2003): 22–29.

———. Interview with Thomas Loeb. *Puntocero* 1 (September 2005–February
2006). http://www.puntocero.de.

———. *La ruina, la utopía.* Curaduría de José Ignacio Roca. Bogotá, Colom-
bia: Banco de la República/Biblioteca Luis Ángel Arango, 2000.

García, Cristina, ed. *Cubanísimo! The Vintage Book of Contemporary Cuban
Literature.* New York: Vintage, 2003.

———. *Dreaming in Cuban.* New York: Knopf, 1992.

García, Luis Manuel. "Crónica de la inocencia perdida: La cuentística cubana
contemporánea." *Encuentro de la cultura cubana* 1 (summer 1996): 121–27.

García Canclini, Néstor. *Consumidores y ciudadanos: conflictos multiculturales
de la globalización.* Mexico City: Grijalbo, 1995. Trans. George Yúdice.
Consumers and Citizens: Globalization and Multicultural Conflicts. Minneapolis: University of Minnesota Press, 2001.

———. *Culturas híbridas: estrategias para entrar y salir de la modernidad.*
Buenos Aires: Sudamericana, 1992. Trans. Christopher L. Chiappari and
Silvia L. López. *Hybrid Cultures: Strategies for Entering and Leaving Mo-
dernity.* Minneapolis and London: University of Minnesota Press, 1995.

———. *La globalización imaginada.* Buenos Aires and Mexico City: Paidós,
1999.

García González, Francisco. "Lo mío primero." In *Color local,* 36–58. Havana:
Ediciones Extramuros, 1999.

García Márquez, Gabriel. *Cien años de soledad.* Buenos Aires: Editorial Sudamericana, 1967. Trans. Gregory Rabassa. *One Hundred Years of Solitude.* New York: Avon, 1971.

García Meralla, Emir. "Hágase la timba." *Temas* (Havana) 39–40 (October– December 2004): 49–59.

Gavin, Angus. "Heart of Beirut: Making the Master Plan for the Renewal of the Central District." In *Projecting Beirut: Episodes in the Construction and Reconstruction of a Modern City,* ed. Peter G. Rowe and Hashim Sarkis, 217–33. Munich: Prestel, 1998.

Genette, Gérard. *Paratexts: Thresholds of Interpretation* (1987). Trans. Jane E. Lewin. Cambridge: Cambridge University Press, 1997.

Goldberger, Paul. "Annals of Preservation: Bringing back Havana." *New Yorker* 26 (January 1998): 50–62.

González-Abellás, Miguel Ángel. "'Aquella isla': Introducción al universo narrativo de Zoé Valdés." *Hispania* 83:1 (March 2000): 42–50.

———. "La figura de la mulata cubana en el fin del milenio: *Trilogía sucia de la Habana.*" *Hispanic Journal* 22:1 (spring 2001): 251–62.

———. "Sexo transnacional: La cubana como mercancía en la obra de Zoé Valdés." *Alba de América* 22:41–42 (July 2003): 277–85.

González Echevarría, Roberto. "Autobiography and Representation in *La Habana para un Infante difunto.*" *World Literature Today* 61:4 (autumn 1987): 568–74.

———. *The Voice of the Masters: Writing and Authority in Modern Latin American Literature.* Austin: University of Texas Press, 1985.

Gorgoni, Gianfranco. *Cubano 100%.* Foreword by Gabriel García Márquez. Text by Reynaldo González. Milan: Charta, 1997.

Gott, Richard. *Cuba: A New History.* New Haven: Yale University Press, 2004.

Goux, Jean-Joseph. "Cash, Check or Charge?" In *The New Economic Criticism: Studies at the Intersection of Literature and Economics,* ed. Martha Woodmansee and Mark Osteen, 114–27. London: Routledge 1999.

Guevara, Ernesto. *Man and Socialism in Cuba.* Trans. Margarita Zimmerman. Havana: Guairas Book Institute, 1967.

Gutiérrez, Pedro Juan. "Animal literario." Interview with Marilyn Bobes. *La gaceta de Cuba* (Havana) (July–August 2004): 36–40.

———. *Animal tropical.* Barcelona: Anagrama, 2000; Havana: Letras Cubanas, 2002. Trans. Peter Lownds. *Tropical Animal.* Published by arrangement with Faber & Faber UK. New York: Carroll & Graf Publishers, 2005.

———. *Carne de perro.* Barcelona: Anagrama, 2003.

———. *El nido de la serpiente. Memorias del hijo del heladero.* Barcelona: Anagrama, 2006.

———. "El Rey de Centro Habana: Conversación con Pedro Juan Gutiérrez." Interview with Stephen Clark. *Delaware Review of Latin American Studies* 2:1 (December 15, 2000).

———. *El Rey de la Habana.* Barcelona: Anagrama, 1999.

———. *El insaciable hombre araña.* Barcelona: Anagrama, 2002. Trans. John
King. *The Insatiable Spider Man.* New York: Carroll & Graf, 2006.

———. Interview with Kiko Nogueira and Helena Fruets. *Playboy* (São Paulo,
Brazil) August 2001 (accessed August 30, 2001). http://www.2.uol.com.br/
playboy/entrevistas/integra/gutierrez.html.

———. *La realidad rugiendo (Poesía graficada).* Pinar del Río, Cuba: Dirección
Provincial de Cultura, 1987.

———. *Melancolía de los leones.* Havana: Ediciones Unión, 2000.

———. *Poesía.* Edición de 500 ejemplares foliados y firmados por el autor.
Pinar del Río, Cuba, 1988.

———. *Trilogía sucia de la Habana.* Barcelona: Anagrama, 1998. Trans.
Natasha Wimmer. *Dirty Havana Trilogy.* Reprinted by arrangement
with Farrar, Straus and Giroux. New York: HarperCollins, 2002. Trans.
Piotr Fornelski. *Brudna trylogia o Hawanie.* Warsaw, Poland: Zysk I S-ka
Wydawnictwo S.j., 2004.

———. *Vivir en el espacio: Del sueño a la realidad.* Havana: Editorial
Científico-Técnica, 1989.

Hagedorn, Katherine J. *Divine Utterances: The Performance of Afro-Cuban
Santería.* Washington, D.C.: Smithsonian Institution Press, 2001.

Haines, Lila. "Spanish Investment in Cuba: A Second Coming?" In *Identity
and Discursive Practices: Spain and Latin America,* ed. Francisco Domínguez, 107–22. Bern: Peter Lang, 2000.

Hamberg, Jill. *Under Construction: Housing Policy in Revolutionary Cuba.*
New York: Center for Cuban Studies, 1986.

Harvey, David Alan. *Cuba.* Text by Elizabeth Newhouse. Washington, D.C.:
National Geographic Society, 1999.

Hasson, Lillian. "¿Y en Francia, qué?" *Revista Hispanocubana* 12 (2002). July 23,
2002. http://www.hispanocubana.org/revistahc/paginas/numerosframe/
numero12frame.html.

Hernández-Reguant, Ariana. "Havana's *timba*: A Macho Sound for Black
Sex." In *Globalization and Race: Transformations in the Cultural Production
of Blackness,* ed. Deborah Thomas and Kamari Clarke, 249–78. Durham,
N.C.: Duke University Press, 2006.

———. "Radio Taino. The Cuban Culture Industries between Socialism and
Capitalism." Ph.D. diss. University of Chicago, 2002.

Herrera Ysla, Nelson. "De frente y luchando." *Memoria de la postguerra*
(Havana) (November 1993): 12.

Herrero-Olaizola, Alejandro. "Consuming Aesthetics: Seix Barral and José
Donoso in the Field of Latin American Literary Production." *Modern
Language Notes* 115 (2000): 323–39.

Hollander, Paul. *Political Pilgrims: Travels of Western Intellectuals to the Soviet
Union, China, and Cuba, 1928–1978.* New York: Oxford University Press, 1981.

Huertas, Begoña. *Ensayo de un cambio: La narrativa cubana de los '80.* Havana:
Editorial Casa de las Américas, 1993.

Huggan, Graham. *The Postcolonial Exotic: Marketing the Margins.* London and New York: Routledge, 2001.

"Información a la población." *Granma* (Havana), August 29, 1990, 1.

Iyer, Pico. *Cuba and the Night.* New York: Knopf, 1994.

Janowitz, Anne. *England's Ruins: Poetic Purpose and the National Landscape.* Cambridge, Mass.: Basil Blackwell, 1990.

Jorge, Andrés. *Voyeurs.* Mexico City: Alfaguara, 2001.

Kassir, Samir. *Histoire de Beyrouth.* Paris: Librairie Arthème Fayard, 2003.

"La hoguera de las vanidades." Roundtable debate. *El caimán barbudo* (Havana) 30:277 (1996): 2+.

Lanon, Philippe. "Plumes françaises et Castro show." *Libération* (Paris), February 15, 2002 (Culture), 34.

———. "Zoé Valdés, le destin nu." *Libération* (Paris), September 21, 2000 (Livres), 8.

Leal Spengler, Eusebio. *Viaje en la memoria: apuntes para un acercamiento a La Habana Vieja: Plan maestro, revitalización integral de La Habana Vieja.* Havana: Oficina del Historiador de la Ciudad de La Habana; Navarre, Spain: Colegio Oficial de Arquitectos Vasco Navarro, 1996.

Lejeune, Philippe. "The Autobiographical Pact." In *On Autobiography,* ed. Paul John Eakin, trans. Katherine Leary, 3–30. Minneapolis: University of Minnesota Press, 1989.

"Le nombre des romans bat tous les records." *Les Echos* (Paris), September 5, 2000 (Livres), 69.

Lezama Lima, José. *Poesía completa.* Madrid: Alianza, 1999.

Lightfoot, Claudia. *Havana: A Cultural and Literary Companion.* New York: Interlink Books, 2002.

———. "Publishing in Cuba." *Bellagio Publishing Network Newsletter* 22 (July 1998): 10.

Loomis, John. *Revolution of Forms: Cuba's Forgotten Art Schools.* New York: Princeton Architectural Press, 1999.

López Ramos, Rafael. "La guerra ha terminado, Afirma jóven artista cubano." *Memoria de la postguerra* (Havana) (November 1993): 5.

López Sacha, Francisco. *La nueva cuentística cubana.* Havana: Ediciones Unión, 1994.

———. "La pelea cubana entre los ángeles y los demonios." Introduction to *Fábula de ángeles,* ed. Salvador Redonet and Francisco López Sacha, 5–17. Havana: Letras Cubanas, 1994.

———. "Literatura cubana y fin de siglo." *Temas* (Havana) 20–21 (January–June 2000): 155–60.

———. "Tres revoluciones en el cuento cubano y una reflexión conservadora." *La letra del escriba* (Havana) 6 (May 2001): 2–3.

Loss, Jacqueline. "Global Arenas: Narrative and Filmic Translations of Identity." *Nepantla: Views from South* 4:2 (April 2003): 317–44.

──────. "Vintage Soviets in Post–Cold War Cuba." *Mandorla* 7 (spring 2004): 79–84.

Loss, Jacqueline, and Esther Whitfield. *New Short Fiction from Cuba.* Evanston, Ill.: Northwestern University Press, 2007.

Ludmer, Josefina. "Ficciones cubanas de los últimos años: El problema de la literatura política." In *Cuba: un siglo de literatura,* ed. Anke Birkenmaier and Roberto González Echevarría, 357–71. Madrid: Ediciones Colibrí, 2004.

Macauley, Rose. *Pleasure of Ruins* (1953). London: Thames and Hudson, 1966.

MacCannell, Dean. *The Tourist: A New Theory of the Leisure Class* (1967). Berkeley: University of California Press, 1999.

Manolín, el médico de la salsa. "Somos lo que hay." In *De buena fe.* Caribe Productions, 1997. CD.

Marqués de Armas, Pedro. "Boceto de mercado." *Mural* (Guadalajara, Mexico) (November 30, 2002) (Hoja por hoja): 7.

──────. "Ficción y realidad del solar habanero (y breve dossier sobre condiciones de vida en Cuba según la mirada de los higienistas)." *La Habana Elegante* (spring 2007) (accessed September 16, 2007). http://www.habanaelegante .com/Spring2007/Panoptico.html.

Martin, Gerald. "Boom, Yes: 'New Novel,' No: Further Reflections on the Optical Illusions of the 1960s in Latin America." *Bulletin of Latin American Research* 3:2 (1984): 53–63.

Martin de Holan, Pablo, and Nelson Phillips. "Sun, Sand and Hard Currency: Tourism in Cuba." *Annals of Tourism Research* 24:4 (1997): 777–95.

Marx, Karl. *Das Kapital: A Critique of Political Economy* (1867–94). Ed. Friedrich Engels. Condensed by Serge L. Levitsky. Washington, D.C.: Regnery Gateway, 1996.

Más Zabala, Carlos Alberto. "Las nuevas del libro en Cuba." *Revista del libro cubano* (Havana) 3:1 (2000): 49–52.

Mateo, Margarita. *Ella escribía poscrítica.* Havana: Casa Editora Abril, 1995.

Mathey, Kosta. "Informal and Substandard Housing in Revolutionary Cuba." In *Housing the Urban Poor: Policy and Practice in Developing Countries,* ed. Brian C. Aldrich and Ranvinder S. Sandhu, 245–60. London: Zed Books, 1995.

Matús, Álvaro. "El llanero solitario." *¿Qué pasa?* (Santiago de Chile), May 30, 2003 (accessed May 30, 2005). http://www.pedrojuangutierrez.com/ Entrevista_ES_QuePasa.htm.

McLaughlin, Kevin. "The Coming of Paper: Aesthetic Value from Ruskin to Benjamin." *Modern Language Notes* 114:5 (1999): 962–90.

Mejides, Miguel. *Perversiones en el Prado.* Havana: Ediciones Unión, 1999.

──────. "Trópico." *Anuario 1994/Narrativa,* 271–81. Havana: Ediciones Unión, 1994. Trans. Clara Marín. "The Tropics." In *Dream with No Name: Contemporary Fiction from Cuba,* ed. Juana Ponce de León and Esteban Ríos Rivera, 95–112. New York: Seven Stories Press, 1999.

Menéndez, Ana. *In Cuba I Was a German Shepherd*. New York: Grove Press, 2001.

Menéndez Plasencia, Ronaldo. "El gallo de Diógenes: Reflexiones en torno a lo testimonial en los novísimos narradores cubanos." *Encuentro de la cultura cubana* 18 (fall 2000): 215–22.

———. *La piel de Inesa*. Madrid: Lengua de Trapo, 1999.

———. "Money." In *El derecho al pataleo de los ahorcados*, 63–76. Havana: Casa de las Américas, 1997.

Menton, Seymour. *Prose Fiction of the Cuban Revolution*. Austin: University of Texas Press, 1975.

Merrim, Stephanie. *Logos and the Word: The Novel of Language and Linguistic Motivation in Grande Sertão; Veredas and Tres tristes tigres*. New York: Peter Lang, 1983.

Ministerio de Cultura de Cuba. "Producción editorial." February 17, 2005. http://www.min.cult.cu/estadisticas/prodeditoriasl.html.

Monreal, Pedro. "Globalization and the Dilemmas of Cuba's Economic Trajectories." In *The Cuban Economy at the Start of the Twenty-first Century*, ed. Jorge I. Domínguez, Omar Everleny Pérez Villanueva, and Lorena Barberia, 91–118. Cambridge: Harvard University/David Rockefeller Center for Latin American Studies, 2004.

———. "Las remesas familiares en la economía cubana." *Encuentro de la cultura cubana* 14 (fall 1999): 49–62.

Moore, Robin. *Nationalizing Blackness: Afrocubanismo and Artistic Revolution in Havana, 1920–1940*. Pittsburgh: University of Pittsburgh Press, 1997.

Morales, Edel. "Literatura y mercado." *Revista del Libro Cubano* (Havana) 2:3 (1998): 4–8.

Morales, René. "Beyond Insularity/Más allá de la insularidad." In Judith Tannenbaum and René Morales, *Island Nations: New Art from Cuba, the Dominican Republic Puerto Rico and the Diaspora/Islas Naciones: Arte nuevo de Cuba, la República Dominicana, Puerto Rico y la diáspora*, 23–37. Catalog for exhibition at the Museum of Art, Rhode Island School of Design, October 29, 2004–January 30, 2005. Providence: RISD Museum of Art, 2004.

Moraña, Mabel. "El *boom* del subalterno." In *Teorías sin disciplina: Latino-americanismo, poscolonialidad y globalización en debate*, ed. Santiago Castro-Gómez and Eduardo Mendieta, 233–43. Mexico City: Porrúa; San Francisco: University of San Francisco Press, 1998.

Moreiras, Alberto. "The Aura of Testimonio" (1995). In *The Real Thing: Testimonial Discourse and Latin America*, ed. Georg Gugelberger, 192–224. Durham, N.C.: Duke University Press, 1996.

Moreno Fraginals, Manuel. *Cuba/España, España/Cuba: Historia común*. Barcelona: Grijalbo Mondadori, 1995.

Morley, Morris H., and Chris McGillion. *Unfinished Business: America and*

Cuba after the Cold War, 1989–2001. Cambridge: Cambridge University Press, 2002.

Mulvey, Laura. "From 'Visual Pleasure and Narrative Cinema.'" In *A Cultural and Critical Theory Reader*, ed. Anthony Easthope and Kate McGowan, 158–66. Toronto: University of Toronto Press, 1992.

Navarro, Desiderio. "In Medias Res Publicas: On Intellectuals and Social Criticism in the Cuban Public Sphere." *Nepantla: Views from South* 2:2 (2001): 355–71.

Novás Calvo, Lino. "La noche de Ramón Yendía" (1942). In *Cuento cubano del siglo XX*, ed. Jorge Fornet and Carlos Espinosa, 75–93. Mexico City: Fondo de Cultura Económica, 2002.

Numismática cubana: Siglo XVI–Siglo XX. Havana: Museo Numismático/ Banco Nacional de Cuba, 1982.

Obejas, Achy. "From Havana with Love: A New Generation Faces Cuba's Dark Reality." *Village Voice Book Review*, February 2001, 82–119.

Orsenna, Erik. "Sortez-moi de là!" *Le Monde des livres* (Paris), March 31, 1995. *Academic Universe*. Lexis-Nexis (accessed July 23, 2002). http://www.web .lexis-nexis.com.

———. "Volcanique Havane." "Monde des livres." *Le Monde* (Paris), October 17, 1997. *Academic Universe*. Lexis-Nexis (accessed July 23, 2002). http://www.web.lexis-nexis.com.

Ortiz Ceberio, Cristina. "La narrativa de Zoé Valdés: Hacia una reconfiguración de la na(rra)ción cubana." *Chasqui* 27:2 (November 1998): 116–27.

Padilla, Heberto. *Fuera del juego* (1968). Ed. conmemorativa, 1968–98. Miami: Ediciones Universal, 1998.

Padura Fuentes, Leonardo. *Máscaras*. Barcelona: Tusquets, 1997.

———. *Paisaje de otoño*. Barcelona: Tusquets, 1998.

———. *Pasado perfecto*. Havana: Ediciones Unión, 1995.

———. *Vientos de cuaresma*. Havana: Ediciones Unión, 1994.

Panorámica de la edición española de libros. Madrid: El Centro del Libro y de la Lectura, Dirección General del Libro y Bibliotecas, Ministerio de Cultura, 1988–2002.

Pattullo, Polly. *Last Resorts: The Cost of Tourism in the Caribbean*. London: Cassell, 1996.

Paz Pérez, Carlos. *Diccionario cubano de habla popular y vulgar*. Madrid: Agualarga Editores, 1998.

Perdomo, Omar. "Cuban Novel Boom." *Granma International* (Digital Edition), February 3, 1999 (accessed May 30, 2005). http://www.granma .cu/1999/ingles/febrero3/6feb11i.html.

Pérez, Jorge Ángel. *Cándido habanero*. Mexico City: Colibrí, 2001. Also published as *El paseante cándido*. Havana: Ediciones Unión, 2001.

Pérez Firmat, Gustavo. "Cuba sí, Cuba no: Querencias de la literatura cubano/ americana." *Encuentro de la cultura cubana* 14 (fall 1999): 131–37.

Pérez López, Jorge F. *Cuba's Second Economy: From behind the Scenes to Center Stage.* New Brunswick, N.J.: Transaction Publishers, 1995.

Phaf, Ineke. *Novelando la Habana: Ubicación histórica y perspectiva urbana en la novela cubana de 1959 a 1980.* Madrid: Editorial Orígenes, 1990.

Piña, Manuel. *De construcciones y utopías.* Solo exhibit. Havana: Centro de Desarrollo de las Artes Visuales, 1996.

Piñera, Virgilio. *Cuentos completos.* Madrid: Alfaguara, 1999.

———. *La carne de René.* Text set by Antón Arrufat. Havana: Ediciones Unión, 1995.

———. *La isla en peso: obra poética.* Comp. and preface by Antón Arrufat. Havana: Ediciones Unión, 1998; Barcelona: Tusquets, 2000.

———. *Teatro completo.* Comp. and preface by Rine Leal. Havana: Letras Cubanas, 2002.

Ponte, Antonio José. "Carta de la Habana: La maqueta de la ciudad." *Cuadernos hispanoamericanos* 649–650 (July–August 2004): 251–55.

———. *Contrabando de sombras.* Barcelona: Mondadori, 2002.

———. *Corazón de Skitalietz.* Cienfuegos, Cuba: Reina del Mar Editores, 1998. Reprinted in *Un arte de hacer ruinas,* 156–91. Mexico City: Fondo de Cultura Económica, 2005. Trans. Cola Franzen. "Heart of Skitalietz." In *In the Cold of the Malecon,* 81–127. San Francisco: City Lights, 2000.

———. "De 'Un paréntesis de ruinas': Fragmentos de *La fiesta vigilada.*" *Encuentro de la cultura cubana* 37/38 (summer/fall 2005): 111–25.

———. Interview with Anna Solana and Mercedes Serna. *Cuadernos hispano-americanos* 655 (November 2005): 127–34.

———. Interview with Teresa Basile. *Katatay* (Buenos Aires) 1:1/2 (June 2005): 28–36.

———. *La fiesta vigilada.* Barcelona: Editorial Anagrama, 2007.

———. "La fiesta vigilada." In *Cuba y el día después,* ed. Iván de la Nuez, 23–33. Barcelona: Mondadori, 2001.

———. "Un arte de hacer ruinas." In *Cuentos de todas partes del imperio,* 23–40. Angers, France: Éditions Deleatur, 2000. Reprinted in *Un arte de hacer ruinas,* 56–73. Mexico City: Fondo de Cultura Económica, 2005. Trans. Cola Franzen. "A Knack for Making Ruins." In *Tales from the Cuban Empire,* 21–44. San Francisco: City Lights, 2002.

———. "Un arte de hacer ruinas: Entrevista con el escritor cubano Antonio José Ponte." Interview with Néstor Rodríguez. *Revista Iberoamericana* 68:198 (January–March 2002): 179–86.

———. "What Am I Doing Here?" In *Cuba on the Verge: An Island in Transition,* ed. Terry McCoy. Boston: Bulfinch Press, 2003. 14–16.

Portela, Ena Lucía. *Cien botellas en una pared.* Barcelona: Mondadori, 2002; Havana: Ediciones Unión, 2003.

———. "Con hambre y sin dinero." *Crítica: Revista cultural de la Universidad Autónoma de Puebla* (Mexico) 98 (April–May 2003): 61–80.

———. *El pájaro: pincel y tinta china*. Havana: Ediciones Unión, 1998; Barcelona: Casiopea, 1999.

———. "El viejo, el asesino y yo." *Encuentro de la cultura cubana* 16–17 (spring–summer 2000): 133–47.

———. "Literatura vs. lechugitas. Breve esbozo de una tendencia." In *Cuba: voces para cerrar un siglo (I)*, comp. and preface by René Vázquez Díaz. Stockholm: Olof Palme International Center, 1999.

Prieto, René. "Tropos tropicales: Contrapunteo de la frutabomba y el plátano en *Te di la vida entera* y *Trilogía sucia de la Habana*." In *Cuba: un siglo de literatura*, ed. Anke Birkenmaier and Roberto González Echevarría, 373–90. Madrid: Ediciones Colibrí, 2004.

Quiroga, José. *Cuban Palimpsests*. Minneapolis: University of Minnesota Press, 2005.

Rama, Ángel. "El Boom en perspectiva." In *Más allá del Boom: Literatura y Mercado*, 51–110. Mexico City: Marcha Editores, 1981.

Redonet, Salvador, ed. *Doce nudos en el pañuelo*. Mérida, Venezuela: Ediciones Mucuglifo, 1995.

———, ed. *Los últimos serán los primeros*. Havana: Letras Cubanas, 1993.

———, ed. *Para el siglo que viene: (Post)novísimos narradores cubanos*. Zaragoza, Spain: Prensas Universitarias de Zaragoza, 1999.

———. "Ruptura en la narrativa social cubana: Novísimos y Novísimas." Interview with José B. Álvarez. *Torre de papel* (Iowa City) 5:1 (spring 1995): 61–75.

"Resolución No. 80/2004." Havana: Banco Central de Cuba, October 23, 2004. Translated in *Granma International*, October 26, 2004 (accessed February 17, 2005). http://www.granma.cu/ingles/2004/octubre/mart26/44resol-i.html.

Ritter, Archibald R. M., and Rowe, Nicholas. "Cuba: 'Dedollarization' and 'Dollarization.'" In *The Dollarization Debate*, ed. Dominick Salvatore, James W. Dean, and Thomas D. Willett, 425–48. Oxford: Oxford University Press, 2003.

Rodríguez, Juan Carlos. "Abel Prieto: 'No publicamos a Zoé Valdés en Cuba porque es un subproducto literario.'" *La razón* (Madrid), November 15, 2000 (accessed September 25, 2006). http://www.cubanet.org/CNews/y00/nov00/1506.htm.

Rojas, Rafael. *Isla sin fin. Contribución a la crítica del nacionalismo cubano*. Miami: Ediciones Universal, 1998.

———. "Partes del imperio." Review of Antonio José Ponte, *Un arte de hacer ruinas. Encuentro de la cultura cubana* 39 (winter 2004–spring 2005): 251–53.

———. *Tumbas sin sosiego: Revolución, disidencia y exilio del intelectual cubano*. Barcelona: Anagrama, 2006.

Romero, Vicente. *Los placeres de la Habana*. Barcelona: Planeta, 2000.

Roses, Lorraine Elena. *Voice of the Storyteller: Cuba's Lino Novás Calvo.* Westport, Conn.: Greenwood Press, 1986.

Rostagno, Irene. *Searching for Recognition: Latin American Literature in the United States.* Westport, Conn.: Greenwood Press, 1997.

Rowe, Nicholas, and Ana Julia Yanes Faya. "Cuban Monetary Policy: Peso, Dollar or Euro?" In *The Cuban Economy,* ed. Archibald R. M. Ritter, 45–58. Pittsburgh: University of Pittsburgh Press, 2004.

Rowe, Peter G., and Hashim Sarkis, eds. *Projecting Beirut: Episodes in the Construction and Reconstruction of a Modern City.* Munich and New York: Prestel, 1998.

Roy, Joaquín. *La siempre fiel: Un siglo de relaciones hispanocubanas, 1898–1988.* Madrid: Instituto Universitario de Desarrollo y Cooperación Libros de la Catarata, 1999.

Rozencvaig, Perla. "La complicidad del lenguaje en *La nada cotidiana.*" *Revista hispánica moderna* 49:2 (1996): 430–33.

Rubio Cuevas, Iván. "Lo marginal en los novísimos narradores cubanos: estrategia, subversión y moda." In *Todas las islas la isla,* ed. Janett Reinstädler and Ottmar Ette, 79–90. Madrid and Frankfurt: Iberoamericana & Vervuert, 2000.

Rundle, Mette. "The Cuban Diaspora in Spain: Identity Politics and Transnational Imaginaries." Paper delivered at the Fourth Conference on Cuban Studies of the Cuban Research Institute. Florida International University, March 6, 2002.

Sánchez, José Miguel (Yoss). "La causa que refresca." *Encuentro de la cultura cubana* 8/9 (spring–summer 1998): 91–94.

Santana, Mario. *Foreigners in the Homeland: The Spanish American New Novel in Spain, 1962–1974.* Lewisburg, Pa.: Bucknell University Press; Cranbury, N.J.: Associated University Presses, 2000.

Santí, Enrico Mario. "La vida es un salmón con grasa: Entrevista con Zoé Valdés." *Apuntes posmodernos/Postmodern Notes* 7:2 (fall 1998): 2–13.

Santos, Lidia. "Melodrama y nación en la narrativa femenina del Caribe contemporáneo." *Revista Iberoamericana* 69:205 (October–December 2003): 953–68.

Sarkis, Hashim. "A Vital Void: Reconstructions of Downtown Beirut." In *The Resilient City: How Modern Cities Recover from Disaster,* ed. Lawrence J. Vale and Thomas J. Campanella, 281–97. Oxford: Oxford University Press, 2005.

Scarpacci, Joseph L., Roberto Segre, and Mario Coyula. *Havana: Two Faces of the Antillean Metropolis.* Chapel Hill: University of North Carolina Press, 2002.

Schnabel, Julien, dir. *Before Night Falls.* Fineline Features/Grandview Pictures, 2001.

Schwartz, Marcy. *Writing Paris: Urban Topographies of Desire in Contemporary Latin American Fiction.* Albany: State University of New York Press, 1999.

Shell, Marc. *Money, Language, and Thought* (1982). Baltimore: Johns Hopkins University Press, 1993. 47–83.

Shor, Jacqueline. *Nós que ficamos: Contos cubanos.* São Paulo, Brazil: Livraria Nobel, 2001.

Sierra y Fabra, Jordi. *Cuba: La noche de la jinetera.* Barcelona: Ediciones del Bronce, 1997.

Simmel, Georg. "The Ruin." In *Georg Simmel, 1858–1918: A Collection of Essays, with Translations and a Bibliography,* ed. Kurt H. Wolff, 259–66. Columbus: Ohio State University Press, 1959.

Singler, Christoph. "Imagen de Cuba en Francia." Paper delivered at the Fourth Conference on Cuban Studies of the Cuban Research Institute. Florida International University, March 6–9, 2002.

Smorkaloff, Pamela María. *Literatura y edición de libros: La cultura literaria y el proceso social en Cuba.* Havana: Letras Cubanas, 1987.

———. *Readers and Writers in Cuba: A Social History of Print Culture, 1830s–1990s.* New York: Garland, 1997.

Soler Cedre, Gerardo. "Pinos nuevos en la balanza: ¿Ser o no ser?" *La revista del libro cubano* (Havana) 1:4 (1997): 20–23.

Sommer, Doris. *Foundational Fictions: The National Romances of Latin America.* Berkeley: University of California Press, 1991.

———. *Proceed with Caution, when Engaged by Minority Writing in the Americas.* Cambridge: Harvard University Press, 1999.

Sontag, Susan. *Regarding the Pain of Others.* New York: Farrar, Straus and Giroux, 2003.

Sorel, Julián B. *Nacionalismo y revolución en Cuba, 1823–1998.* Madrid: Fundación Liberal José Martí, 1998.

Stone, Elizabeth, ed. *Women and the Cuban Revolution: Speeches and Documents.* New York: Pathfinder Press, 1981.

Strausfeld, Michi. "Isla-Diáspora-Exilio: Anotaciones acerca de la publicación y distribución de la narrativa cubana en los años noventa." In *Todas las islas la isla: Nuevas y novísimas tendencias en la literatura y cultura de Cuba,* ed. Janett Reinstädler and Ottmar Ette, 11–23. Madrid: Iberoamericana; Frankfurt: Vervuert, 2000.

Suárez. Karla. *Silencios.* Madrid: Editorial Lengua de Trapo, 1999.

Sutton, Philip Christian. "The Laughter of *Tres tristes tigres*: An Ideological Production of Despair." In *Ensayos de literatura europea e hispanoamericana,* ed. Felix Menchacatorre, 549–56. San Sebastián: Universidad del País Vasco, 1990.

"Tesis y resolución del Primer Congreso del Partido Comunista de Cuba. Diciembre 1975." In *Política cultural de la Revolución cubana: Documentos,* 81–133. Havana: Editorial de ciencias sociales, 1977.

Thomas, Hugh. *Cuba, or the Pursuit of Freedom.* New York: Da Capo Press, 1998.

Torralbas Caurel, José Mariano. "Último tren a Londres." In *Los últimos serán los primeros,* ed. Salvador Redonet, 90–97. Havana: Letras Cubanas, 1993.

Unión de Escritores y Artistas de Cuba (UNEAC). *Anuario 1994/Narrativa.* Havana: Ediciones Unión, 1994.

Valdés, Zoé. *Café Nostalgia.* Barcelona: Planeta, 1997.

———. "Cannes, ou l'émotion poétique." *Le Monde* (Paris), May 26, 1998. *Academic Universe.* Lexis-Nexis (accessed July 23, 2002). http://www.web .lexis-nexis.com.

———. *La hija del embajador.* Barcelona: Emecé, 1996.

———. "La infancia ultrajada." *El Nuevo Herald* (Miami), December 19, 1999, 25A.

———. *La nada cotidiana.* Barcelona: Emecé, 1995. Trans. Sabine Cienfuegos. *Yocandra in the Paradise of Nada.* New York: Arcade, 1997.

———. *Sangre azul.* Havana: Letras Cubanas, 1994; Barcelona: Emecé, 1996. Trans. Michel Bibard. *Sang Bleu.* Arles: Actes Sud, 1993.

———. *Te di la vida entera.* Barcelona: Planeta, 1996. Trans. Nadia Benabid. *I Gave You All I Had.* New York: Arcade, 1999. Trans. Liliane Hasson. *La douleur du dollar.* Arles: Actes Sud, 1996.

Valdés Figueroa, Eugenio. "Trajectories of a Rumor: Cuban Art in the Postwar Period." In *Art Cuba: The New Generation,* ed. Holly Block, 17–23. New York: Abrams, 2001.

Vega, Jesús. "Wunderbar." In *Wunderbar, ¡maravilloso!,* 5–8. Havana: Letras Cubanas (Colección Pinos Nuevos), 1994. Trans. Claire Haskins. "Wunderbar." In *The Voice of the Turtle: An Anthology of Cuban Stories,* ed. Peter Bush, 333–36. New York: Grove Press, 1997.

Vega Serova, Anna Lidia. "Billetes falsos." In *Catálogo de mascotas,* 128–33. Havana: Letras Cubanas, 1998.

———. "Erre con erre." In *Catálogo de mascotas,* 99–115. Havana: Letras Cubanas, 1998. Trans. Mary Berg. "Peter Piper Picked a Peck." In *Open Your Eyes and Soar: Cuban Women Writing Now,* 38–52. Buffalo: White Pine Press, 2003.

———. "La encomienda." In *Catálogo de mascotas,* 16–22. Havana: Letras Cubanas, 1998.

———. *Noche de ronda.* Tenerife: Baile del sol, 2001; Havana: Ediciones Unión, 2003.

Venegas Fornias, Carlos. "Havana between Two Centuries." *Journal of Decorative and Propaganda Arts* 22 (1995): 12–35.

Vicent, Mauricio. "El oscuro encanto de Cuba." *El país* (Valencia, Spain), July 30, 2000 (Internacional), 5.

Villaverde, Cirilo. *Cecilia Valdés o La Loma del Ángel: Novela de costumbres cubanas* (1882). Mexico City: Porrúa, 1986.

Weiss, Jason. "Introduction: The Lure of Paris." In *The Lights of Home: A Century of Latin American Writers in Paris,* 1–13. New York: Routledge, 2003.

Woodmansee, Martha and Mark Osteen. *The New Economic Criticism: Studies at the Intersection of Literature and Economics*. London: Routledge, 1999.

Woodward, Christopher. *In Ruins*. New York: Pantheon Books, 2001.

Yáñez, Mirta, ed. *Cubana: Contemporary Fiction by Cuban Women*. Trans. Dick Cluster and Cindy Schuster. Boston: Beacon Press, 1998.

Index

Created by Eileen Quam

Esther Whitfield is assistant professor of comparative literature at Brown University, where she teaches Latin American, Caribbean, and European literature. She is editor of a collection of Antonio José Ponte's fiction, *Un arte de hacer ruinas,* and coeditor, with Jacqueline Loss, of *New Short Fiction from Cuba.*

(continued from page ii)